THE NEW TRANSATLANTIC AGENDA

The G8 and Global Governance Series

Series Editor: John J Kirton

The G8 and Global Governance Series explores the issues, the institutions, and the strategies of the participants in the G8 network of global governance, and other actors, processes, and challenges that shape global order in the twenty-first century. Many aspects of globalisation, once considered domestic, are now moving into the international arena, generating a need for broader and deeper international co-operation and demanding new centres of leadership to revitalise, reform, reinforce, and even replace the galaxy of multilateral institutions created in 1945. In response, the G8, composed of the world's major market democracies, including Russia and the European Union, is emerging as an effective source of global governance. The G8 and Global Governance Series focusses on the new issues at the centre of global governance, covering topics such as finance, investment, and trade, as well as transnational threats to human security and traditional and emerging political and security challenges. The series examines the often invisible network of G8, G7, and other institutions as they operate inside and outside established international systems to generate desired outcomes and create a new order. It analyses how individual G8 members and other international actors, including multinational firms, civil society organisations, and other international institutions, devise and implement strategies to achieve their preferred global order.

Also in the Series

Guiding Global Order
G8 governance in the twenty-first century
Edited by John J. Kirton, Joseph P. Daniels and Andreas Freytag
ISBN 0 7546 1502 2

Shaping a New International Financial System
Challenges of governance in a globalizing world
Edited by Karl Kaiser, John J. Kirton and Joseph P. Daniels
ISBN 0 7546 1412 3

Hanging in There
The G7 and G8 summit in maturity and renewal
Nicholas Bayne
ISBN 0 7546 1185 X

The G7/G8 System
Evolution, role and documentation
Peter I. Hajnal
ISBN 1 84014 776 8

The G8's Role in the New Millenium
Edited by Michael R. Hodges, John J. Kirton and Joseph P. Daniels
ISBN 1 84014 774 1

New Directions in Global Economic Governance
Managing globalisation in the twenty-first century
Edited by John J. Kirton and George M. von Furstenberg
ISBN 0 7546 1698 3

The New Transatlantic Agenda
Facing the challenges of global governance

Edited by
HALL GARDNER and RADOSLAVA STEFANOVA

Ashgate

Aldershot • Burlington USA • Singapore • Sydney

Published by
Ashgate Publishing Limited
Gower House
Croft Road
Aldershot
Hampshire GU11 3HR
England

Ashgate Publishing Company
131 Main Street
Burlington, VT 05401-5600 USA

Ashgate website: http://www.ashgate.com

British Library Cataloguing in Publication Data
The new transatlantic agenda : facing the challenges of
    global governance. - (The G8 and global governance series)
    1.Group of Eight (Organization) 2.Europe - Foreign
    relations - United States 3.United States - Foreign
    relations - Europe
    I.Gardner, Hall II.Stefanova, Radoslava
    327.4'073

Library of Congress Control Number: 2001092645

ISBN 0 7546 1780 7

Printed and bound by Athenaeum Press, Ltd.,
Gateshead, Tyne & Wear.

Contents

List of Contributors

Dana H. Allin is Editor, *Survival*, International Institute for Strategic Studies, London, England.

Yves Boyer is Deputy Director, Strategic Research Foundation, Paris.

David P. Calleo is Dean Acheson Professor and Director of European Studies at the Johns Hopkins University, Paul H. Nitze School of Advanced International Studies, Washington D.C.

Anne Deighton is Lecturer in European International Politics and Course Director of the M. Phil. in European Politics and Society, University of Oxford, England.

Hall Gardner is Professor and Chair, Department of International Affairs, The American University of Paris, France.

John Ikenberry is Professor of Government and International Affairs, Georgetown University, Washington, D.C.

Bernhard May is Senior Researcher, Deutsche Gesellschaft für Auswärtige Politik (DGAP), Berlin.

Volker Perthes is Senior Researcher, Stiftung Wissenschaft und Politik, Berlin, Germany.

Radoslava Stefanova is Head of the South-East Europe program, Istituto Affari Internazionali, Rome, and Researcher at the European University Institute, Florence, Italy.

Karsten D. Voigt is Coordinator for German-American Cooperation at the Foreign Office of the Federal Republic of Germany, Berlin.

Jan Zielonka is Associate Professor and co-chair of the Robert Schumann Center at the European University Institute, Florence, Italy.

Introduction

HALL GARDNER and RADOSLAVA STEFANOVA

The main objective of *The New Transatlantic Agenda: Facing the Challenges of Global Governance* is to analyze the new developments in Euro-Atlantic relations in view of the changing nature of the European Union and the United States. The aim is also to identify and examine in detail the main political processes in the transatlantic alliance, which condition the benchmarks of the origin and evolution of its policy formation. In addition, the book seeks to evaluate the prevalent new trends in transatlantic relations with strategically important third countries and regions, such as Russia, China, the Balkans, and the Middle East, as well as EU and U.S. relationships with key international organizations, such as NATO, the UN and the G-7/8. Finally, a major objective of the project has been the formulation and rationalization of plausible policy recommendations with the purpose of contributing to the successful transformation, strengthening, and continuity of the transatlantic relationship.

The editors would like to acknowledge the institutional support provided by *Istituto Affari Internazionali* (IAI), a major Italian think-tank based in Rome, which greatly facilitated the completion of the book. They are also very grateful to the German Marshall Fund of the United States, the U.S. Embassy in Rome, and the WEU Institute for Security Studies in Paris, whose generous support at the early stages of the project was fundamental. Hall and Radoslava would also like to thank the IAI's Deputy Director, Ettore Greco, for having conceived the idea of a book on transatlantic relations. Armend Reka and Agnieszka Ignaczak from the American University of Paris helped with formatting and proofreading respectively. The editors would also like to thank their families. The Gardner family has now suffered the birth pangs of a fourth major project. On Radoslava's side, Ettore's unvaried support was also important, as was Hall's experience and guidance in the editing process. Both editors look forward to the possibility of future collaboration on a number of possible projects!

The first three chapters of the book by David P. Calleo, John Ikenberry and Yves Boyer, focus on the U.S./NATO-European relationship that has been in a stage of metamorphosis since the end of the Cold War.

In the first chapter, "Imperial America and its Republican Constitution", **David P. Calleo** identifies five major factors that have been pushing Europe towards becoming a political and economic superpower. Each of these factors imply that Europe can no longer depend absolutely upon the United States but now needs to develop its own political, military and economic autonomy. Calleo moreover argues that building a serious European security and defence capability would benefit not only Europe's own security, but it would also permit the United States to begin to re-examine its increasingly disjointed decision making process, and thus re-focus upon its own domestic and foreign policy.

In the second chapter, "Strengthening the Atlantic Political Order", **John Ikenberry** identifies two basic shifts in the world situation that reinforce the views of an increasingly troubled Atlantic relationship. The first is the end of the Cold War and the Soviet threat that helped foster cohesion between Europe and the United States; the second is the emergence of American unipolar power. Ikenberry thus argues that if American-European relations are to be strengthened, political leaders on both sides of the Atlantic must understand how this order has worked to dissolve the tensions and insecurities that result from the shifting disparities of power between America and Europe through distinctive institutional practices that integrate and bind together the United States and Europe in ways that make American power more restrained and less provocative. These bargains and institutional practices have also helped both foster European unity and connect Europe with the outside world order.

In third chapter, "NATO Forever!", **Yves Boyer** argues that there remains a generally held assumption that NATO will last forever, despite the radically significant changes in the post-Cold War global system. For Boyer, NATO permits European countries "to mask the hollowness of their military posture". He argues that as Europe moves into the 21st century, that "it would be a mistake, if not a collective suicide", for Europe to assume non-military responsibilities and leave NATO as the sole security actor. He accordingly calls for Europe to develop greater autonomy, "l'Europe puissance", a power endowed military capabilities ranging from the ability to engage in multinational peacekeeping to high intensity military operations.

The next three chapters, by Karsten D. Voigt, Anne Deighton, and Jan Zielonka, analyse intra-European Union relations, and more closely examine European efforts to achieve a Common European Security and Defence Policy.

In the fourth chapter, "The European Security and Defence Policy: Birth Pangs of a New Atlanticism", **Karsten D. Voigt** argues that existing Euro-American frictions are "not a sign of imminent failure, but rather an unavoidable side effect of the transatlantic success". Voigt examines Europe's complex institutional problems and progress over the past decade, noting that the Union is about to become more autonomous, and hence a more reliable ally of the United States. On the one hand, the very Europeans who call for Europe's greater autonomy from the United States are also those who demand that the United States defend Europe when the going gets tough. On the other hand, the very Americans who harbour reservations about the ESDP often call upon Europeans to play a greater role in joint operations in and around Europe, or even to tackle European crises on their own. This shows that differences in analysis often do not just exist between Europe and America but also within Europe and the United States.

Anne Deighton's fifth chapter "Why St. Malo Matters" outlines the complex nature of the EU's emerging new defence project, and argues that the Common European Security and Defence Policy will require much more than a mere technical and bureaucratic implementation. The "militarising" of the EU will, in fact, open up new and more vehement debates in regard to three essential areas: What constitutes EU culture; over the nature and capabilities of security that the EU intends to develop; and at the strategic level, over the very conception of "community" and Europe's present relationship and interaction with the future nature of the European, Atlantic and global communities. Deighton argues that the Pandora's box of security projection has already been opened and there is no telling if the EU can hold itself together as it attempts to cope with new dilemmas of the post-Cold War order.

Jan Zielonka in his chapter, "Transatlantic Relations: Beyond the Common Foreign and Security Policy", takes what appears to be an even more pessimistic forecast. He argues, quite bluntly, that the CFSP of the EU has made only a marginal impact on transatlantic relations and remains in a state of paralysis. On the one hand, the EU not tried to tackle any major crisis through this mechanism on the other, the CFSP does not even deal with the most crucial problems on the transatlantic agenda, which include the primary issue of the spread of western European institutions into the countries of central and eastern Europe. It is furthermore not clear that the CFSP will be able to co-ordinate strategy in regard to the largely separate European defence identity that appears to be emerging since the December 2000 Nice summit. The United States is thus right to point to the EU's many weaknesses. The EU is ill-suited to cope with military and defence issues; but it can cope with "the post-modern agenda of cascading interdependence, mass communications, cross-cutting institutions and multiple cultural identities".

Transatlantic relations in regard to the Balkan region, the Middle East, and then in regard to Russia and China are examined by Radoslava Stefanova, Volker Perthes and Hall Gardner respectively.

Radoslava Stefanova, in "Balkan Clutter: American and European Handling of a Powder Keg" portrays some notable differences in U.S. and European policies in regard to crisis management in the Balkan region. In particular, she examines the U.S.-EU interaction in the Bosnian war and in the Kosovo conflict, considering also the evolution of transatlantic policies towards Belgrade. Continued instability in southern Yugoslavia, and the new security challenge in the Former Yugoslav Republic of Macedonia (FYROM), are also addressed. Besides revealing and criticising a general policy of an ad hoc and short-term involvement, as well as a notable lack of coherence and unity of approach on the part of the transatlantic allies' conflict management and peace-maintenance in the Balkans, she also identifies a number of serious challenges to the EU-U.S. relationship, which were particularly revealed by the Balkan crises. She concludes by stating that fragmented and incoherent strategies on the part of the allies are likely to contribute to the erosion of regional stability in the Balkans, a development that has negatively influenced the transatlantic relationship.

Volker Perthes in "The Advantages of the Complementarity: The Middle East Peace Process" examines the transatlantic relationship in regard to the Middle East. He argues that U.S.-European differences over the Middle East have to be characterised as differences of priorities and approach, rather than differences of purpose or vital interests. Needless to say, EU states are not always in full agreement in regard to their particular policies towards the region, and the United States is no entirely a decisive and unitary actor either. Yet despite their differences, the EU and United States can work to achieve a certain complementarity between the EU's multilateralist emphasis on social and economic assistance and a more balanced approach in regard to states of the region in contrast to the U.S. emphasis on power projection and its primary focus on one or two regional states.

Hall Gardner in "Russia and China: The Risks of Uncoordinated Transatlantic Strategies" argues that NATO and the EU need to take more substantial and carefully calculated steps toward an amelioration of the NATO-EU-Russian relationship. While most attention has been focused on the Balkans, NATO and the EU need to pay greater attention to the Baltic region and to Russian Kaliningrad in particular, where a potentially significant crisis is brewing. The largely uncoordinated NATO-EU "double enlargement" could well lead to the isolation of Russia and/or the formation of a much tighter Sino-Russian entente or alliance. To prevent the formation of such an alliance, NATO and the EU will need to forge a concerted strategy intended to bring Russia into a new form of NATO-EU-WTO "full" membership and simultaneously coordinate their geostrategic and political economic policy toward China, but without leading to the estrangement of the latter, if possible.

The final two chapters examine transatlantic interactions with two key international regimes, the UN and the World Trade Organization.

Dana H. Allin in "Uneasy Triangle: Transatlantic Partnership and UN Governance" provides a critical analysis of the U.S. relationship with the United Nations, and describes both liberal internationalist and neo-conservative American thinking in regard to the UN in an effort to explain the "sources of American UN bashing". He argues that greater support for the UN may need to come from a more united Europe, and that it is largely up to the EU to promote "multilateralism" (albeit an inadequate expression for such a unique international regime!) and to show how to implement it, as the EU continues to rise in world prominence. He argues that the crucial question for the success or failure of global governance and the UN will soon be determined by how, and whether, the United States can stave off trends toward neo-conservative isolationism.

In chapter 11, "New Challenges for Transatlantic Economic Relations", **Bernhard May** discusses changing economic relations between the United States and EU as the latter develops a common currency, the Euro. Despite the fact that the United States and the European Union are their most important economic partners, and despite an impressive record in economic integration, there are currently some potentially serious trade disputes between the two transatlantic partners making the headlines and creating a potentially serious political backlash on both sides of the Atlantic. These trade disputes make up only about one per cent of the total transatlantic trade volume. Yet if they are not solved in a timely and acceptable fashion, even minor disputes could create a major transatlantic crisis with global implications. And it is still not clear if the two sides are willing to work out a compromise.

The conclusion examines key points raised by each of the contributors, makes a number of policy recommendations, and raises a number of important questions for the future of the transatlantic relationship and the global system in general.

1 Imperial America and its Republican Constitution

DAVID P. CALLEO

For more than half a century the western world has depended on American power for its security. The United States has acted as a sort of benevolent Roman Empire for its allies. The Cold War justified this hegemonic role, both to the European powers and to the Americans themselves. The end of the Cold War raised the question of whether this American role should, or could, continue. The 1990s have given a rather ambiguous response. NATO enlargement suggests a very positive answer, whereby America's new commitments since the Cold War are geographically, at least, much greater than during it. Yet despite this firm reassertion and extension of NATO's role, European experience with the American alliance in Bosnia and Kosovo has proved seriously disturbing. For some Europeans, the lesson of Bosnia is that the United States cannot be relied upon to engage itself on Europe's behalf in a timely fashion, and cannot be relied upon to back Europe loyally in its own efforts. For some, the lesson of Kosovo is that when the United States does intervene in European affairs, it does not necessarily do so in a fashion that is effective, or pleasing to European interests. In recent years, moreover, Europeans have grown sensitive to America's swelling official triumphalism. Some Europeans find visions of the United States as the "indispensable superpower" in a unipolar world irritating and alarming rather than reassuring. In addition, the United States has enjoyed an extraordinary prosperity in the 1990s, whereas they were difficult years for European economies. The American tendency to vaunt its economic superiority, and give economic lessons to the world in the name of "globalisation," has not proved endearing to many Europeans, particularly in conjunction with America's unilateral and increasingly imperious behaviour in trade disputes.

Europe's reaction has helped it to achieve the Euro and now encourages a more autonomous security system. Initiatives like CFSP and ESDI have stirred up the familiar struggle between those who want to work vigorously for a stronger and more autonomous Europe, and those who prefer not to disturb their traditional American protector. But while the debate is longstanding, its balance seems to have shifted. On this matter, the United Kingdom has ostensibly joined the Europeanist ranks. No one can be sure how seriously to take this new adhesion, given Britain's traditional role as NATO's booster, and given the still very strong anti-European sentiment rampant in British politics. Nevertheless, things seem to be moving along. Even the Germans, hitherto extremely diffident, have been moving toward military forces that would allow them to take a real role in an autonomous European defence.

Behind the apparent drift toward a collective and more self-sufficient European defence are certain trends in the post-Cold War era—characteristics that appear to make Europe's traditional Cold War dependency on the United States less and less probable or healthy. Among these is our topic today: America's own constitutional evolution. But before discussing this trend in detail, it would perhaps be useful to mention some of the others, since they form a good part of the general context for America's evolution as well as that of Europe.

First among these trends is the changing nature of Europe's security problems. In the Cold War, the greatest threat to Europe was obvious and external. A malevolent superpower on Europe's edge, with a large army in Europe's middle, constituted an urgent threat, justifying U.S. leadership and heavy military presence to Europeans and Americans alike. A malevolent superpower called naturally for importing a compensating and friendly superpower. Today, Europe's security problems are much more domestic—ethnic neighbourhood warfare, stampedes of terrorized populations, gangsterism, drug trafficking, and large-scale criminality in general. In many respects these are police problems, and it is not comfortable or efficacious to have such problems managed by an outside power, however well intentioned. Furthermore, the United States is not very good at such matters. Understandably, Americans lack the intimate knowledge or constant attention needed to deal with them. Often, the best tools are political and economic, rather than strictly military. In comparison with the EU states, the United States often lacks comparable means for effective intervention.

A second major trend pushing Europe toward more autonomous defence is the growing divergence of transatlantic strategic interests, particularly in regions on the edge of Europe. The differences stem mostly from geography. To paraphrase de Gaulle, Europe is the cape of a continent, whereas the United States is another world. As a result of both its greater military power and its geographical distance, the United States is much more inclined toward confrontation with some of Europe's more difficult neighbours than are the Europeans themselves. Where the United States sees "rogue states", Europeans tend to see neighbours with important economic assets and prospects. Europeans tend to believe it is more efficacious to engage constructively with these neighbours rather than to punish and thwart them. Above all, this is true of Europe's relations with Russia. Europe's long-term prospects depend heavily on a happy and productive Russia. It seems in Europe's long-term interest not to antagonize Russia during its period of exceptional weakness. Furthermore, stable security in regions like the Balkans seems more probable with a cooperative, rather than an antagonistic, Russia. Following NATO's enlargement, and given

America's propensity to emphasize NATO's abrasive military predominance, it is counterproductive for the Europeans to let the United States take the lead in managing their relations with Russia, but for Europe to have a more autonomous Russian policy seems to require a more autonomous collective foreign security and defence policy as a precondition.

A third major trend is America's increasing preoccupation with Asian security. Whereas Europe seems, in theory, capable of taking primary responsibility for its own security problems, there seems no real alternative for containing a rapidly rising China, other than for the United States to reaffirm its role as Asia's security manager. As China becomes a more serious nuclear power, the United States will very likely be forced into a strategy of flexible response – to containment based primarily on conventional defence. This was, of course, the evolution of strategic doctrine in Europe once the Russians developed the capacity to seriously endanger the American homeland. A flexible response in Asia against China will very likely prove very expensive. Embarking on it will eventually reverse America's low defence budgets of the 1990s. It will sharpen burden-sharing issues with Europe, issues tied more than ever to competition in high technology.

This brings us to a fourth trend pressing Europe toward a more autonomous defence. The evolution of Europe as a political and economic superpower, a development symbolized rather dramatically by the Euro, makes it more and more anomalous that the Europeans should depend so completely on America for security. To put the matter bluntly, a Europe whose money is challenging the dollar around the world will be unlikely to remain comfortable as a U.S. military protectorate. Among other things, the Euro, as a major alternative reserve currency, seems likely to affect significantly America's capacity to manipulate the dollar in order to finance its habitual deficits, fiscal or external. As the Euro forces Americans to pay more to finance their deficits, the burden-sharing issue will grow more seriously divisive. The logical solution, particularly given the other trends we are discussing, is for Europe to take over the primary responsibility for its own defence.

Alongside these four trends pressing toward a more autonomous European defence, there is certainly a fifth: the evolution of the American political system. On the whole, it does not give comfort to those expecting the United States to produce a coherent, consistent, long-term foreign policy, sensitive to the needs of its allies. Constitutionally, America's capacity to produce that kind of foreign policy has always depended on a strong presidency, presiding over a powerful and disciplined executive branch, with the legislative and judicial branches deferential in matters of foreign policy. Such was the nature of our imperial constitution during the Second World War. The Cold War prolonged it, and the Kennedy and Johnson administrations proved its climacteric. The erosion of the imperial presidency began with the attacks on Lyndon Johnson and continued apace throughout the troubled presidency of Richard Nixon. Both Johnson and

Nixon were effectively forced from office. The assault on Nixon was something more than an upsurge of populist opposition to an unpopular war. It involved collaboration between the other two branches of government. The judiciary stripped away presidential prerogative and removed the veil of legal protection over the president's servants. Meanwhile, the House of Representatives impeached and the Senate stood prepared to convict. The imperial presidency never recovered. The next two presidents—Ford and Carter—were weak and lasted no more than one term. While Reagan enjoyed widespread popular support, and was easily re-elected in 1984, his whole second term was plagued by a legal assault over the Iran-Contra affair. Several of his closest aides lived under persistent threat of indictment. The same conditions plagued the Bush administration, despite his smooth handling of America's role in the end of the Cold War and his highly successful conduct of the Gulf War. That war, it bears remembering, came within one vote of being disavowed by the American Senate. The public, and the rest of the political system, gave little credit to the administration for its impressive foreign policy accomplishments. Instead, they faulted Bush for not paying enough attention to domestic needs and the voters repudiated him at the first opportunity. In this context, the acute, if singular, problems of the Clinton administration do not seem so unusual. Over the past three decades, the Congress, the courts and the states have frequently combined to cut the presidency down to size. Nothing illustrates this trend more than Clinton's ordeal. Despite the President's continuing popularity with the electorate, and his impressive achievements in the economic field, his presidency was subjected to the most savage constitutional attack since Nixon's time.

What are the consequences for American foreign policy of this weakened presidency? They form the familiar litany of complaints: Foreign policy, dominated by Congress, pursues an incoherent aggregate of private agendas. In trade legislation, congressional unilateralism regularly defies not only presidential authority, but also the country's treaty obligations. In defence spending, congressional pressure greatly affects not only decisions about arms purchases and military organisation, but basic strategic doctrine – as, for example, when the Senate refused to ratify the Test-Ban Treaty, or now, as it apparently forces the administration to pursue missile defence, along with a renegotiation of the ABM Treaty. The list goes on. In diplomacy, professionalism is at a discount as appointments are routinely held hostage to the Senate's own agenda. Continual congressional interference and witch-hunting have long ago demoralized the professional quality of the intelligence services. And there is Congress' captious antipathy toward international organizations, with highly disruptive consequences for the UN, the IMF, the World Bank, and the WTO.

This unhappy picture of American behaviour does not indicate that the United States has grown isolationist, i.e., turned its back on the world. The United States has not, for example, dismantled the great foreign policy bureaucracies established during the Cold War—the huge military and its attendant industrial complex, or the huge intelligence bureaucracy, or the very large diplomatic establishment, or indeed the large semi-academic establishment linked to foreign policy. These institutions survive but, in the absence of presidential authority, they have become "privatised". In the United States, as in Russia, the great state enterprises of the Cold War have been taken over by their managers and colonized by political and economic special interests. In America, this makes the great government departments no longer serviceable instruments for a coherent national foreign policy, professionally conducted and attuned to the realities of a complex world, let alone to the interests and sensitivities of allies.

To be sure, this sort of constitutional bazaar of politicians and interests is hardly unknown elsewhere. Indeed, many people would describe it as the essence of democratic politics. But it is not the kind of governmental machinery that seems well adapted to what might be called the Roman function in a globalised world system. It does not seem the proper way to govern the "indispensable superpower"—the manager of security in Europe and Asia, the consumer of last resort in the world economy, or the creator and manager of the world's principal money. In other words, there is a profound tension between the United States as a national democracy and the United States as a global hegemon.

The United States is not, of course, a national state like others. It is a state on a continental scale. It is ethnically and culturally more diverse than any other advanced democratic state. The United States used to be thought a "melting pot", where ethnic and cultural differences dissolved in a common national culture. Today, it seems more a mixing bowl, where the parts of the salad remain distinct, even if covered by a common sauce—itself an emulsion of incompatible elements. On top of its rich European mixture of the nineteenth century, and a substantial black population inherited from slavery, the United States has now acquired a large Hispanic population that resists abandoning Spanish for English, even as an official language. There is also now a large Asian population, whose distinct presence is a more and more striking feature in America's universities.

In short, the United States, in some respects, resembles the EU as a whole rather than any one of its member states. Like the EU, the United States is continental in scale and multinational in character. Like the EU, the United States has tremendous resources but some considerable difficulty in mobilizing them for common purposes. Mr. Kissinger used to complain that he never knew what telephone number to call to discover what was Europe's policy. It would be interesting to know what this telephone number might now be in Washington. Given America's size and diversity, the present disorder, rather than the imperial presidency of the Cold War, might seem America's normal condition. The philosophy that informed the American Constitution at the start was not that of Rousseau or Mazzini. Rather, it was the philosophy of James Madison of Federalist Paper Number 10. The avowed aim was not to create enough of a legitimate general will to hold the country together. Rather, it was to prevent any single interest or combination of interests from dominating the state. It carried into politics the philosophy of the free market: things work out for the best so long as no concentration of power – no monopoly – blocks competition among self-seeking interest groups. Arguably, there is nothing wrong with this view as a philosophy of government—for Switzerland—but it is not very adaptable to the needs of the world's "indispensable superpower".

All this being said, the history of the last century suggests an obvious riposte: The United States did, after all, play its leading global role in World War II and the Cold War with outstanding success. It defeated the Axis, met the Soviet threat and stabilized nuclear deterrence. It helped post-war Europe to recover and to begin the process of integration. It also fostered the growth of an integrated world economy, with dramatic results for Asia. And even with today's anarchical politics, the Clinton administration managed some major accomplishments in foreign policy – in the trade field especially. In other words, the past demonstrates that American resources can be mobilized effectively for a consistent long-term foreign policy. Nevertheless, as I have tried to argue, this effectiveness depends on the strength of the presidency within the constitutional balance of power. The prospects of the United States as a successful global manager thus depend greatly on the future of the presidency within the evolving American constitutional system. Obviously, the personality, skill and character of whoever holds the office does matter a great deal – a matter of absorbing interest in the early months of the administration of George W. Bush, Jr. At this point, it must be said that the circumstances of his election do not, in themselves, bode well for a strengthening of the presidency. In any event, deeper factors are at work. Presidential power has been in decline through the previous seven administrations and began well before the Cold War was over. A long view of American history indicates several cycles where presidential power has waxed and waned. What insights does this history offer? Does it suggest how presidential power can be stabilized sufficiently to permit the United States to play the international world role that many still hope for, and play it well enough to be a positive and stabilizing force in the world?

Let me suggest three approaches to explaining the rise and fall of presidential power. These I would label: The pathological approach, the cyclical and cultural approach, and the internationalist approach. The pathological approach is the most straightforward. According to this view, the current weakness of the presidency is a disease resulting from the colonization of the American government by swarming private interests. The colonization, to some extent inseparable from representative democracy, has now reached so acute a form that it constitutes a pathological condition, with a perverse linkage between democracy, corruption, and special interests. As a consequence, a good deal of American foreign policy is conditioned heavily by the financial or electoral rewards held out to politicians by special interests. Thus, military and strategic policy is increasingly dominated by arms manufacturers, diplomacy by ethnic pressure groups, and trade policy by special business or labour interests. A large part of the American public believes this condition is a very serious degeneration of the democratic process, whose principal cause is the excessive intrusion of money into politics. The case is not difficult to make. Individual campaigns for seats in the House of Representatives, for example, cost roughly one million dollars and have to be waged every other year. Financing on such a scale offers lavish opportunities for personal enrichment. The situation is made worse by the anarchical nature of the political process. Since parties are exceptionally weak, every representative or senator becomes a private entrepreneur in the political marketplace. From this perspective, it will be difficult to have a coherent and effective foreign policy without serious campaign reform. But while campaign reform is often popular with the electorate, its principal advocates during the recent presidential campaign all lost out to rivals with more ambivalent views. In the early days of the new Congress, Senator McCain attempted to initiate reform of campaign finance. It remains to be seen how far the project will succeed. The interests opposing it are massive and all pervasive.

The second approach, cyclical and cultural, is a view popularized by the American historian Arthur Schlesinger, and is now being written about very interestingly by two old friends: Warren Zimmermann, former U.S. ambassador to Yugoslavia, and John Harper, my colleague in Bologna. The cyclical approach links the ups and downs of presidential power not only to changing international or domestic circumstances, but also to basic and contending traditions of American foreign policy. To me, three traditions seem critical and I would label them isolationist, imperialist, and realist. All three appeared at the very start of the republic at the end of the eighteenth century and, according to changing circumstances, have continued to contend with each other ever since.

Isolationism is normally identified with Jefferson, and tends to see the United States as an exceptional nation, whose virtues can only be undermined by prolonged engagement with European power politics. As many people point out, isolationism does not necessarily mean ignoring the world. Nor does it prevent the United States from using its power to promote its own interests abroad. Rather, it means refusing to engage with other sovereign states in any systematic and limiting fashion. Thus, isolationism easily becomes "unilateralism", making the United States a gigantic rogue state in the international arena.

Imperialism is identified with Alexander Hamilton in the early Republic, and later with turn-of-the-century imperialists and "neo-Federalists" like Theodore Roosevelt, Admiral Mahan or Henry Cabot Lodge. Subsequently, World War I brought the Wilsonian school—a sort of Jeffersonian imperialism, with Hamiltonian policies explained in Jeffersonian or neo-Kantian rhetoric. All elements of this imperial tradition share the view that the United States is a country with huge prospects that destin it for world leadership. In the twentieth century, many imperialists believed the United States was fated to inherit the British global role, and in the twenty-first, some believe it is fated to lead Eurasia as well. In effect, the imperialist tradition sees the United States as a new global

Rome – engaging with others to lead the world into a global system of order and prosperity.

The realist tradition is a blending of the two others. From the imperialists, it takes the view that the United States is a power in the world and cannot ignore what goes on there. From the isolationists, it takes the view that America's domestic balance and freedom preclude a national career of world domination. The particular realist blend depends on the circumstances of the time—from Washington's "Farewell Address" to the strictures of Morgenthau, Lippmann, Kennan, or Niebuhr against the war in Vietnam.

From the overall cyclical-cultural perspective, the current weakness of the presidency is part of the natural ebb and flow of the constitutional elements. In the twentieth century, the imperial presidency reached a high point with Theodore Roosevelt and Woodrow Wilson, and then collapsed after World War I. It revived under Franklin Delano Roosevelt, whose powers were quasi-dictatorial by normal standards, reached a post-war high point in the Kennedy administration and has been declining ever since. Vietnam's reversal has been further accelerated by the end of the Cold War. The pendulum seems unlikely to reverse itself sharply until there is some new threat that restores legitimacy to presidential hegemony within the constitutional order. That threat might be terrorism from "rogue states" an economic disaster or perhaps growing tension with China.

Finally, let me suggest an internationalist perspective on the question of presidential power. Here, there is a lesson for the United States from Europe's experience over the past half-century. The health of any national constitutional system depends greatly on the international setting that forms the country's environment. European states have achieved a remarkable stability in their internal affairs since the end of World War Two, thanks not only to the benevolent presence of their American protector, but also, and increasingly, thanks to the structured environment they have created for themselves collectively. With the European Union, European states have entered into intimate forms of cooperation unimaginable in the pre-war setting. Countries – Italy, for example – have created a sort of super-ego for themselves, compelling behaviour in the name of Europe that would otherwise be difficult to manage in a purely national context. This European structure, moreover, has not meant the end of Europe's nation-states. In many respects, their practical sovereignty has increased rather than decreased. States, realizing that national policy formulated and implemented in isolation has little chance of success, have learned that bargaining together greatly increases their real control over their own environment.

In other words, intimate and continuous structured cooperation significantly increases their practical, as opposed to their theoretical, sovereignty. And despite its theoretical constraints on sovereignty, the European structure has not threatened national independence. At the start of post-war integration, not one country was in a position to dominate the others. Germany was effectively constrained by the Americans and Russians. As decades have passed, an inherent balance of power has consolidated itself within the EU: Between France and Germany, between big states and small states, and between north and south. There is, to be sure, a hegemony of sorts to provide broad leadership for Union – a hybrid hegemon created out of the Franco-German couple. But a remarkably civilized bargaining process of rules and habits finely balances this hegemony. And these rules are sustained by an inherent balance of power, no doubt reinforced by the American presence, but no longer dependent upon it. This internal balance is in sharp contrast to the internal dynamics of NATO and the security system. In NATO, the security structure with its American hegemon required a Soviet threat to maintain its own inner balance. By contrast, the European structure has evolved an inner balance of its own.

What are the relevant lessons of this European experience? To begin with, the EU certainly demonstrates how engagement in interstate organizations can favour stability, rational policies and intelligent compromises, not only within a state system, but also within the states themselves. The present situation in NATO and in the strategic realm generally—where the United States still has enormous military power but no balancing antagonist—is not only disquieting for the world, but dangerous for the United States—for its own inner constitutional balance and sanity. Hence, the increasing signs of imperious unilateralism. One obvious remedy is to restore balance in the security sphere—not, presumably, by recreating the Soviet threat, but by building a more balanced transatlantic system. As Europe seems already to have learned in the trade field, the proper response to American unilateralism is firm, principled, and efficacious European resistance. Without such responses it is difficult for Americans to keep their own wayward political system under control. Obviously, it is hard for Europe to sustain such responses, so long as it is so completely dependent on the United States to manage its security. Thus, building a serious European security and defence capability is a benefit not only for Europe's own security, but also for the inner balance of the American polity. The presence of a friendly but cohesive and strong Europe should encourage a corresponding refocusing of policy-making in the United States itself—in short, a stronger presidency.

Perhaps there are some further lessons for world order in the future. The European Union suggests the advantages of shared hegemonies within a larger system. France and Germany have been able to lead Europe far more effectively together than either has ever been able to do alone. This is not only because together each is stronger, but because in reaching a common view, their leadership becomes more representative of the whole. Each has its own special friends and clients among the smaller states and its own particular and complicated relations with the other major powers of the EU—Britain and Italy. Arguably, this kind of shared hegemony may have broader uses in the world. American leadership shared with the EU should be more representative and less captious, as well as backed by greater resources.

As we peer into the future, it seems unlikely that the world will continue to seem unipolar. Europe is gradually evolving into a more complete and autonomous world power. Russia is also transforming itself – painfully, to be sure – but will not remain weak indefinitely. And the great states of Asia are rapidly modernizing. These trends are unlikely to be reversed. They imply a great challenge: how to construct a world order that makes room for new powers, but contains them in a rules-based system of shared risks and responsibilities. This will hardly be an easy task. The West cannot simply impose such an order; indeed, the relative power of the West seems fated to decline. This prospect indicates the urgent need for the West to get its own inner relations in order. A Europe, enabled through the EU to become a serious global partner should benefit, not only itself, but the United States and the rest of the world as well.

In summary, the health of national systems depends greatly on the international context within which they find themselves. The European Union, in creating a shared framework of rules and norms and consolidating a balance of power that encourages habits of cooperation, has vastly improved the internal stability of its member states. The end of the Cold War poses a new Pan-European challenge to the EU. So far, the net effect has been to encourage deeper and fuller integration, rather than to undermine the Union already achieved. What happens with enlargement remains to be seen. But the 1990s, at least, can be counted a highly productive decade for the stability and constitutional evolution of the European Union and its member states, despite a difficult period economically.

For America's constitutional progress, the decade is less encouraging, despite record economic prosperity. The end of the Cold War has brought new danger to the American constitutional system. After years of creating and mobilizing great power to contain a great enemy, the sudden disappearance of that enemy leaves the United States with excessive power. At the same time, it removes the pressure for constitutional discipline. The combination of excessive power and governmental indiscipline is not good for the United States, the West, or the world in general. The United States needs to be contained—not by an enemy, but by a friend.

2 Strengthening the Atlantic Political Order

JOHN IKENBERRY

Introduction

By some accounts, relations between Europe and the United States are in serious disrepair. Rising trade disputes, NATO strains over the war in Kosovo, disagreements over national missile defence, European preoccupation with monetary union, and American worries about a European defence pillar under the EU umbrella – these and other tensions have been the grist for what some observers see as an increasingly troubled Atlantic relationship.[1] Comments made by the Bush foreign policy team during the campaign about America's peacekeeping commitment to Kosovo raised doubts about the new administration's larger commitment to Europe. The agreement reached by European governments in Nice to move forward with a European security capability raises questions as well about the future of Atlantic security ties. Are these signs of Atlantic drift?

Two basic shifts in the world situation reinforce these worries. One is the end of the Cold War, eliminating the Soviet threat that helped foster cohesion between Europe and the United States. The Cold War provided "glue" that helped hold the Atlantic partnership together. The allies were thrown together in securing their common defence and this spilled over into wider political and economic arenas of cooperation. Economic gains by one country were seen as good for the larger alliance, so economic disputes were kept in check. The United States was more willing to forego short-term and domestic-driven economic interests and focus on the longer-term good of the Atlantic world. The Cold War also fostered a common identity - the so-called "free world" – which strengthened Atlantic bonds and ensured stable relations.[2] In the view of some scholars, without the old Soviet threat, Europe and the United States have started to drift apart and disputes have become more acrimonious.[3]

The second shift is the emergence of American unipolar power. The present disparities in economic and military capabilities between the United States and Europe (and the rest of the world) have widened - and American predominance is without historical precedence. No state in the modern era has ever enjoyed such a dominant global position. The decline in rival ideologies and the economic failings of other major states have added to the reach and pervasiveness of American power. "The United States of America today predominates on the economic level, the monetary level, on the technological level, and in the cultural area in the broad sense of the word", the French Foreign Minister, Hubert Vedrine, observed in a speech in Paris in early 1999. "It is not comparable, in terms of power and influence, to anything known in modern history".[4]

The problem with American unipolar dominance is that it is a potential threat to other states if it is exercised in an arbitrary and exploitive way. Unilateral trade restrictions, such as the Helms-Burton and Super 301 legislation, are manifestations of what some see as the abusive use of American power. The United States has also failed to ratify various multilateral agreements and conventions dealing with land mines, environmental protection, and the proposed International Criminal Court.[5] In its relations with the United Nations, the United States went for years failing to fully pay its UN dues and it acted in what many observers thought was a heavy-handed manner to prevent Secretary General Boutros Boutros-Ghali from returning for a second term. The frequent American military interventions in recent years – Somalia, Haiti, Iraq, and Kosovo – also underscore America's singular capacity to project military power with few international constraints.

This pattern of American unilateralism leads some to openly worry about what looks to be an increasingly unrestrained world power. A French former ambassador remarked in the spring of 1999 that the great menace in world politics was the American "hyperpower". During the Cold War the United States and the Soviet Union restrained each other, whereas now "the U.S. can do anything it wants".[6] Even an American ally, German Chancellor Gerhard Schröder, has raised concerns. "That there is a danger of unilateralism, not by just anybody but by the United States, is undeniable".[7]

The argument advanced here is that if American-European relations are to be strengthened, political leaders on both side of the Atlantic must recognize and preserve the aspects of Western political order that have made it stable and successful. The first step is to recognize that the United States and Europe have over the last fifty years indeed built a political order. The United States and Europe do not just have "relations", but rather share a common political order that they jointly created over half a century – and it is a political order that requires that they operate in particular ways to ensure its continuation. Despite the vagaries of economic and security relations between the Western allies, these states have built an Atlantic world – a regional world order that extends into Asia and the Western Hemisphere – that has provided more physical security and economic prosperity for more people than any other political order in history. It is also an order that is distinctive – built around open, legitimate, reciprocal, and highly institutionalised relations. In contrast to most of the rest of the world, it is an order where the use of violence to resolve disputes is essentially unthinkable. Understanding the sources and logic of this order is essential for political leaders to act in ways to make it last. This order was not simply a result of the Cold War but was created with a more positive vision of relations among the Western democracies.

The second task is to understand how this order has worked to dissolve the tensions and insecurities that result from the shifting disparities of power between America and Europe. The Western order has developed distinctive institutional practices that integrate and bind together the United States and Europe in ways that make American power more restrained and less provocative. These bargains and institutional practices have also helped both foster European unity and connect Europe with the outside world order. NATO is the cornerstone of this elaborate system of institutions that provide reassurance and credible commitments. If the United States had not endeavoured to build the array of regional and global institutions that it did in the 1940s, it is difficult to imagine that American power would have had the scope, depth, or longevity that it in fact has had. International institutions can make the exercise of power more restrained and routinised but they can also make that power more durable, systematic, and legitimate.[8] This is a lesson that the United States – along with Europe – need to relearn as they work to preserve the Atlantic world in the new century.

The United States and Europe need to remember the institutional roots of Western order – and seek to strengthen and expand these institutions. The United States needs to remember that its power is made acceptable to the rest of the world when it is manifest within regional and global multilateral institutions. If it decides to operate in a more unilateral or disengaged manner, the rest of the world – including Europe – will respond accordingly. And Europe needs to look for ways to forge new institutional bargains with the United States and connect the European Union more directly to the Atlantic world.

The Atlantic World Order

NATO is at the heart of the Western order. It provides the most formal and durable link between Europe and the United States. But the alliance – together with the larger array of formal and informal economic and political institutions – are not simply products of the Cold War. The political construction of Western order after 1945 was facilitated by the Cold War but the visions and principles of that order predated and emerged semi-independently of the Cold War.

Even the birth of the Atlantic pact in April of 1949 had a positive vision behind it as reflected in British Foreign Minister Ernst Bevin's call in December 1948 for a "spiritual union" of the Western democracies. That is, NATO was part of Western community building and not just a military alliance. John Foster Dulles made the same point in 1954 when he argued that the major emphasis of the Atlantic alliance was "on cooperation for something rather than merely against something".[9] It is this democratic community impulse that must be recalled when searching for the underlying bases of Western order.

Indeed, it is useful to remember that there were two orders that were created after World War II. One order is what could be called the "containment order".[10] This order was the most direct manifestation of the Cold War. It was built around superpower competition, extended deterrence, the doctrine of containment, and intense ideological competition. This is the order that most people associate with the late-1940s and celebrated in the ideas and policies of the early post-war American diplomats, such as George Kennan, Dean Acheson, and Paul Nitze. The containment order is what was swept away after 1991.

Yet, at the same time, another order took shape that was focused on building a new set of relations among the Western democracies. This order was not directed at countering Soviet power and the fears of communism but was aimed at solving the problems of the 1930s – the economic breakdown and competing geopolitical blocs that paved the way for world war. This Western democratic order was a less explicit and coherent entity but it too reflected a vision of world order after 1945. That vision found its way into a sequence of founding agreements. The first was the Atlantic Charter of 1941 that spelled out a view of what the Atlantic and wider world order would look like if the allies won the war. This agreement was followed by the Bretton Woods agreements of 1944, the Marshall Plan in 1947, and the Atlantic pact in 1949. Together these provided a framework for a radical reorganisation of relations among the Atlantic democracies. The emerging Cold War gave this Western-oriented agenda some urgency and the American congress was more willing to provide resources and approve international agreements because of the threats of communist expansion that lurked on the horizon. But the vision of a new order among the Western democracies pre-dated the Cold War, and even if the Soviet Union has slipped into history, some sort of new order would have been built across the Atlantic.

This order among the democracies was built around four ideas. One basic commitment was that there would be economic openness among the regions. That is, capitalism would be organised along international, and not national, regional, or imperial lines. In many ways, this was what World War II was fought over. Germany and Japan each had built their states around the military domination of their respective geographical regions. Russia was also an imperial power unto itself. Even Great Britain had the imperial preference system and this was also a threat to an open world economy. During the 1930s in the United States, the debate among scholars and policy thinkers was about the implications of a world of regional blocs for the United States. The debate was really settled by the time the United States entered the war – the United States could not be a great power and survive only in the Western hemisphere. The country would need to have access to trade and resources from the vast Eurasian regions. Capitalism would need to be organized on a global basis.

At Baylor University in 1947, Truman gave voice to his view by speaking of the lessons the world must learn from the disasters of the 1930s. "As each battle of the economic war of the thirties was fought, the inevitable tragic result became more and more apparent. From the tariff policy of Hawley and Smoot, the world went on to Ottawa and the system of imperial preferences, and from Ottawa to the kind of elaborate and detailed restrictions adopted by Nazi Germany". Truman reaffirmed American commitment to "economic peace", which would involve tariff reductions and rules and institutions of trade and investment. In the settlement of economic differences, "the interests of all will be considered, and a fair and just solution will be found". Conflicts would be captured and domesticated in an iron cage of multilateral rules, standards, safe guards, and dispute resolution procedures. According to Truman, "this is the way of a civilised community".[11]

The British were not eager to give up their preference arrangements but they were committed to a generally open world economy. There was wide agreement that if the industrial Western democracies were to avoid a return to strategic rivalry and war, they would need to ensure openness and access to world markets. Many Western leaders drew this lesson from the failures of Versailles in 1919. Peace and political cooperation needed to be built on an economic foundation.

The second idea behind Western democratic order was that the new arrangements would need to be managed through international institutions and agreements. It was not enough simply to open the system up. There would need to be an array of trans-governmental and international organisational institutions that would bring government officials together on an ongoing basis to manage economic and political change. This was the view of the economic officials who gathered in Bretton Woods in 1944. Many of them took the lesson from the heightened role of governments during the economic downturn of the 1930s. Governments would need to play a more direct supervisory role in stabilizing and managing economic order. New forms of intergovernmental cooperation would need to be invented. Indeed, it is no accident that the most ambitious era of international institutional building took place after 1945 – bilateral, multilateral, regional, global, economic, political, and security-oriented. The democratic countries would enmesh themselves in dense institutional relationships.

The third idea was that a new social bargain would underlie the Western democratic order. This was the message that Roosevelt and Churchill communicated to the world in the Atlantic Charter of 1941. The industrial democracies would provide a new level of social support – a safety net – under the societies of the Atlantic world. If the citizens of these countries were to live in a more open world economy, their governments would help stabilize and protect their people with the welfare state. Job insurance, retirement support, and other social protections were to help the industrial democracies operate in a free trade system. An open system would provide both winners and losers. Economists argue that in such a system, the winners always win more than losers lose, and if there is a compensation mechanism it is possible for the whole of society to benefit. It was the building of such a compensation mechanism – the modern welfare state – that provided a fundamental support to an economically integrated Western democratic order.

Finally, the West was to be tied together in a cooperative security order. This was a very important departure from past security arrangements within the Atlantic area. The idea was that Europe and the United States would be part of a single security system. Such a system would ensure that the democratic great powers would not go back to the dangerous game of strategic rivalry and balance of power politics. It helped, of course, to have an emerging Cold War with the Soviet Union to generate this cooperative security arrangement. But the goal of cooperative security was implicit in the other elements of Western order. It is not clear that, without the Cold War, a formal alliance would have emerged as it did. Probably it would not have taken on such an intense and formal character. Yet a security relationship between Europe and the United States that lessened the incentives for these states to engage in balance of power politics was needed, and probably would have been engineered. A cooperative security order – embodied in a formal alliance institution – ensured that the power of the United States would be rendered more predictable. Power would be caged in institutions thereby making American power more reliable and connected to Europe (and to East Asia).

The Western order that emerged after 1945 was built upon these institutions and principles. It is difficult to identify a single grand design or a specific statement by a Western leader that articulated the full image of Western democratic order. But across the realms of economics, politics, and security such an order did in fact emerge. European and American leaders in the 1940s and after created a shared order that was built on institutions, commitments, habits, and organisational principles that together produced a remarkable political order. When relations between Europe and the United States enter a period of conflict, it is important to return to the founding logic of the order.

Binding Institutions and Restraints on Power

Behind this Western order is a distinctive – and pioneering – set of binding institutions that keep the exercise of power predictable and restrained. NATO is at the centre of this complex set of institutions that cut across the Atlantic and provide these basic elements of restraint and reassurance. These same institutions provide mechanisms for weaker and junior partners of the Western order to have regular access to the hallways of economic and security policy making. It is precisely this institutional complex – anchored in the Atlantic alliance – that mitigates the insecurities that arise when states of unequal power are operating within a single political order.

When Lord Ismay made his famous remark that NATO was created to keep the Russians out, the Germans down, and the Americans in, he was getting at the multifaceted way in which a binding security pact would stabilize order in the West. In fact, the security alliance was key to the building of an elaborate set of institutional arrangements that provided strategic restraint, reassurance, and integration among the Atlantic democracies. To be sure, the alliance was meant to deter Soviet aggression and the evolution of the NATO pact did reflect shifts in the perceived balance of power between the Soviet Union and the West. It was only after the Korean war and the advent of the Soviet bomb that an integrated military structure took hold and the American military commitment became permanent.

But the Atlantic pact has had additional purposes. One was to tie Germany to Europe – which revealed the logic of security binding. The idea was to tie potentially threatening states to each other and thereby reduce the incentives to balance against each other. This is precisely what France and Germany did after the war – even if Paris was somewhat reluctant about it. Post-World War II Europe and the United States recognised the problem: An unrestrained Germany could destabilize Europe. John McCloy, the High Commissioner to Germany captured the idea in 1950: "Whatever German contribution to defence is made may only take the form of a force which is an integral part of a larger international organisation.... There is no real solution of the German problem inside Germany alone. There is a solution inside the European-Atlantic-World Community". NATO has always been as much about knitting Germany into Europe and the Atlantic world as it has been about keeping the Soviets out.

Another purpose of the Atlantic pact is to institutionalise the American commitment to Europe. Britain and France were quite explicit in the late-1940s: they would only agree to bind themselves to Germany, if the United States agreed to bind itself to Europe. The United States was very reluctant to make this commitment and the actual process of doing so was a rolling one with incremental steps toward a full commitment. When the NATO pact was signed in 1949, American officials did not see this new security commitment as absolute or permanent. NATO was modelled after the Rio Pact – it was a commitment with an escape clause. Only after the Cold War escalated – after 1952 – when German rearmament was deemed necessary did the United States fully commit itself with the permanent stationing of troops and an integrated command. At each step, the rebuilding and reintegration of Germany was matched by an expansion of the American commitment.

The final purpose of NATO was to serve as a vehicle to commit European countries to European- wide unity and integration. This was clearly seen by American officials as a critical rationale for the alliance. The United States insisted that the Brussels Pact – which entailed commitments by the core European states to each other – be launched before it would negotiate an Atlantic pact. NATO's purpose was to lend support to European steps to build stronger economic, political, and security ties within Europe itself.[12] In this sense, the NATO agreement was a continuation of the Marshall Plan strategy: To extend assistance to Europe in order to improve the chances that Europe would succeed in reviving and integrating itself. Even the strongest advocates within the Truman administration of a security treaty with Europe understood that European unity was a necessary component of an Atlantic security pact. Many anticipated that once a confident and unified Europe emerged, the Atlantic alliance would recede in importance or even lapse.[13] American officials made it clear that a security commitment hinged on European movement toward integration. One State Department official remarked that the United States would not "rebuild a fire-trap".[14] American congressional support for the Marshall Plan was also premised, at least in part, on not just transferring American dollars to Europe but also on encouraging integrative political institutions and habits.

Overall, the political organization of post-World War II relations among the industrial democracies was driven by this process of reciprocal institutional binding. The United States did seek to remain as unencumbered as possible after the war. At the same time, American officials pursued a remarkably sophisticated agenda aimed at binding the Europeans together and tying western Germany into a more unified and integrated Europe. At first, this agenda was driven by the demands of post-war economic renewal and the need for some solution to the German problem. These represented imperatives that existed independently of the worsening of relations with the Soviet Union – although the Cold War did raise the stakes and speed up the process. Yet at each stage in this process, European officials insisted that the binding together of Europe was only acceptable if the United States itself made binding commitments to them as well. At each stage, the United States conceded as much commitment as was needed to keep the Europeans on their path toward integration and reconstruction. Restraint, reassurance, and commitment were the price the United States had to pay in order to achieve its order building goals in Europe and elsewhere.

The Europeans engaged in a similar trade off: They agreed to steps towards European integration and accepted western Germany back into Europe, in part, because in exchange they got a more institutionally restrained and connected post-World War II America. The full measure of this binding of American power to Europe occurred relatively late after the war – only after 1950 and in response to a heightening of the Soviet threat – with the integration of NATO forces and the permanent stationing of American troops in Europe. This institutionalisation of Atlantic security relations provided reassurances to Europe by making the exercise of American power more certain and predictable, and by creating institutional mechanisms for these partner states to gain access to American policy making. Together, these institutional arrangements were critical in giving shape to the order among the Atlantic states and overcoming the insecurities otherwise inherent in highly asymmetrical power relations. The rise of the Soviet Union reinforced Western solidarity, but that solidarity was imagined and acted upon before Cold War hostilities broke out.

Unipolar Power and Cooperation

American power is made more acceptable to other states because it is institutionalised power. There are limits on the arbitrary and indiscriminate exercise of this power. NATO and the other security treaties establish some limits on the autonomy of American military power, although these limits are only partial. Other regional and global multilateral institutions also function to circumscribe and regularise America's power in various economic and policy realms. Restraints are manifest through some institutionalised limits on policy autonomy and mechanisms that allow other states to have a voice in policy. As one former American State Department official described the operation of this post-World War II order: "The more powerful participants in this system – especially the United States – did not forswear all their advantages, but neither did they exercise their strength without substantial restraint. Because the United States believed the trilateral system was in its interest, it sacrificed some degree of national autonomy to promote it".[15] The implication of this argument is that the more that power peeks out from behind these institutions, the more that power will provoke reaction and resistance.

The lesson of American order building in this century is that international institutions have played a pervasive and ultimately constructive role in the exercise of American power. Traditional realist theory misses the way institutions relate to power. The conventional view is that they tend to be antithetical: More of one entails less of the other, and because power is the ultimate determinant of outcomes in international relations, institutions do not matter. But power and institutions are related to each other in a more complex way. Institutions can both project and restrain state power. If the United States had not endeavoured to build the array of regional and global institutions that it did in the 1940s, it is difficult to imagine that American power would have had the scope, depth, or longevity that it in fact has had. International institutions can make the exercise of power more restrained and routinised but they can also make that power more durable, systematic, and legitimate.

When American power holders bridle at the restraints and commitments that international institutions often entail, they might be reminded that these features of institutions are precisely what has made American power as durable and acceptable as it is today. If the American post-war order persists in the new century, it will be due in no small measure to the way power and institutions operate together to create stable and legitimate order.

A New American-EU Pact?

To return to the roots of the Atlantic order is not simply a historical or academic exercise – it is essential to understand the underlying logic of American-European cooperation if we are to preserve and expand that cooperation. This complex and highly institutionalised system of restraint, commitment, and assurances has operated for most of the last fifty years under the shadow of the Cold War. The Atlantic system operated almost as a by-product of this struggle. Today, it will be increasingly necessary to make the system of restraints, commitments, and assurances more explicit and formal if the system is to last without the Cold War's shadow.[16]

Taken together, a new American-European pact might include the following elements. First, the United States and Europe do need to reaffirm the post-war bargain. This bargain has several aspects. The United States agrees to exercise its military and political power in concert with Europe and through regional and global multilateral and intergovernmental institutions. The United States both restrains the most excessive expressions of unilateralism and arbitrary power and commits itself to extended deterrence. In return, the Europeans pursue an agenda of continental integration and cooperation that is deeply compatible with regional and global openness. Europe also agrees not to organise its security affairs in a way that lays the groundwork for strategic rivalry between itself and the United States.[17] The two units agree to a binding security pact that trumps all other security arrangements. Just as the solution to Franco-German rivalry is "solved" through binding security ties and deep economic integration – so too, the American and European rivalry is "solved" through security binding and economic interdependence. This bargain must be acknowledged, celebrated, and reaffirmed.

The George W. Bush administration sent mixed signals during the campaign regarding the institutional bargain. One of George W. Bush's advisors, Condolezza Rice, created a stir when she hinted that the United States might want to reduce its commitment to the NATO peace keeping operation in Kosovo – and this raised a larger concern in foreign capitals about whether the United States would continue to provide leadership in the world's trouble spots. But the same foreign policy team has made "listening to our allies" a major theme. It remains to be seen which tendency comes to dominate the new administration and whether it is willing to renew the institutional bargain with Europe.

Second, the United States and Europe need to push forward with engagement on their many transatlantic disputes. David Aaron recently indicated that there are about thirty issues – mostly in the trade area – that are in play between Brussels and Washington.[18] He also suggests that there needs to be more self-conscious efforts to develop routine ways to resolve these disputes and identify emerging disputes before they overwhelm political leaders. Many of these disputes are more difficult to resolve than, say, similar disputes between the United States and Japan, simply because there are so many more layers of complexity in the bargaining process. But a search for institutional reforms that make bargaining and compromise easier would be most welcome. At the same time, we should not get too excited about these disputes – and put them in wider perspective. There is over $1 trillion in trade and investment that cross the Atlantic. It would be surprising, indeed, if thorny issues and economic disputes did not arise. The genius of the Atlantic order is that the allies have found ways to contain and diffuse these controversies. These institutional mechanisms must continuously be upgraded.

Third, the EU and the United States need to continue to search for new institutional innovations that will facilitate joint leadership. It is not enough to rely on the annual US-EU summit, the G-7 process, or NATO to provide the *ad hoc* structure in which the leaders of Europe and the United States steer their regional and global agenda. It would be useful, perhaps, if a high-level commission were set up to look into the adequacy of inter-government consultation and coordination mechanisms. In some areas, such as finance and security, there are well-established institutional mechanisms for joint policy making. But in others – such as the new transnational issues and more general political matters – the two entities are not well connected.

Fourth, one of the sources of stability in the Atlantic region is the dense set of private transnational relations and networks. These should be fostered. Of course, even without encouragement, the societies of Europe and the United States will continue to interweave. The more infused the Atlantic world is with transnational groups and organisations, the more these countries are likely to cooperate and act with a common purpose. Private groups operating across the democratic world foster stronger common political identity. This is the classic phenomenon of cosmopolitanism. The Trilateral Commission, the Atlantic Council, Atlantic business councils, and hundreds of other organisations have an accumulative impact. Moreover, these private transnational groups act as a sort of private political system conveying views and building political coalitions that favour cooperation. Sometimes private transnational groups can work out common policy goals and collaborate to push those goals on their respective governments. To the extent they foster a common political identity, this process reinforces the prospects for cooperative security relationships.[19]

Fifth, the leaders of the Atlantic world must redouble their efforts to talk about the Atlantic world as a distinct political community. As I argued earlier, this is a critical source of stable order in the Atlantic – we think of this region as united by a common set of values and a common political identity. The region may be held together by "interests", but it will be more durable if it is also held together by "identity". Europe would not be able to pursue such a profound agenda of political and economic unity if the various countries of Europe only had geography in common. It is history, culture, and values that these countries have in common. But identities are not simply given by nature. They are constructed. Europe and the United States must continuously act to construct this common identity. Political engineering is made easier if the political identities of the parts are similar and congruent.

Finally, the United States must deal with its unipolar power problem. American power has become more provocative and it is increasingly an obstacle to cooperation. The United States must realise that the asymmetries of power that have long marked the post-World War II political landscape have been rendered more acceptable when that power was institutionalised. The United States between 1944 and 1951 pushed for a post-war order that was built around institutions. Other countries were willing to cooperate with the United States because they were able to conclude that the United States would not exploit or abuse its power position. Of course, abuses did occur. There has always been a low-grade American parochialism and periodic departures from rule-based multilateralism. American allies have rolled their eyes and complained, but the unilateralism and abusive dominance was never sufficiently extreme to trigger a wholesale reordering of the post-war order.

The question today is not whether the United States has too much power to maintain the stability of the post-war Atlantic order but whether that power remains sufficiently institutionalised to keep the order stable. The important point for European and American leaders to remember is that they have fifty years of institutions and practices that have kept the order.

Notes

1   "The widening gulf between the self-images and aspirations of the United States and Europe emerge almost daily now in disputes over cashmere sweaters and bananas, the human costs of U.S. warplanes barrelling over Alpine ski resorts, and the debility of allied diplomacy in the Cold War's long aftermath". Jim Hoagland, "Prepare Together for Different Trans-Atlantic Relations", *International Herald Tribune*, 10 March 1999.

2   On the importance of the Cold War for the creation of an open post-Cold War economic order, see Robert Gilpin, *The Challenge of Global Capitalism* (Princeton: Princeton University Press, 2000).

3   See Stephen M. Walt, "The Ties that Fray: Why Europe and America Are Drifting Apart", *The National Interest*, No. 54 (Winter 1998/99), pp. 3-11.

4   Quoted in Craig R. Whitney, "NATO at 50: With Nations at Odds, Is It a Misalliance?", *The New York Times*, 15 February 1999, p. A 7.

5   See Laura Silber, "Divisions are Deep over New War Crimes Court", *Financial Times*, 6 April 1998.

6   Flora Lewis, "Uncomfortable With U.S. Power, Real or Illusory", *International Herald Tribune*, 14 May 1999, p. 5.

7   Whitney, "NATO at 50", *The New York Times*, 15 February 1999, p. A 7.

8   This argument is developed in G. John Ikenberry, *After Victory: Institutions, Strategic Restraint and the Rebuilding of Order After Major War* (Princeton: Princeton University Press, 2000).

9   Quoted in Mary N. Hampton, "NATO at the Creation: U.S. Foreign Policy, West Germany, and the Wilsonian Impulse", *Security Studies*, Vol. 4, No. 3 (Spring 1995), p. 625.

10 This argument is made in G. John Ikenberry, "The Myth of Post-Cold War Chaos", *Foreign Affairs*, Vol. 75, No. 3 (May/June 1996).

11 Truman, "Address on Foreign Economic Policy", Baylor University, March 6, 1947.

12 See "Statement on the North Atlantic Pact, Department of State", 20 March 1949, *Foreign Relations of the United States*, 1949, IV, pp. 240-1.

13 This point is made in Peter Foot, "America and the Origins of the Atlantic Alliance: A Reappraisal", in Joseph Smith, ed., *The Origins of NATO* (Exeter: University of Exeter Press, 1990).

14 "Minutes of the Fourth Meeting of the Washington Exploratory Talks on Security", 8 July 1948, *Foreign Relations of the United States*, 1948, III, pp. 163-69.

15 Robert B. Zoellick, "21st Century Strategies of the Trilateral Countries: In Concert or Conflict? The United States", paper presented at annual meeting of the Trilateral Commission, Spring 1999, p. 5.

16 It is widely agreed that the Cold War facilitated Atlantic cooperation. But it is also true that many of the most contentious issues in U.S.-European relations in the post-World War II era were related to the conduct of Western security policy toward the Soviet Union. The Euro-missiles controversy, Star Wars, sanctions controversies, and other security matters troubled the Atlantic pact. The two regions may have less reason to cooperate - but they also have fewer reasons to disagree!

17 The delicate matter of Europe's common foreign and security policy must be rendered compatible with the long-term preservation of the Atlantic alliance.

18 David L. Aaron, "The Need for a Transatlantic Early Warning System", *European Affairs*, Vol. 1, No. 2 (Spring 2000), pp. 24-28.

19 This is the argument in Bruce Cronin, *Community under Anarchy: Transnational Identity and the Evolution of Cooperation* (New York: Columbia University Press, 1999).

3 NATO Forever!

YVES BOYER

Introduction

In almost every Chancellery in Europe, in most forums of discussion on European security within "informed circles" the present nature, the role and the place of NATO are considered as an intangible given. The present security arrangement linking the two sides of the Atlantic looks as robust as the walls of Jericho before they broke down.

Unnoticeably however, the dynamics of the international system are transforming the context that gave NATO its past resilience. Perceptions of the future consequences of that evolution on the Alliance now even resound in the United States. Reflecting on the summit commemorating the 50th anniversary of the Washington treaty, a renown editorialist from the Washington Post commented that "several score presidents and prime ministers will parade noisily in the reflected glory of the transatlantic unity while the termites of discord gnaw quietly at the cultural and economic foundation of history's most successful international joint venture".[1] Richard Haas has pointed out the uncertainties in regard to NATO's fate: "Alliances depend on clear foes and obvious scenarios for their cohesion. It is precisely the absence of such clarity and predictability that capture the emerging nature of post-Cold war politics".[2]

However, for some European countries NATO has acquired a holistic dimension, a systemic function. It allows them to succumb into a comfortable torpor in buying, from the United States, security protection at the cheapest cost. They, thus, mask the hollowness of their military posture and clothe their international impotence behind the illusion of still weighing on international security affairs through their heavyweight proxy. Indeed, with the exception of Britain, Germany and France, which amount for almost 80% of the military spending of EU's countries, one can notice that European members of NATO have lost their cold war military strength. Their overall military capabilities no longer represent a coherent system of forces. Still having valuable assets in specific domains, their military apparatus is largely fragmented and dramatically over costly for what they can achieve. The solution chosen to overcome growing global military inefficiency has been finding niches in the overall system of forces brought by the United States.

In this manner, many European members of NATO answer the admonishments coming from America whose future presence in Europe would largely be linked to "the ability of the European countries to be engaged in high tech; [it] is going to be a central part of maintaining the strength of the alliance".[3] In a very sophisticated manner, the United States has been keen to provide to their consenting European allies those niches and also sometimes reward faithful allies. During the Kosovo crisis, the Netherlands Air Force, performed very well in Air defence missions, having been given the same high tech electronic devices that only the U.S. Air Force F 16's possessed at that time. Such bonus, parsimoniously attributed, do largely explain the conservatism and the positive if not the very warm appreciation that many European military circles express to their American counterparts.

This posture has however its costs in economical, military and political fields. In military affairs the implicit arrangements, i.e. protection through integration in the overall U.S. military architecture, annihilate most of the margin of manoeuvre Europeans countries have when guns are used. The war in Kosovo has exemplified this situation. As stated by Admiral Leighton Smith, a former NATO commander in chief in Bosnia in 1996, "the United States squeezed its NATO partners so hard during the Kosovo air war that many came away with a never-again attitude towards joining another American-led offensive operation outside alliance borders".[4]

The Balkans crisis and noticeably the Kosovo war however awoke Europeans about the state of their respective military apparatus, their dependency on U.S. goodwill and more generally on EU's lack of ability to adequately respond to such type of event. A phase of redeeming gave impetus within the EU to develop the embryo of a EU political-military capacity. The process started, in December 1998, between France and Britain with the Saint-Malo declaration on defence. Few months later in the midst of the Balkans crisis, the German government having, at that time, the EU's presidency had been going along the same lines. At a EU informal meeting, Joschka Fischer set forwards ideas about a common European security and defence policy that would enable the Union to take and implement quick military decisions in crisis without recourses to the assets and capabilities of the U.S.-dominated NATO alliance.[5] Immediately after the air campaign against the Yugoslav Federation, during their first meeting in 4 years, British and Italian Prime ministers Blair and D'Amato unveiled a proposal "to set criteria for improved and strengthened Europeans defence capabilities".[6] Almost at the same time, it was agreed that a high-ranking European public figure with responsibility for dealing with Common Foreign and Security Policy (CFSP) problems be appointed. This paved the way, in June 1999, to the designation of M. Javier Solana, a former Secretary General to NATO, as "Mr. CFSP". His nomination could have been seen as a rapprochement, if not a form of vassalage, of the EU's CFSP with NATO. A view rapidly dismissed by French European affairs minister, Pierre Moscovici who, then, used a metaphor borrowed from a football game, "when an important club succeeded in acquiring a champion, the one which is weakened is the club which loses his champion".[7]

In June 2000 when presenting French goals of the EU's presidency, Jacques Chirac, declared that the ambition of France was "to make Europe a major global player...our ambition should be to make Europe a leading political player in tomorrow's world, and we must make sure that this ambition has wide popular support".[8] He added that

> Any of the fifteen members of the Union who wish to become part of this commitment will be welcome. But those who do not wish to make the same commitment, either because they do not have a tradition of alignment or because they do not wish to commit the necessary resources, should not prevent the bolder members from advancing. It is only natural that there should be front-runners in any group that make faster progress towards a mutually agreed goal. I think defence is an area where it is natural for more far-reaching co-operation to exist within a small group of countries.[9]

Almost at the same time, Joschka Fischer, the German Foreign affairs minister made proposals that, by and large, were going in the same direction as the French ones. Stating that the European unification process was the most important challenge confronting the Europeans, he advocated the creation of a European Federation adding that if it proved to be impossible, he would then favour the creation of an "avant-garde" comprising few Sates, forming a "centre of gravity" deciding to move forwards.[10] As an echo, few weeks later speaking at the Reichstag in Berlin, president Chirac evoked the idea, he already mentioned in his Elysée palace speech, of a pioneer group of States moving ahead of the other members of the Union in integrating their policies particularly in the field of defence.

One can draw from the consistency of French, as well as from German attitudes, that EU's efficiency has to be preserved whatever be the new parameters of an enlarged Union because there is an irrepressible need to weight on world affairs in order to "make the EU both a model and a player in the effort to control globalisation".[11] In that short sentence, the French Foreign Affairs minister summarized a vision for the future of the EU that should not be rapidly dismissed because of its French origin. The EU can become: 1) a magnet for the rest of Europe which brings peace, stability and prosperity through its extraordinary achievements accomplished in the last fifty years; 2) a power centred around a core group of countries capitalizing from EU developments and capabilities to bear upon international affairs in a multipolar world. Accordingly, defence has to be gradually included in the inner perimeter of the Union.

The process launched within the EU for a first round of building a rapprochement on defence culminated with the "headline goals" conference in Brussels (November 2000) and the Nice summit of the EU (December 2000) where it was collectively agreed by the 15 to create permanent politico-military structures for crisis management and a Rapid Reaction Force. This process has been undertaken with pragmatism (moves have been made step by step; quarrels on principles were put aside; the architecture was inspired by NATO), efficiency (concrete needs Vs institutional questions) and solidarity (the progresses made at Cologne, Helsinki, Santa Maria de Feira and Nice summits have been collectively prepared and agreed). This is a successful first round of developments of EU's defence policy. It shall lead by 2003 the Europeans to possess a political-military structure giving the EU autonomous capacity of assessing a crisis situation and possibly use a rapid reaction force. According to the French Defence minister, this force could be employed after approval by the EU's Council either on the European scene or within the framework of a UN resolution on another theatre of operation.[12] These achievements were in coherence with the qualitative transformation of the Union where members states decides and implement common policies on a wide range of domains that now includes defence matters ranging from strategic intelligence to defence industries.

How can it go differently when increasingly the international environment will leave no chance for countries like Belgium, Sweden, Austria, Portugal, Greece (not to mention other smaller countries) which respective population is as big as half of Mexico city or even for bigger EU's nations, to exert influence on events which may deeply affect security in Europe? Shall Europeans continue to stick to past obsessions or habits: Russian threat, Baltic instability, maintenance of U.S. leadership on European security affairs, etc. when their common horizon is made of uncertainties ranging from a wide variety of risks, by example, terrorism, mass migration, the spread of AIDS, provoking the collapse of large part of Africa with its tremendous potential repercussion in security matters, and, last but not least, to the apparition of superpowers with a global reach such as Brazil, India or China? In moving into the 21st century, it would be a mistake if not a collective suicide for Europe, to bend to an apparent easy solution in security and defence that may lead to a division of labour: Europe would assume non-military responsibilities and NATO would be left as the sole security actor.[13]

The Pressing Need for "*L'Europe Puissance*"

Initially, the European project was aimed at definitively putting to an end fratricidal wars that, twice in the last century, have devastated, wounded and weakened Europe. Later, it became implicit that the partial abandonment of sovereignty, without which the European project would not take substance, could not be politically sustained in the long term if it was not also aimed at collectively acquiring more strength and capacities to weight on world affairs.

Indeed, the disappearance of the Soviet threat that bound together Western democracies has opened the gates to an international landscape that is disconcerting in many ways. In Europe, fifteen new states have appeared in the 1990s. On the one hand, greater regional or trans-national integration (APEC, ASEAN Regional Forum, OSCE, EU, NAFTA, etc.) help increase stability and growing interdependence. On the other hand, disintegration or fragmentation of state structures are provoking tensions and upheavals as seen in the former Yugoslavia, Caucasus, South-East Asia or in Africa.

The many consequences of these evolutions are indeed far from being totally appreciated. Their influence on international relations is combining with a series of deep economical, technological and societal transformations that raise the question of defining adequate European roles and interests for the years ahead. Among those transformations, it is worth mentioning the shift in the centre of gravity of world competition from arms race to high-tech economic development and market access.

This evolution is blurring the traditional pattern of alliances that, for the West, were aimed during the Cold War at building a common unified defence under U.S. leadership against the same threatening adversary. The threat disappeared, diverging geopolitical interests and economic competition, which were toned down, are now surfacing among allies. At the same time, the changing nature of the European construction – whatever painful be the process – with the single currency, the implementation of the goals defined by the Maastricht treaty, and the perspective of enlargement of the European Union, is affecting the balance of power within the Atlantic alliance. In this context, it is obvious that the EU and NATO cannot be placed on the same ground. Relationship between the EU and NATO has to take into account the difference of nature of the two structures. EU is a complex and profound political endeavour. NATO is a traditional alliance, unequal in its functioning which binds, with increasing difficulties, the two sides of the Atlantic.

What will be then the meaning of U.S. leadership when military affairs– where Washington still enjoys a clear supremacy – have lost their past importance in European affairs, when the goal of European monetary union is to act on the world market on equal footing with the dollar, the other instrument of American leadership, and when European defence is on the rise?

In addition, new risks stemming out from the development of terrorism, ethnic rivalries, and the spreading of "grey zones", where order is no longer guaranteed by national or international control, are proliferating with direct or indirect consequences on European society. Accordingly, European security is no longer solely the domain of military forces but will require, for this type of risks, co-ordinated measures and, integrated at the EU level, actions by intelligence, custom, police (and possibly military forces) as one begins to witness among the EU nations part of the Schengen agreement.

In order to be able to adequately respond to changes on the world arena, the EU needs to develop the its military capacities. It has to possess enough forces for high-intensity operations using high-tech weapons systems integrated in the framework of innovative concepts and doctrines of employment. At the other end of the spectrum of military capabilities, a whole new range of options are emerging. They derive from the growing role that preventive diplomacy is expected to play in that it is altering significantly the ways by which armed forces have to be employed. Peacekeeping operations are multinational in essence and compel European armed forces to define adapted doctrines and equipment to complex situation mixing a variety of tasks about belligerents with regard to whom neutrality shall prevailed in most cases. Adequate military instruments for intervention to help stabilizing situations in Europe or in adjacent zones, particularly in the Mediterranean Basin have to be set up by the Europeans. This has begun with measures agreed in Nice. In themselves, these recent evolutions are good examples as to why the EU shall going in the direction of *"l'Europe puissance"*.

"L'Europe Puissance" and the American Question

The development of EU's monetary, technological and military capabilities is challenging an Atlantic order based on a covenant established fifty years ago between the United States and European countries when the Soviets posed an existential threat to Western democracies. Such an order was based on few principles such as: a shared democratic order; economic openness; institutional arrangement to facilitate the solution of disputes; a co-operative security order with NATO at its centre.

Nowadays, even if most of those principles remain valid by and large, a malaise has appeared between the two sides of the Atlantic. Contrary to a view widely spread in the United Sates, a so-called imbalance of power between the two sides of the Atlantic is not at the roots of the malaise. Indeed, if one takes the economic domain, the EU's economy is in a state of recovery and prosperity, its fundamentals in economy are sane, while the United States suffers from being the world's most important debtor. In the monetary domain, the preponderance of the dollar is in jeopardy with the venue of the euro. As stated by Joschka Fischer "if the Euro does not come, the United States will define the developments of a globalised economy in the 21st century. Decision will be made in Washington and in New York".[14] The threat posed by the euro has been implicitly acknowledged in Washington as illustrated by the many attempts made to limit the influence of the Euro countries in the executive body of the IMF.[15]

In the technological field, contrary to a superficial assumption, the discrepancy between the two sides of the Atlantic is not so dramatic at the detriment of the Europeans. It suffices to mention in the civilian sector, Airbus, Ariane space launcher or the cellular phone, are domains where the Europeans are surpassing the United States. In the military field, according to a survey made by French defence officials, with European counterparts, after the war in Kosovo, on forty-seven critical military technologies, the United States is ahead in fifteen domains, the Europeans in three and parity does exist for the remaining twenty nine. Addressing this issue during a visit in the United States, the French Defence minister underlined the fact that very often the gap concerns capacities more than technologies, adding that the example of the civilian sector shows that Europe is not lagging behind America.[16] In the social domain, here again, the EU may be proud of its achievements. Before the visit of then president Clinton to Germany, in June 2000, Chancellor Schroeder was keen to point out the success of the European social model which, did he say, was far advanced than the American one.

If the malaise is not due to an imbalance of power, at least in the civilian domain, what is the reason for the difficulties in the transatlantic relations? Probably because after having experienced together the existential threat posed by the former Soviet bloc, each side of the Atlantic has now a specific agenda. On the European side, after the collapse of the Soviet empire ones have had the perception of entering a long period of strategic transformation and, that the future balance of power in the new world shall encompass the European Union as a player.[17]

On the U.S. side, the stakes that are confronting the United States are no longer the same than in Europe as exemplified by the National Missile Defence program.[18] In fact, the difficulties between the two sides of the Atlantic are largely due to the European integration project itself that, according to a senior member of the Council on Foreign Relations, "poses a head-on challenge to American habits of leadership. U.S. leaders have been raised with a sense of pre-eminence and an expectation that friends will usually follow the U.S. lead".[19] A basic U.S. interest continues to be that of continental Europe not being dominated by a single rival power, yet today that power is the European Union itself.

At the same time, the transformation of the internal scene in U.S. politics affects transatlantic relations. Foreign countries have indeed experienced growing difficulties in dealing and negotiating with Washington because of the excessive impact of domestic considerations on U.S. foreign and security policy. In trade areas, by example, U.S. position has been increasingly entangled with internal dispute. The Executive Branch of the U.S. government has been overtaken by initiatives coming from the Congress and is unable to stop them before they complicate relationship with Washington's trade partners. The Helms-Burton and D'Amato legislation highlighted this shift of political influence over the course of American trade position. Not only does it mean that it becomes increasingly difficult to negotiate with America on these matters but, to reverse the famous question asked by Henry Kissinger years ago if there would ever be a single phone to call in Europe, the same question can now be raised to Washington where *"the phone numbers are multiplying"*.[20] It also means that U.S. internal politics has a global reach with significant consequences, albeit not always with legitimacy, with to foreign countries. This evolution was underlined by U.S.

observers like William Pfaff commenting that: "The Congress [has] predilection for attempting to legislate foreign policy for others countries".[21] Commenting the presidential campaign, the *Financial Times* expressed its fears that America may move towards unilateralism.[22] The latter in foreign policy is tempting for Washington: In the international security domain it is particularly worth noting the apparent determination expressed by the new administration and whatever be the attitude of other powers to develop a national missile defence (NMD).

Does American unilateralism represent an excess of power that is leading the United States to thus be willing to assert its political, economical and strategic interests? Or does it, on the contrary, represent the fact that the United States, which contains only 5% of the world population and 20% of the world wealth, possesses a growing sense of uncertainty about the future role to be played by America in an international environment where it is hard to discern the line of force? Is it not the result of an evolution in the relationship between the Executive and the Legislative branches in the United States when, increasingly, U.S. foreign policy is tinted for internal reasons with unilateral decisions at the international level?

At a time when Washington has a dominant position in military, cultural and technological domains, greater unilateralism in U.S. foreign policy provokes uneasiness. In France, this uneasiness has been underscored by President Jacques Chirac and his Foreign Affairs Minister Huber Védrine. Both leaders outlined that this unilateralism could possess a perfume of hegemony from a *"hyper-puisance"*. Such posture would be largely related to the absence of other centres of power at the world level. This vision is also exposed in a document written by the EU Commissioner Chris Patten:

> les États-Unis ne sont pas isolationnistes mais sont enclins à l'unilatéralisme – et cette tendance sera renforcée si l'Europe ne montre pas qu'elle en fait plus pour elle-même. L'unilatéralisme des États-Unis accroît également le champ de la contribution que l'UE, dans un monde qui s'efforce d'élaborer un cadre économique, juridique et politique multilatéral efficace pour contenir les passions des États, aider à gérer leurs relations et contribuer à la globalisation maîtrisée.[23]

Conclusion

Undoubtedly, the development of the EU has modified the very nature of the covenant established between the United States and Western Europe fifty years ago. EU success promises Europe eventual parity with America and an escape from the role of junior partner to which it was relegated. This evolution has been constantly fought by the United States. To limit or to contain this nascent EU's international role, various recipes have been implemented in the United States with very limited results. Sometimes, the U.S. "internal card" has been used: if the Europeans do not take care of the consequences of their choices on transatlantic relations, the U.S. Congress may decide to leave Europe alone; sometimes it has been the "German card": Washington guarantees against any temptation from Germany to play alone; the "seduction card" has also been used highlighting the benefits Europeans may draw from collaborating under U.S. leadership in political, commercial or technological fields; lastly the "division card" has also been used as exemplified in spring 2000 when U.S. Senator Phil Gramm proposed that the UK join NAFTA.

Nothing stemmed out from those various attempts because the centre of gravity of the new Europe is henceforth focused on developing the EU, rather than on NATO, which has lost the centrality it used to have during the cold war. Even if Washington remains a key ally, the U.S. card is no longer the most important parameter when looking at Europe's future. The future belongs to the Europeans themselves. Their collective resources are impressive, their common will to further develop the EU has been a constant and key feature in EU's nations for at least fifty years for the six initial members of the family. What is now lacking is a psychological transformation aimed at adjusting their behaviour and their representation of the world to this new reality on the world stage that represents the European Union.

Notes

1   "Prepare together for different Trans-Atlantic relations", Jim Hoagland, the *Washington Post*, 10 March 1999.
2   Richard Haas, "What makes a Legend? Some foreign policy tips?" *International Herald Tribune*, 26 September 1997.
3   Robert Hunter, U.S. representative to NATO, "USA warns of 3 tier NATO technology drift", *Jane's Defence Weekly*, 1 October 1997.
4   Admiral Leighton Smith quoted in "Kosovo has been hard on NATO", George Will, *International Herald Tribune*, 21 April 2000.
5   "EU may need own military staff to act without NATO, says Bonn", *Financial Times*, 15 March 1999.
6   "UK and Italy in call to defence group", *Financial Times*, 19 July 1999.
7 . Pierre Moscovici, interview with the TV cable network LCI, 7 June 1999.
8   Speech by Jacques Chirac to the Presidential Committee of the WEU Parliamentary Assembly and the Auditors from the IHEDN, Elysée Palace, Paris, May 30, 2000.
9   Ibid.
10 Joschka Fischer, speech at Humboldt University, Berlin, 12 May 2000.
11 "On course of the French presidency of the European Union", article by Hubert Védrine, minister of Foreign Affairs, published in the European press, Paris, 28 June 2000.
12 Press Conference of the French Defence minister, M. Alain Richard, Brussel, 20 November 2000.
13 On that issue see by example the declaration of the Chairman of the Defence commission   at the French National Assembly, Paul Quilès, interview with *Le Monde*, 1 December 1998.
14 J. Fischer, in "German Green Leader backs EMU", *Financial Times*, 12 August 1997.
15 "Rubin seeks to limit Europe's influence", *Financial Times*, 26 April 1999.
16 Speech by Alain Richard, CSIS, Washington, 18 February 2000.
17 See Lionel Jospin, Prime Minister, speech at the Saint-Mandrier naval station, 4 March 1998.

18   On the relationship between NMD and European defence, see "Le projet de bouclier antimissile américain: un Cheval de Troie américain?" *Le Figaro*, 9 March 2001.

19   "Drifting apart", Daniel Tarullo, *International Herald Tribune*, 12 December 1999.

20   Pascal Lamy, Trade Commissioner of the European Union, speech to the American Enterprise Institute, Washington, 18 December 2000.

21   William Pfaff, "U.S. ambitions outstrip its domestic appetite", *International Herald Tribune*", 10 July 1997.

22   *Financial Times*, editorial, 15 december 2000.

23   "Relations Extérieures: Exigences, Contraintes et Priorités", Chris Patten, 10 juin 2000.   "The United States is not isolationist, but is inclined to unilateralism, and this tendency will be reinforced if Europe does not demonstrate that it can do more for itself. American unilateralism also increases the range of contribution in which the EU, in a world that continues to attempt to implement an efficient multilateral economic, legal and political framework in order to contain the passions of states, helps to manage EU-U.S. relations and contribute to the taming of the processes of globalisation". (Translation by Hall Gardner.)

4 The European Security and Defence Identity: Birth Pangs of a New Atlanticism

KARSTEN D. VOIGT

Introduction

Europe and America are bound closer today more than ever before by shared interests cultural and economic ties and, above all, by modern means of communication. This growing closeness opens up new opportunities, but also leads to the emergence of new sources of friction. This friction is not a sign of imminent failure, rather an unavoidable side effect of the transatlantic success. If we use these opportunities to renew relations between the two sides of the Atlantic, this growing integration could lead to a new Atlanticism and a Euro-Atlantic community marked by democratic stability and economic prosperity.

The most important challenge and task facing the Euro-Atlantic partnership today is to jointly shape and manage globalisation in all its forms. The EU and the United States are each other's most important partners and their concerted action is indispensable.

Changes in America

Over the last decade Europe and America have changed drastically, as have their respective roles in the international system. The United States is the only remaining superpower and, for the first time in history, has neither opponents nor rivals of equal stature. It is the only country in the world that is in the position to make lasting global projections of military strength. It has the strongest economy in the world. It is easier for the United States than for any other country to impose its own ideas as worldwide norms, in isolated cases even going it alone. Many Europeans still harbour feelings of cultural superiority over the United States; but the days when this was justified are long gone. The United States has long been setting standards on a worldwide basis, not just for the general populace, but has also been leading the field in the traditional cultural spheres, for example in research and teaching, or film and modern art. Its global role is rooted in an unprecedented blend of economic power, the ability to set the global cultural agenda and military superiority. Never before has American self-esteem had less reason to use benchmarks other than its own as the guiding principle for worldwide action.

Changes in Europe

Europe has changed too. It is in the process of turning into a player with a single voice on the world stage which, although far from being as powerful as the United States in military terms, can nevertheless play in the same league, particularly in trade, economic and monetary policy.

The enlargement of the EU to include Sweden, Finland and Austria as well as the territory of the former GDR and the launch of accession negotiations with now twelve, out of thirteen, additional candidates will mean that the EU – with the exception of Russia and Ukraine in particular – will increasingly be able to speak for Europe as a whole. The deepening of integration, including the involvement of further political spheres such as domestic, legal and asylum policy, and the increased use of majority voting have particularly strengthened the EU's internal ability to act. The completion of the European internal market on 1 January 1993 and the introduction of the Euro have made Europe an equal partner of the United States in economic and monetary issues, enjoying almost equal influence, not just on paper but also in reality, and thus quite rightly also increasingly self-confident.

In the field of Common Foreign and Security Policy (CFSP) a comparable development will not be possible in the foreseeable future. However, there has been considerable progress in this sphere during the last few years, as the elaboration of the European Security and Defence Policy (ESDP) clearly shows. The determination of Europeans to do more here was a natural progression from the painfully clear European weaknesses during the military action in Bosnia and Kosovo. It is, however, also in line with the logic of the European integration process.

Within Europe, the self-perception and the role of Germany have also changed. This was where the East-West conflict was at its strongest, the dependence on United States protection at its greatest and the number of stationed troops and nuclear weapons at its highest. Today, unified Germany is surrounded by friends and cooperation partners and no longer feels its territorial security to be threatened. Its troops have been drastically cut, the foreign troops stationed on its territory completely, or at least largely, withdrawn. For the foreseeable future, Germany will, to a much lesser extent, need the transatlantic partnership to protect it from external threats. Instead, Germany needs it so that it can, together with the United States, secure democracy, security and economic prosperity in the whole of Europe, even beyond the current borders of NATO and the EU. In other words, Germany is no longer solely a consumer but primarily a producer of stability and security in Europe.

The European Interest in Transatlantic Cooperation

In contrast to the Cold War years, during which all NATO states were exposed to a common massive threat, the question of the joint reaction to regional conflicts in Europe, either out of area, or in the immediate vicinity of Europe, is now at the top of NATO's agenda. The current momentum for Europe's and America's joint security actions is primarily being generated by questions of regional stabilization, crisis prevention and crisis management, stabilization through political and economic integration and multilateral cooperation. The question is whether and how the United States and Europe can cooperate within the 'security framework' encompassing NATO, the EU, the UN and the OSCE, in order to prevent or deal with regional crises and conflicts in Europe and on its periphery. Common strategies on the multilateral incorporation and integration of Central, Eastern and South-Eastern Europe need to be developed.

Worldwide, the transatlantic partners must contain security risks in the broadest sense, in particular through cooperation in preventing the further proliferation of weapons of mass destruction and their delivery systems, but also in environmental hazards, international terrorism or organized drug trafficking, to name a few examples.

With regard to collective defence and American involvement in Europe, we now only have to cover the residual risk. Moreover, the U.S. presence in Europe continues to act as an additional safeguard against the resurgence of rivalries within Europe. Good transatlantic relations - including an ongoing American presence in Europe - are thus also in the interests of Europeans, particularly Germans.

U.S. security policy dominance is not set to diminish in the foreseeable future – even after the successful launch of a common ESDP. Germany supports the strengthening of the EU in security and defence policy, not to cut ties between Europe and the United States but to ensure that Europe remains fit for a true partnership with the United States.

While some in the United States eye the ESDP with suspicion – particular with regard to France – there are also calls for Europeans, above all from Congress, to finally implement a system of real burden-sharing, to take more responsibility for crisis management in Europe and not to simply always call for American leadership in an emergency. On the one hand, the very Europeans who call for Europe's greater autonomy from the United States are also those who demand that the United States defend Europe when the going gets tough. On the other hand, the very Americans who harbour reservations about the ESDP often call upon Europeans to play a greater role in joint operations in and around Europe, or even to tackle European crises on their own. This shows that differences in analysis often do not just exist between Europe and America but also within Europe and the United States.

The European Security and Defence Policy

The Aim of the ESDP

The Treaty of Amsterdam and the subsequent decisions taken in Cologne, Helsinki, Feira and Nice on the development of a common ESDP all aim at rendering the EU capable of being able to contribute to international security, thus further advancing the EU on its way towards a political union that is truly able to act. Once these decisions are fully implemented, the EU will marshal a considerable range of both civil and military means to engage autonomously and efficiently in crisis prevention and crisis management.

However, to emphasize the matter right away, European collective defence is, and will remain, only NATO's responsibility. The European Council in Helsinki 1999 clearly spells out that EU-led operations shall only take place "where the Alliance as a whole is not engaged".

The development of a common ESDP was only possible because, firstly, the Balkans crises showed that such a policy was needed to complement the task of collective defence as covered by NATO, and, secondly, because the non-Alliance EU members redefined their own security identity in such a way that they could subscribe to the Petersberg tasks themselves.

To act on the whole range of crisis management scenarios, the EU needs to have the necessary operational capacities at its disposal, both in the civilian and in the military field. This purpose is served by the headline and capabilities goals developed for the military and non-military spheres, whose implementation is intended to ensure that the EU has the means at its immediate disposal for operations in a crisis situation.

This also involves developing decision-making mechanisms, so that the EU bodies will be equipped with the ability to react quickly in deciding on, and carrying out, an operation. On the institutional side, we want to concentrate discussions on instances of crisis management in the standing Political and Security Committee (PSC), which is about to be formally set up in early 2001. This body shall be advised on military matters by the future Military Committee and on civilian matters by a Committee on Civilian Aspects of Crisis Management. These bodies will be supported in their conduct of operations, planning and coordination on the military side by the future Military Staff (and by NATO), and on the civilian side by the Coordinating Mechanism for Civilian Aspects of Crisis Management established in the Council Secretariat.

Institutional Questions

The PSC will deal with all CFSP questions, including ESDP, under the umbrella of the EU's unified institutional framework. In case of a crisis, the PSC will assume political control and strategic direction of crisis management operations in accordance with the guidelines laid down by the General Affairs Council. A Military Committee tasked to counsel the PSC and a Military Staff is about to be established in early 2001. The Committee on Civilian Aspects of Crisis Management was already set up as a permanent body in May 2000.

In the meantime, since March 2000 an interim PSC, which as a standing Political Committee (under the direction of the PC in capital city formation) has been discussing general CFSP questions and, in particular, elaborating recommendations for a further development of the ESDP. Also, an Interim Military Body (IMB) has been established as a precursor of a future Military Committee. Furthermore, military experts have been seconded to the Secretariat of the Council, who are to form the core of the future Military Staff.

Status of the High Representative (HR)

Apart from the tasks defined in Article 26 of the Amsterdam Treaty, Helsinki gives High Representative Solana a special mandate to advance the work on the ESDP, in cooperation with the Presidency. In times of crises, the HR will chair the PSC.

Military capabilities

It is especially in this field that astonishing progress, at least measured by EU decision-making standards, has been achieved in the short time period since the Cologne European Council in June 1999. This underlines the seriousness of the efforts undertaken in the field of ESDP.

In line with the headline goal agreed upon in Helsinki in December 1999, the EU should be capable, by 2003, of deploying troops up to corps-sized level (between 50,000 and 60,000 troops, plus appropriate air and naval elements) within 60 days for a crisis management operation and to sustain such an operation for at least one year. It is considered particularly urgent that serious deficits in the fields of command and control capabilities, reconnaissance and strategic transport (known as collective capability goals) be addressed. One element that should be mentioned in this context is the creation of a European air transport command, as suggested by Germany and confirmed by the Franco-German Summit of 30 November 1999.

The EU's Foreign and Defence Ministers are responsible for the fulfillment of headline and capability goals. This will include an explicit reference concerning the recourse to NATO defence planning, including the planning mechanisms valid for PfP partners.

Improving military capabilities is of central importance, as this will not only enhance the EU's capabilities, but also contribute significantly to the strengthening of those of NATO, especially in the area of non-Article 5 operations. At the Capabilities Commitment Conference held in November 2000,

EU member states, non-EU European Allies and states who are candidates for accession to the EU pledged their first contributions to the headline and capabilities goals. This implementation of the ESDP decisions is the most obvious expression of the commitment of the European member states of both NATO and the EU toward a better burden sharing within the Alliance and, at the same time, also a contribution to the implementation of the Defence Capabilities Initiative adopted by the NATO summit in Washington.

EU-NATO relationship

On the basis of decisions taken in Helsinki and Washington in 1999, EU and NATO took up work on the establishment of permanent arrangements for consultation and cooperation between EU and NATO, as well as on arrangements on EU access to NATO assets and capabilities ("Berlin plus"). At Nice, the European Council endorsed the EU's proposals for such arrangements. December's NAC in ministerial session welcomed the EU's proposal on permanent EU/NATO arrangements. However, the EU's proposal on "Berlin plus" – in particular the EU's demand for assured and automatic EU access to NATO planning capabilities – did not meet the approval of all Allies. Therefore, work will have to continue on all aspects of EU/NATO relations, as "nothing is agreed until everything is agreed".

Participation of European Non-EU NATO Member States
and Associated Members

In this area, too, tangible progress has been achieved in translating the mandate of Cologne into reality. The fixed basic rules on third-country participation in EU-led operations go far beyond the legal position, which NATO foresees for states participating in NATO-led non-Article 5 operations. For example, all states that participate in a EU-led operation are granted co-decision rights within the framework of the day-to-day management of the operations (paragraph 23). (Note: this area still requires a clearer regulation on the relationship between PSC and Operations Committee. This regulation will also further clarify the extent of co-decision rights). Furthermore, although the second sentence of paragraph 20 and paragraph 25 do not express this with sufficient precision, structures will be created that will permit consultations with these states, ahead of every Council decision regarding operations.

On 11 May 2000 meetings of the PSC with representatives of third states took place for the first time in the "15 + 15" format (EU member states, the 13 accession candidates, as well as Iceland and Norway), as well as the "15 + 6" format (EU member states, as well as the 6 non-EU European NATO members).

Civilian crisis management

The action plan on the improvement and strengthening of the EU's non-military capabilities adopted at the Helsinki European Council is intended to guarantee that the EU has at its disposal the full range of capabilities, non-military and military, and that the military option is thus only used as a last resort. The strengthening of the EU civilian crisis management capacities shall not only enable the EU to carry out autonomous missions, but, even more so, shape the EU-contribution to UN- and OSCE-led operations in such a way as to make them more effective and to provide for a higher EU profile in this context.

With the establishment of a Committee for Civilian Aspects of Crisis Management by the General Affairs Council on 22 March 2000 we have achieved a key goal in the development of the EU's civilian crisis management capabilities. The new committee will advise the PSC and other bodies on all-important issues relating to non-military crisis management and also have a coordinating function with other players in this field. The Coordinating Mechanism for civilian aspects of crisis management established in the Council Secretariat has already begun to operate and to advance the work on civilian crisis management. It has set up a database on civilian police and is now compiling data on experts on the rule of law.

In June 2000 the EC Feira Summit defined four priority areas in which the EU will strengthen its civilian capacities: Police, strengthening of rule of law and civilian administration, and civil protection. Feira also adopted concrete targets for police: By 2003, the EU wants to be able to provide up to 5,000 police officers, within this target, or at least 1,000 officers within 30 days for civilian missions. Under French presidency, work has concentrated on the implementation of the concrete targets for police – to which Germany has made a substantial contribution – as well as on the second priority "strengthening of rule of law". The Committee of Civilian Crisis Management has established contacts to the UN, OSCE and Council of Europe offices responsible for civilian crisis management.

At Nice, SG/HR Javier Solana and the European Commission presented a common report on improving the coherence and effectiveness of European action in the field of conflict prevention. Under the new Swedish presidency (in January 2001), we expect that work on all four priorities of civilian crisis management defined in Feira will progress. Germany will support the coming presidency in order to achieve a substantial result also in the next half a year.

Summary

To sum up, the outlines of the political and military structures for a European crisis management within the framework of the EU have been sharpened after the Amsterdam Treaty and the Summits in Cologne, Helsinki, Feira and Nice. The EU member states have proven their desire and ability to implement and further develop the basic decision of Cologne – to integrate the field of security and defence policy into the common activities under the institutional umbrella of the EU. Collective defence continues to be a task for NATO, because the ESDP, as initiated last year, limits itself to crisis management within the framework of the so-called Petersberg tasks. We do not intend to develop the EU into an organization that will compete with NATO. The EU will only carry out operations "where the Alliance as a whole is not engaged". However, in those fields it must be willing and able to act.

Nothing of what we have decided since Cologne is competing with NATO. On the contrary, the ESDP will strengthen the European pillar of NATO and enhance our ability to be a real partner for the United States. We neither want to act against NATO, nor do we want an unnecessary duplication of NATO structures. However, we Europeans must be able, in the medium term, to contribute to security on our own continent, at least in the case of smaller crises.

Furthermore, the agreements on consultations with third parties concerning the ESDP, and their participation in EU-led operations, do not aim at the complete adoption of the existing participation rights of WEU-associated states by the EU. In other words, there cannot be a direct integration of WEU into the EU. However, the new EU bodies will ensure effective consultation. Should third countries make available a considerable number of troops to a EU-led operation, they will have the same rights and obligations in the running of such an operation as the participating EU member states. The possibilities for the participation of these states will therefore not be merely limited to contributing troops.

Transatlantic Conflicts

The discussion on the ESDP is not the only difference in the field of international security between the two sides of the Atlantic. Differences of opinion are also emerging on the National Missile Defence (NMD) and on the importance of multilateralism.

National Missile Defence

I have lately heard European politicians occasionally ask whether the United States, which rightly demands a satisfactory European answer to its worries and questions concerning the ESDP, would be willing to react with equally constructive openness to European worries and questions concerning the U.S. concept to introduce NMD systems.

I personally am one of those in Europe who have been pointing out that the United States has legitimate and understandable reasons for introducing NMD systems. However, this does not change the fact that Europeans have their own legitimate reasons for their questions and worries relating to NMD.

These mainly concern the risk analysis connected to NMD, i.e., the possible consequences for arms control, for the non-proliferation of nuclear arms, for the cohesion of NATO, for the threat to Europe, as well as for the relationship of the transatlantic partners with third countries.

Multilateralism

Recently, a difference in opinion between the two sides of the Atlantic concerning the basic principles according to which America and/or Europe define their international relations has come increasingly to the fore. This difference in opinion is sometimes wrongly interpreted as one between "multilateralism" and "isolationism".

It is clear that the aim of U.S. foreign policy operations remains the worldwide enforcement of American values and interests. However, the kind of foreign policy action used to achieve this goal varies. In American foreign policy, a mix of selective multilateralism, and occasional recourse to unilateral action, has gained ground. The leitmotif is "America first". It is first and foremost the United States itself which decides when, with what means, and with the help of which institutions, that it will further the global breakthrough of its self-defined values and interests of universal application.

This approach does not necessarily represent consensus within America because there are also strong advocates of multilateralism. The followers of an "America first" option also favour the formation of a multilateral coalition under American leadership to solve international problems or to implement a norm with international application – whether within the UN, NATO, occasionally the OSCE, or a "coalition of the willing and able". But in recent years, there has been growing acceptance of the idea that America can also legitimately use its power without the support of its partners, or even without their agreement, should national interests require it. The awareness of a unique moral and military superiority reinforces this reflex.

In Europe by contrast – since 1945 – multilateralism has transpired as the preferred form of foreign policy action. This is shown particularly clearly in the process of European integration and in Europe's attitude to collective security and defence, especially in Germany which, given its history and geographical location, has made multilateralism an indispensable foreign policy norm. This is an expression of more than two hundred years of negative experience of the rivalries among European nation-states and the principle of the "balance of powers". From its history, Europe has learned the lesson that only the multilateral integration of power, and the multilateral channelling of international conflicts of interest, can bring lasting regional stability and give all states concerned a feeling of real security.

There is a host of topics which show this European-American contrast in the choice of foreign policy strategies: American UN policy, the rejection of the

CTBT Treaty by the American Senate, the American debate on the ABM Treaty, NMD, the International Criminal Court and the Landmine Convention, or the U.S. attitude to the Climate Convention and the Kyoto Protocol.

Although differences between Europe and the United States, especially regarding the priorities of their interests and values, do exist, their common interests and values far exceed these differences. The differences have become more a matter of public attention because the transatlantic partnership is increasingly assuming a quasi-domestic character. The differences by no means justify the talk about a political and cultural divide between Europe and the United States. No other global partnership can boast as many points in common and the levels of integration as the transatlantic partnership. Nevertheless, we have to work the partnership to keep it fit for the 21st century.

The difficulties we are experiencing are the typical symbols of a period of transition. We are actually witnessing the birth pangs of a new Atlanticism.

5 Why St. Malo Matters

ANNE DEIGHTON

Introduction

The signature of the Treaty of Nice in December 2000 confirmed the EU's intention to acquire military tools for its security policy. As ratification proceeds, the next practical challenge is to operationalise the project, but this will not just be a phase of technical implementation. The issues involved are far wider: A battle of ideas will underpin any battles over administrative arrangements. This is because, unlike the burden-sharing and two-pillar debates of the Cold War period, these modifications are taking place in a changed international context, in which the old certainties have gone.

We can identify three battlefronts. The first is over contested agendas about *culture* and the working ethos within the EU itself. Militarising will change the EU's own culture as an international institution. The second concerns what *security* now means for the Europeans, and how this relates to territorial defence in a world of rapidly developing technology, and the institutional implications that this will have for the EU's own pillared structure. Third, at the strategic level, the notion of *community* will require re-examination in the context of the shape of the future European, Atlantic, and global community and the EU's relations with other international organisations, in particular NATO. We will examine these in turn. But first, what is the CESDP?

The Common European Security and Defence Policy (CESDP)

This emerging security system is derived from the EU's Maastricht (1993), Amsterdam (1999) and Nice (signed 2001) Treaties, which are themselves based upon the St. Malo declaration, the EU's Council's Cologne Summit (June 1999), Helsinki Summit (December 1999), and Feira Summit (June 2000) reports, and supported by the NATO communiqués of April and November 1999.[1] It is intended to grow out of EU Pillar II, and the Common Foreign and Security Policy (CFSP).

It was almost in passing, given the other debates at the fraught Nice Summit of December 2000, that the necessary sanction was given to these changes. Two Articles, 17 and 25, were appropriately modified; the detail of the changes is described at length in the French Presidency Report. Article 17 reiterates the decisions agreed to at Maastricht and Amsterdam concerning the nature and scope of the CFSP, and consolidates this as being set firmly within the NATO context as well as the particular constitutional arrangements of individual member states, and any particular bilateral arrangements.[2]

Institutionally, the Western European Union (WEU) will be brought to an end as a functioning international organisation, either totally, or in part. The Nice Treaty does not go so far as to close it down, not least because of the complexities of what to do about Article V, which guarantees automatic support by WEU members if one of them is attacked. NATO's Article 5 is not so powerfully worded, and also, not all members of the EU are members of the WEU and NATO.[3] The Union itself now has: "...a capacity for autonomous action backed up by credible military capabilities and appropriate decision-making bodies.... The Council of the European Union ...[will] thus be able to take decisions on the whole range of political, economic and military instruments at its disposal when responding to crisis situations".[4] The Petersberg Tasks of humanitarian and rescue work, peacekeeping missions, and tasks of combat forces in crisis management including peacemaking, define the work of the new initiative. Regular meetings of the General Affairs Council have been established to include Defence Ministers. A Military Committee has now been created, and composed of the Chiefs of Defence, which will give military advice, and make recommendations to the Political and Security Committee (PSC), and its Chair will be entitled to attend Council meetings, if necessary. Military Staff from the EU member states will provide expertise. Certain categories of countries, which are not members of the EU, but which might wish to participate militarily in an action, will be involved in this process. However, the core decision for action is to be made by the European Council alone. The decision-making associated with this exercise is to be taken in conformity with the EU's own procedures, both ensuring consistency and coherence.

Article 25 deals with an issue that may yet come to have important implications. It concerns the Political and Security Committee (PSC). This article states that the PSC will monitor the situation in the areas covered by the CFSP, and contribute to the definition of such policies by delivering opinions, if asked by the Council, or on its own initiative, as well as monitoring the implementation of such policies. The Article goes on to state that that the PSC "shall exercise, under the responsibility of the Council, political control and strategic direction of crisis management operations". The Council may also "authorise the Committee [PSC], for the purpose and for the duration of a crisis management operation, to take the relevant decisions concerning *the political control and strategic direction of the operation*".[5] The PSC, an un-elected body, is therefore given considerable authority to act collectively during a crisis. This clause is an important one as, hitherto, there was some doubt about the constitutionality and possible legality of such actions, unless this kind of decision-making procedure for a committee had been incorporated into the Treaty structure. That the PSC is composed of senior national officials at ambassadorial level is considered as an additional state-based input.

Regarding capabilities, a common European Headline Goal has been adopted for readily deployable military capabilities, and collective capability goals in the fields of command and control, intelligence and strategic transport, to be formulated through voluntarily coordinated national and multinational efforts for the Petersberg tasks agenda. An inventory of tools available has been drawn up, based on a WEU audit. The tasks would be carried through a mandating agency like the UN or OSCE, or, "where appropriate, in autonomous EU actions". The Headline Goal as articulated at the Capabilities Commitment Conference of November 2000 is that, by 2003, cooperating together voluntarily, the EU would be able to deploy rapidly, and then to sustain forces capable of the full range of Petersberg tasks in operations up to corps level (15 brigades, or 50,000–60,000 persons). They thus range from low-level work to war, which is not territorial defence within the remits of Article 5 (NATO) and Article V (modified Brussels Treaty). The forces generated should be militarily self-sustaining, deployable within 60 days, and have smaller units ready for even quicker deployment. Forces should be able to remain in the field for at least a year (actually requiring preparation for between 100,000–200,000 troops). This is the rapid reaction force, or Military Security Pool (MSP), which lies at the heart of the operational changes.[6]

Legal language rarely conveys drama, and these Articles are no exception. Yet to implement these changes successfully will carry great significance for the development and tasks of the European Union, in the three areas mentioned above.

Cultures

Militarising the Union presents a challenge to cultural diversity in the Union itself, and for its member states. The Union has, until recently, prided itself on its civilian culture. This is hardly surprising, given its historical origins. Formed in the wake of Europe's second devastating war in thirty years, and cradled by the protective defence umbrella of NATO, neither the issue of European military instruments, nor the inclusion of European military procurement was perceived as central to the early agenda of the EU. Non-military questions have naturally dominated, and security changes will take place in the context of competition for political space and financial resources, as the whole mission of the Union has, hitherto, been driven by civilian policy priorities. Presently, these include enlargement and the transition to a European Single Currency. Nevertheless, the Union has proved itself to be greedy for new competencies and to be a very resilient international institution. The WEU – Europe's only military institution –

has, to all intents and purposes, already been disposed of, and the EU now plays a key role as a powerful institutional partner for the OSCE and the Council of Europe on the European continent. But implementing a foreign and security policy with military instruments represents a new and qualitatively different task that takes the Union into a taboo area of policy.

Cultures between the member states of the EU have always varied, and this has been most apparent in the national interpretations and implementation of legal instruments, approaches to European parliamentary elections, and differing priorities for the political and economic agenda. Member states have very different military and quasi-military traditions, and different concepts of civil-military tenets at the domestic level (the gendarmerie concept and conscription). All countries have been examining the mainsprings of their military and quasi-military sources of power (for example, the re-examination of neutrality, or non-alignment, in the light of the end of the Cold War; Finland's considerable concern for issues of national territorial defence). European countries are beginning to move towards a closer approximation one to another (Ireland's membership of NATO's Partnership for Peace is a good example); and some are already cooperating closely (as the Eurocorps and other multinational military groupings show). Others have been positioning themselves rather differently: Denmark, for example, has opted out of the St. Malo process.

It is not clear what the Europeans can, or wish, to deliver within their existing defence budgets, or whether the much heralded 'peace dividend' of the post-Cold War may soon be eroded. Any new debate on budgetary requirements designed to meet the needs of the MSP will take place in the context of very different national military cultures, levels of defence expenditure (for example, France, $708 per head; Spain, $196), and the need for increased role specialisation. Germany, naturally a lead player, given its size and geographic position, is going through a debate on ending conscription, and reducing its defence budget, which, at 1.4% of GNP, is already lower than that of the U.S. (3.2%), UK (2.8%), or France (2.6%). How ending conscription may play into domestic politics, national consensus, and military budgets remains unclear.[7]

Merger, or very close cooperation between institutions, is a novel development in the international system, and will have inevitable cultural consequences. The WEU acted as an institutional buffer between the Union and NATO, particularly after the end of the Cold War. In 1996, the then Secretary-General, Javier Solana, felt able to call the WEU the institutional pivot between the EU and NATO. Yet at the same time, the absorption of the WEU's place in the European institutional architecture into the EU was proceeding incrementally but steadily, with the double-hatting of the new High Representative with the Secretary-General of the WEU, and with the dovetailing of the WEU and the EU Presidencies by the mid-1990s. The role of the WEU as an institutional shock absorber may only be appreciated when it loses its role in the security architecture.[8]

Thus, when Javier Solana welcomed the first committee of uniformed military officers to the interim military body of the EU in March 2000, this represented a radical change. Many of these officers are themselves double-hatted, with an additional NATO role, and import a different decision-making culture. In relation to questions of security, transparency and decision-making, the civilian culture of the EU, and particularly that of the Commission, has proved to be very different from that of NATO. There are complaints that the EU is importing the secrecy of decision-making associated with NATO, and that the culture of the EU, its lack of administrative security, and the growing recognition of the need for administrative transparency, makes the sharing of confidential information difficult. Force planning is becoming one of the major areas in which competing ideas are causing problems.

The question of how to involve those countries, which are not members of both institutions, in decision-making is also crucially important in what is trumpeted as an inclusive process, for: "...the EU project is open. If there is to be efficient crisis management, the European Union wishes to receive contributions from the non-EU European NATO members and other countries which are candidates for accession to the EU".[9] Each group has different problems. First are the non- EU/ NATO members: Turkey, Norway, Poland, the Czech Republic, Hungary and Iceland. For most of these countries, while membership in the EU may be an ultimate aim, the immediate issue is to balance the needs of the EU with those of NATO. Parallel security reforms, and the NATO Defence Capabilities Initiative, add yet another strand to the sensitive inter-institutional negotiation. The difficulties, which Turkey is now confronted, have at least some connection with those cultural reasons that explain the EU's reluctance to proceed with enlargement towards Turkey.

Then there are those that are not yet members of either institution, especially Slovenia, Romania, Slovakia, the Baltic States, and Ukraine. The under-sung work that the WEU performed with its Associate Partners cannot easily be incorporated into any new structure.[10] However, the procedures for pre-Council decisions – "upstream" – and post-Council decisions – "downstream" – participation is in place. This means that non-member states may participate in decision-making except at the moment when the decision is taken by the European Council. This procedure is being coupled with a proposal to incorporate a committee on the Associate Partner committee model of the WEU: Such moves are both inclusive and politically astute.

From this perspective, the creation of a EU Military Security Pool for Petersberg tasks will challenge the ingenuity and sensitivity of the 15 member states, with their different national practices, languages and cultures. Foreign and security policy belongs to the arena that is most closely identified with the core *raison d'être* of the state. National pride, sensitivities and interests will never be far from the debating table. Recent reports indicate that there are fears, not that states will go too far, but that they may stall because of the national changes that will be required for member states to meet the MSP criteria.

Securities

The St. Malo initiative reflects a transformed international system and environment, and therefore it is qualitatively different from the burden-sharing and two-pillar debates of the Cold War period. The policy agenda presents another sort of challenge to the EU. Perceptions about what is meant by security, and the nature of the challenges to security, have been immeasurably widened since the end of the 1980s. Security now means more than stability, or non-war. It is clear, even from its "Petersberg" definition, that security is not just about violence and the application of military instruments. It embraces a societal, and even, individual dimension. It covers environmental, criminality, and human rights issues, as well as those involving the illegitimate use of violence.

Security is indivisible in the sense that internal and external security issues are related to each other; it is, furthermore, indivisible in that the instruments required to deal with security threats – although very varied – cannot be neatly pigeon-holed one from another.[11] Indeed, consideration of what is now meant by territorial defence cannot forever be avoided, as the line between security and defence is unclear – the CESDP contains the D, but what does this mean in practice, and where in the Petersberg tasks, is the "D" represented? There is a logic of security that will drive both institutional developments, and the policy toolbox that the EU is developing. This policy logic is slowly being realised in Europe.

First, let us consider internal security and the projection of security. A state, or the EU, cannot project security without itself being secure, and it may be necessary to project a security policy to preserve internal security, or for reasons of altruism. Thus, environmental security requires domestic (or EU) legislation and may also obligate intervention to prevent external environmental disasters, which may have consequences at home.[12] The consequences of instability in a neighbouring country may be an influx of migration, so legislation to manage immigration may require military measures to calm that instability. Such an observation reflects on the institutional structure of the Union. The activities in Pillar III have consequences for a more general security policy and its projection, and the notion of "cross-pillar" activity in Pillar III external actions is under active consideration.[13] The CFSP, for all its current weaknesses, has been a good "shock-absorbing mechanism – protecting outside conflicts from causing problems internally".[14] The Military Security Pool should, eventually, allow the EU to possess the internal cohesion and the tools at its disposal to project military security, thereby increasing the Union's own security.

It follows that, if security threats are multi-dimensional, then many different instruments to deal with them need to be easily available. The EU's Pillar structure was a political compromise engineered during the months leading up to the Maastricht Treaty, and it acts as a deliberate restraint upon policy coherence. Many of the instruments that can be used to try and sustain security are those that already belong to the Commission in Pillar I, including economic instruments, humanitarian aid, and sanctions. Therefore, the Commission already has a robust role in the EU's overall external policy. Much of the early writing on functional "spill-over" was discredited by events during the mid-1960s and the 1970s. However, the Commission received a boost to its capacity to act with the Single European Act, and the drive to revive the single market principle that had underpinned the Treaty of Rome.[15] Now, within Pillar II, the Commission has the right, but not the sole right, to propose initiatives, to sit in at Council meetings on CFSP, and to ensure their implementation. It is arguable that the EU, led by the Commission, is seeking to reduce what Christopher Hill has called the "capabilities-expectation" gap in the security sphere, without openly challenging the sacredness of an inter-governmental Council decision to use military force.[16]

The new security agenda has been seized upon by the EU, which emphasises the indivisibility of security issues. Following the Feira European Council, a Civilian Headline Goal has been put in place to cover police, strengthening the rule of law, strengthening civilian administration and civil protection. This includes police officers, a database of contribution capabilities of member states, the involvement of NGOs and other international organisations, and consideration of civilian aspects of crisis management. The intention of this policy is to "develop a coherent European approach to crisis management and conflict prevention; [and] ensure the synergy between civilian and military aspects of crisis management".[17] An integrated EU planning process is considered essential to the success of its security policy.

External Relations Commissioner Chris Patten takes "an expansive view of the scope of the Commission to contribute ideas and proposals, whether or not it has the exclusive right of initiative, with the aim of ensuring a single and coherent EU position on the major international issues of the day". He argues that security is a broad concept, of which military force is only its ultimate dimension. As he said to a joint gathering of NATO and European parliamentarians, the Commission "with its own restructuring, has shown that it, too, is determined to step up a gear – or two, or three".[18] Patten also mentioned the Commission's potential to progress with a European armaments policy by looking at ways of creating a single armament policy in the EU.

It is clear that the CESDP will not quickly become like any other Union policy arena given its current CFSP Pillar II framework, the need for unanimity in the European Council, and the preferences of member states in this most state-like role of exercising military power. But both the nature of the post-Cold War security problem, and the historical experience of spill-over and extension of

Commission competencies over time, indicate that further change is inevitable. The responses required for security issues are often unclear and controversial, and the timing of these responses is even more difficult to gauge. The moment at which non-military forms of intervention may need to be supported, or supplanted by military forms, is not easy to judge. The precision of the boundaries between Pillar I, Pillar II, and Pillar III will be increasingly challenged: They will have to become more fungible as the indivisibility of external actions in the realm of security becomes more apparent. This is particularly true given that security decisions frequently require speed, as well as secrecy. The Kosovo campaign showed all too clearly that international consensus is difficult to secure, and even more difficult to sustain as events on the ground develop. It could never be wished that necessary, and perhaps humanitarian, actions were hampered because of clumsy decision-making.

Thus, from a policy perspective, the increasing participation of the Commission in the military-security dimension is logical. The Commission remains the only permanent bureaucracy to monitor and act across all external policy, whether in Pillar I or Pillar II. Indeed, the treaties themselves have re-iterated the need for Union coherence in the framing of external policies (Article 3, consolidated Treaties, 1999). The fungibility of the boundaries between the Pillar I – trade, enlargement, aid and humanitarian actions; Pillar II – CFSP including CESDP; and Pillar III – policing – will surely, over time, be increasingly obvious, as the indivisibility of actions in the realm of security becomes more apparent.

Such security logic will play into the wider current debates about the overall structure and purpose of the EU, and the balance of powers between states and the Union, as well as between the Pillars of the Union. Part of the success of the EU over time has been derived from a general acceptance of the ambiguity of the role, or mission, of the EU itself. Since the 1950s, the notion of a *finalité politique* has been avoided by member states. The idea of an "ever closer union" has masked the essentially ambiguous purpose and place of the EU, and its relation to its member states. Those who have taken decisions about the EU, and those who have written about it, have largely contented themselves with ad hoc or *sui generis* explanations. The driving idea of spill-over, first and most eloquently expounded by Ernst Haas in the 1960s, implied an internal momentum that would lead to greater integration over more areas, as time passed. At the same time, there has developed a more inter-governmental set of explanations as to how major change takes place within the EU. This has favoured the idea that states will cooperate and integrate when this is perceived to be in the "national interest". With EMU, enlargement and now a new security dimension, the need to try to define more clearly the scope and limits of the EU itself has intensified.

The Fischer-Chirac-Blair discourse has reopened this debate. At Nice, a charter was accepted, but not woven into the constitutional fabric of the Union. However, it was also agreed at Nice that a major inter-governmental conference would revisit the question of some kind of constitution for the EU, although this is going to be a very fraught exercise. "Doing" has animated the direction of the EU, so it has been possible to avoid the core question of the "final aim" of the member states. Earlier tacit compromises about the balance of decision-making within the EU and its ultimate direction have become increasingly unsustainable. Effective provision of security will play into the wider constitutional debate about the "constitution" of the Union.[19]

Communities

The European security debate has taken place in an Atlantic context, in which it has been argued that the Cold War Atlantic Alliance represented more than a defence alliance, and was part of a value-based security community for its members.[20] However, we cannot forget that it is the failure of NATO to adapt effectively since the end of the Cold War that has created the environment for the St. Malo initiative. NATO alone cannot meet the new security dilemmas that the post-Cold War world poses, both because of its structure, and because of the changing perceptions about the nature of security in the twenty-first century. At the same time, the EU has been steadily expanding its remit.

The Atlantic Community worked as a concept when its prime concern was territorial defence in the face of the Soviet threat. Is this still salient? What are the mainsprings of a European, an Atlantic or a "Western" Community in the post-Cold War era? Do they spring from the UN, or from national declarations and speeches (like that of Tony Blair in Chicago in April 1999)? Is there a European community of values that is qualitatively different from an Atlantic Community (for example regarding the legitimacy of the death penalty)? Do only the national interests of states determine their place in a Security Community? Do we have common expectations about the role of intervention, the expectations we place upon peacekeepers, about protectorates and state building, and about the role of the UN and OSCE? This debate is far from being resolved. Yet there are some aspects that can usefully be established at this stage, for these strategic questions and their implications for the relations between the Military Security Pool, NATO and the United States, as the world's only superpower, will underpin the technical discussions of the next few years.

First, the political interface between the EU and NATO has to be addressed. At the moment, the EU relationship with NATO is complex and turbulent. Tensions have run high over the last two years in Brussels and in national capitals on both sides of the Atlantic. The relationship between the two has been one of intense competitiveness since the end of the Cold War, despite declarations of cooperation, mutual interests, and similar value structures. Both aspire to military security functions, and a collective cooperative security agenda; both are engaged in enlargement programmes. The St. Malo declaration was initially badly received by the six non-EU NATO members, with responses ranging from Turkey's threats, to Canada's lament that it was the seventh member of the six non-EU NATO members. Public and private discussions have ranged beyond the Petersberg tasks to the general direction of EU-NATO relations; U.S. relations with European powers; procurement questions; and the general health of the Atlantic Alliance. It is not always clear whether the United States is distressed by the possibility that the St. Malo project will collapse, or that it will be too successful and be the thin end of the wedge to the end of NATO.

This cusp of the EU/NATO interface has now settled on the military autonomy of the EU. Despite protestations – especially from the British government – that NATO will not be unwillingly marginalised, the French Presidency Report insists upon equality between the institutions, and the ability of the EU to decide strategy and planning in times of crisis. It is worth quoting this section, as it pinpoints the dilemma faced on both sides of the Atlantic. "Having determined the initial general options, the Staff [EU Military Staff] *may* call upon external planning sources, in particular the guaranteed access to NATO planning capabilities, to analyse and refine these options.... *Should the Union intend to look more closely at an option calling for predetermined NATO assets and capabilities*, the PSC will so inform the NAC [North Atlantic Council]".[21] It is at this moment of planning, as well as the yet un-agreed access mechanism to NATO C^3 resources, that the fears about decoupling lie. Whether the Military Security Pool will be able to act parallel to NATO, or only with prior NATO agreement – or first right of refusal – is the point at issue. In practice, of course, given the NATO membership of many EU countries, an initiative that disregarded NATO as an institution is only likely to happen if the viability of NATO had collapsed anyway.

Yet this inter-institutional debate is at root about Euro-Atlantic relations, and particularly the role of the United States in sustaining and promoting security both in Europe (in its widest sense), and beyond. There are two contradictory trends at work, which are creating political tension, and which reflect the ways in which institutions battle for space during a period of international structural change. The first – *transatlantic drift* – is based upon the premise that the international structural underpinning of the Cold War will, over time, be eroded. The argument here is that the St. Malo process is, in part, a response to this drift, but that it will also exacerbate the drift. Instead of a more mature partnership between the United States and its European partners, the Europeans may increasingly see the parallel work being done to re-invent NATO simply as the institutional floundering of a dying Cold War Atlantic Community. The EU will become the new centre of energy through which European-centred security problems will be addressed. The United States will slip into indifference to European security issues, including – infamously – escorting Bosnian children to kindergarten – and concentrate its energies upon its autonomous role, and, indeed, on National Missile Defence. Dominique Moïsi wonders whether we are not entering an era when "the United States will be less willing to protect the world from itself and more inclined to protect the United States from the world".[22] This perspective is reflected in the shifting attitude in the United States towards international institutions generally, a sense that the United States is too big for positive membership in international institutions, fears about military over-stretch, and the constraints of domestic, and particularly, American Congressional politics. The prospect of transatlantic drift raises the question of whether NATO only worked when there was strong American leadership, and when American leaders conflated European, or Western interests, with those of America in the face of a Soviet threat.

Given the above scenario, the NMD debate could not have come at a worse time. It has created a bizarre environment for some kind of potential trade-off with the CESDP that distorts the roots and purposes of both projects and is potentially very de-stabilising. The United States cannot argue that they bear the burden of Europe's defence, complain when the Europeans try to change this, and then unilaterally set a quite different security agenda. British Prime Minister Tony Blair should know better than to lull the United States into thinking that NMD becomes a better idea if the United States gives backing to the CESDP. This irrational "bargain" also gives the impression of a strange division of human and technological labour between the United States and Europe, resulting from a different prioritisation of present and future threats.

A second, and quite different, perspective is that of future increased *transatlantic participation*. Institutional change may give the United States an even stronger presence in Europe, leading perhaps to some kind of convergence between EU and NATO membership – a Transatlantic Defence and Security Community. NATO parliamentarians have been invited to sit in on European Parliamentary sessions and certain European players are even toying with the idea of offering a seat to NATO at some of the EU Council meetings that are concerned with the new security policy.[23] In policy terms, it is almost impossible to think of anything more than a very low level Petersberg-type task over which the United States would not wish to keep an interest, especially if U.S. (NATO) equipment was being lent or leased for such a task. He who pays the piper, calls the tune. U.S. economic interests in Europe, and a desire to dominate the armaments sphere, may yet challenge any exclusively European armaments provision and flood the market with American products, with an inevitable extension of U.S. leverage. The recent revived commitment made by U.S. Secretary of State Colin Powell to the continued presence of the United States in the Balkans, "NATO came into this together, and we will leave together", is a sign that the United States itself realises that complaints about European behaviour are less clever than an effort to re-cement the practical aspects of the transatlantic dimension.

The fault line between these Europeanist (drift) and Atlanticist (participation) interpretations of a post-Cold War security community is typified by Anglo-French competitiveness, despite the apparent bilateral sponsorship of this "inter-governmental adventure" at St. Malo. The 1999 Anglo-French Summit declaration that "we expect NATO and the EU to develop a close and confident relationship", represents, in reality, as much hope as description. There is an on-going tension: About the word "autonomous," about access to NATO military equipment, about the future of the WEU's Article V, as well as about the intentions of the world's only superpower. Some in Britain think that the French have now to realise that the furniture of European security has moved, but that only the Ministry of Defence has yet appreciated this. (Why don't the French re-join the NATO military command structure?) French opinion remains wedded, at least in public, to fears about power, and is suspicious of British Atlantic policy, for example, over the Echelon spy satellite affair. (How to explain UK policy towards Iraq?) In 1998, some in France feared that perfidious Albion would drag them back into NATO, and some in Britain that the French might drive a wedge between the UK and the United States. These distorted visions represent a microcosm of alternative Atlantic and European communities.

The working relationship with the United States is redolent with practical and political landmines. Most European officials and politicians appear to be working hard to reassure the United States that the Europeans have the leadership and political will to carry through the reforms required, but that these reforms are still set firmly in the context of NATO. The Europeans – as well as the Americans – must assess the future role of Russia in these changes – for neither the threat of NMD, nor the minimal force projection of the MSP are, alone, adequate solutions. Last, to give security credibility, to gather support for cultural change, and to "reinvent" a community, whether it is with, or alongside, the U.S./NATO, public support is going to be essential to secure legitimacy and consent. A genuine community that is concerned with a wide range of security tasks cannot expect to survive long unless it secures this democratic legitimation.

Conclusion

CESDP could yet fail for the EU because of a lack of political will, resources, vision, or understanding about the depth of the issues it exposes to public debate. The cultural-structural implications for the EU itself are immense, yet there are no European-wide certainties about what we are doing, and where we wish to go. Key states – Britain and France in particular – have enormous responsibilities. Britain has, once again, to square the circle between its attachment to the United States and its role in Europe, and the French have to assess whether greater autonomy in this sphere will actually help their own European "leadership" mission. The military-security role of Germany, potentially the largest European player of all, is in very early stages of development (in particular given, on the one hand, the successful civilianisation of German political culture since the Second World War, and, on the other, its potential as an alternative Fylingdales-type base for U.S. initiatives). Divisions between the U.S. State Department and the Pentagon are already creating further confusion for the Europeans. Meanwhile, the practical problems – the real-time security problems – of peacekeeping, and state building dominate Europe's Balkan borders, giving lie to any notion that this debate is simply hypothetical or theological. The Pandora's Box of security projection in the post-Cold War world is irreversibly opened.

Notes

1   For a fuller account, Anne Deighton, *Militarising the EU* (Notes de Recherche no. 15, Centre d'études des politiques étrangères et de sécurité, Montreal, 2000).

2   Treaty of Nice, SN 1247/01, January 2001, www.fco.gov.uk. French Presidency Report, Annex VI, SN 400/1/oo ADD 1 REV 1, pp. 37-95, contrasts with the brevity of the relevant Treaty clauses. (The Treaty also states that the "progressive framing of a common defence policy will be supported, as Member States consider appropriate, by cooperation between them in the field of armaments", which opens the door to possible further integration or cooperation in this important area. Enhanced cooperation procedures in Pillar II do not apply "to matters having military or defence implications".)

3   For the complex institutional architecture, see the International Institute for Strategic Studies' *Strategic Survey, 2000* (Oxford: Oxford University Press, 2000), which tabulates the institutional affiliation of states.

4   Cologne European Council (EU), 3-4 June 1999, Council of the European Union.

5   Emphasis added. The detail is fleshed out in the French Presidency Report, Annex III to Annex VI.

6   The misleading phrase, "European Army" is inaccurate (or, very remotely, premature); the more widely adopted phrase "Rapid Reaction Force" is confusing given the use of the phrase for other European military groupings. See further, Anne Deighton, "The Military Security Pool: Towards a New Security Regime for Europe?", *The International Spectator*, XXXV, No. 4, December 2000, pp. 41-54.

7   "German Military Weakness Complicates European Security Futures". www.stratfor.com/, 24 March 2000.

8   Jean-Félix Paganon, "Western European Union's Pivotal Position between the Atlantic Alliance and the European Union", in Anne Deighton (ed.), *Western European Union, 1954-1996: Defence, Security, Integration,* (Oxford: 1997), pp. 93-102. Until very recently, EU and NATO officials made the point that, although both institutions had headquarters in Brussels, the lines of communication between them were virtually non-existent.

9   French Presidency Report, Annex VI, III.

10   For the best accounts of the role of the WEU, see the remarkable corpus of work by Alyson Bailes, including, "European defence: another set of questions", *RUSI Journal,* No. 1, 2000; "A defence and Security Policy for Europe", *CIDOB Yearbook,* Barcelona, 2000.

11   Barry Buzan, *People, States and Fear,* (London: 1991); Lawrence Freedman, "International Security: Changing Targets", *Foreign Policy,* Spring 1998, pp. 48-62.

12   The case of the submarine Kursk is one such example.

13   Council of the European Union, "EU priorities and policy objectives for external relations in the field of justice and home affairs", 7653/00, June 2000

14   Knud Eric Korgensen, "The European Union's Performance in World Politics: How should We Measure Success", in Jan Zielonka (ed.), *Paradoxes of European Foreign Policy* (London: Kluwer Law International, 1998), pp. 90-1.

15   It is worth remembering that the potential of the SEA was completely underestimated at the time: The Italian Parliament was reluctant to ratify the Treaty as it was considered too minimalist; given the scale of he debate surrounding its creation, it was called the "elephant that gave birth to a mouse".

16   Christopher Hill, "The capability-expectations gap, or conceptualising Europe's international role", *Journal of Common Market Studies*, Vol. 31, No. 3, 1993, pp. 305-28. For excellent overviews of CFSP, Fraser Cameron, "Building a common foreign policy", pp. 59-76, Helene Sjursen, "Missed opportunity or eternal fantasy?: The idea of a security and defence policy", pp. 95-112; Christopher Hill, "Closing the capabilities-expectations gap?", pp. 18-38, in Helene Sjursen and John Peterson, *A Common Foreign Policy for Europe?: Competing Visions of the CFSP* (London, 1998).

17   French Presidency Report, Annex VI, II.

18   Joint meeting of European Parliament Foreign Affairs Committee with members of the NATO Parliamentary Assembly, Brussels, 22 February 2000, (http://www.europa.int).

19   Jolyon Howorth, *European Integration and Defence: The Ultimate Challenge?*, Chaillot paper, No. 43, November, 2000; Venusberg *Group's Enhancing the European Union as an International Security Actor* (Bertelsmann Foundation, 2000); Charles Grant, *Europe: 2010* (Centre for European Reform, 2000); European Policy Centre, "From Biarritz to Nice and Beyond", October 2000, (http://www.TheEPC.be).

20   Thomas Risse Kappen, *Cooperation among Democracies: The European Influence on United States Foreign Policy* (Princeton University Press, 1995).

21   French Presidency Report, Annex VII to Annex VI, emphasis added.

22   *Financial Times*, 11 February 2001.

23   *The Independent*, 17 February 2000.

6 Transatlantic Relations: Beyond the Common Foreign and Security Policy

JAN ZIELONKA

Introduction

The Common Foreign and Security Policy (CFSP) of the European Union (EU) has only a marginal impact on transatlantic relations.[1] This is partly because the CFSP remains in a state of paralysis: No major international crisis has so far been tackled effectively by this instrument. But it is also because the CFSP proper does not deal with the most crucial problems on the transatlantic agenda, that is, economic relations and the spread of Western institutions into countries of Eastern and Southern Europe. The newly emerging European defence identity, while formally "in support of" the CFSP, also has a separate and largely independent dimension. It is in these three crucial fields: Defence, economics and institutional enlargement, that transatlantic partners are likely to interact most intensely in the foreseeable future.

Will this interaction mean cooperation or conflict across the Atlantic? Much will depend on the ability to bridge diverging interests and to utilise the different assets of the two transatlantic partners. Both the EU and the United States have vested interests in maintaining a liberal international order in Europe and beyond. However, creation of such an order is incompatible with a selfish definition of mutual interests. It will be argued that the attitude to legal rules and international institutions in different functional fields will be crucial. Moreover, the EU and the United States are very different international actors in terms of structure, instruments and ethos. Comprehending, accepting and utilising mutual strengths, rather than only bashing mutual weaknesses, is the key to successful transatlantic relations.

CFSP: A Dormant Institution

The CFSP was created by the Treaty of Maastricht a decade ago. The idea behind it was quite plausible. Individual members of the EU could no longer effectively run all sorts of foreign policies on their own. Should they resign themselves to the idea that the United States was best suited to run foreign policies on Europe's behalf or should they rely on a new type of great power "*directoire*" to do the job? For most Europeans the answer to these questions was "neither", which explains the CFSP's basic rationale.

In other words, the CFSP makes sense, but provided that it is well designed and works in practice. Unfortunately, the latter is hardly the case. This was especially evident in the first years of the CFSP's operation, when the Union pretended to be in charge of the Balkan crisis and utterly failed to match its rhetoric with action. In 1995, the European Commission admitted: "(T)he experience of the common foreign and security policy has been disappointing so far".[2] Criticism from independent observers at the time was usually much more sharp and candid.[3] As a consequence, the EU's ambitions concerning the CFSP were scaled down. When European countries decided to intervene in Albania, and later in Kosovo, the CFSP institutional framework was hardly utilised.

Of course, CFSP officials and national delegates continue to be very active, they meet and talk quite frequently about foreign and security issues, they sponsor initiatives, nominate mediators and distribute economic rewards and sanctions. However, the relationship between this (hyper)activity and its output is rather disappointing. The CFSP's "common actions" or "strategies" are either too vague to make any real policy impact or concentrate on second rank challenges.[4] As a special report of the Bertelsmann Stiftung observed: "While these actions have been useful, they have not led to increased EU visibility nor really decisive action. The scope has been modest and the added value of CFSP not always apparent".[5]

The list of weaknesses of the CFSP is long and worrying. Weaknesses range from operational to conceptual problems. The Union is either unable to formulate its policies or unable to implement the policies adopted. Sometimes procedural and institutional difficulties are at the core of CFSP failures. At other times, the Union is simply faced with the reluctance of member states to have any common policy whatsoever. The unilateral policies of member states and their failure even to consult other EU partners have been notorious and striking. The Union's inaction in crisis situations has been frequent and especially damaging to the CFSP's reputation. Reform of the initial structure of CFSP could help fortify some of its weaknesses. But as the 1997 Amsterdam European Council demonstrated, the Union is willing and able to adopt only small incremental changes that do not give much hope for the CFSP's smoother functioning.[6]

Of course, this criticism ought to be qualified. The CFSP's paralysis has not been total. Yet, there have been only a few successes and the exact impact of the CFSP on the outcomes is unclear. For instance, the EU's policy towards South Africa certainly contributed to the collapse of the Apartheid regime there, but so did many other factors – most notably domestic ones.[7] Moreover, there is no point in criticising the Union for failing to live up to some imagined (absolute) standards. All international organisations suffer from slow and clumsy decision-making. Even individual states, including such great powers as the United States, are not immune to cumbersome procedures and conflicts of competency. The foreign policy of any national or international actor is usually of a neutralising nature (that is, reactive) rather than of a progressive one (that is pro-active). Finally, it is difficult to disagree with Knud Eric Jøergensen's argument that the utility of the CFSP should not be judged only on its external impact, but also on its internal impact, however ambiguously that is expressed. As he put it: "While the CFSP may be less successful in solving problems outside the EU, it has been very successful as a shock-absorbing mechanism – protecting outside conflicts from causing problems internally".[8]

All these and other possible qualifications apart, it is difficult to deny that the Union is unable to live up to its Treaty commitment concerning the CFSP, let alone broader public expectations.[9] The question is: Why is this so and what are the implications? The latter question will be tackled later. The answer to the former question is partly political and partly institutional.

In institutional terms, the Union's problem is not so much a lack of sufficient policy instruments but an in-built difficulty to arrive at a collective decision, especially when they it really matters.[10] In political terms, the problem is not so much in the persistent divergence of national interests, but in the weak legitimacy of European foreign policies. Despite all their divergence, the national policies of EU states are increasingly geared towards Europe. For individual European governments, EU institutions are becoming the most important means for coping with global pressures and local problems. The EU political agenda increasingly dictates national agendas, and not the other way around. The EU framework has become the central point where most agreements and disagreements concerning foreign policy are being debated and made. The problem is that the common policies of the Union do not really enjoy genuine legitimacy. Europeans do not have a high degree of natural affinity towards these policies and they have little chance of controlling them. The CFSP is not based on spontaneous social links, communal solidarity or shared traditions that would justify broader, cross-national support. It is not very clear who the "consumers" and "producers" of these policies are, just as it is unclear what their broader strategic purpose is. This does not mean that the electorate should directly determine the foreign policies of the European Union. But if people in various countries do not identify with European policies, their governments can hardly get these policies off the ground. The people of Europe are apparently quite happy to endorse the CFSP when asked some vague and general questions by Eurobarometer pollsters. However, there are few indications so far that they are willing to underwrite European foreign policies with their chequebooks, let alone with their blood, sweat, and tears.

From a Common Foreign Policy to a Common Defence

The EU's decision to initiate a European defence project was prompted by the CFSP's weakness. During the war in Kosovo, in particular, some European leaders could not hide their frustration with being total dependent on American capabilities, decisions and actions. There was a feeling that Europe ought to be able to do more in the defence field, and the historic 1998 Saint Malo agreement between France and Great Britain paved the way for the broader European initiative articulated in the Helsinki Declaration of the European Council.

The basic rationale behind the initiative is again plausible. The combined European military potential is not negligible, but the EU cannot really conduct any military operation due to practical and procedural constraints. Moreover, Washington often indulges in unilateral policies and often has a peculiar understanding of European interests.[11] Putting an end to reliance on the American capacity to perform peacekeeping operations in Europe's volatile backyard seems to be a well-conceived proposition.

However, the fact that the European Security and Defence Policy (ESDP) stems from the CFSP's weaknesses, rather than its strengths, already presents a problem. One cannot help but ask whether a common defence policy of the Union is possible without a workable common foreign policy? After all, it is important to know how, when and for what purposes the Union is going to use its soldiers. If a common foreign policy is often in a state of paralysis, especially when faced with a crisis, how will a common defence policy ever be able to work?

Of course, one can argue that creation of a common defence policy may itself improve the functioning of the CFSP. In other words, there might be a positive spill-over from the defence field into the field of diplomacy. The history of integration shows that European cooperation in various fields proceeds at different speeds without any given sequence or logic. For instance, the development of an independent military capability could make it more difficult for the Europeans to wait for American leadership in a crisis. Just before the European Council in Nice, Member States had offered military contributions that would allow the Union to meet the original commitment agreed to at the Helsinki European Council. At the Nice Summit as such, the permanent military and political structures of the ESDP have been spelled out in great details and the erection of these structures has already begun. The Nice European Council also agreed to strengthen EU capabilities for civilian aspects of crisis management and worked out consultation and co-operation procedures with non-EU European NATO members and with NATO as such.[12] However, putting in place military capabilities does not guarantee their use in a timely and effective manner. In particular, it is hard to agree with the kind of reverse determinism popular in some European circles that says that European cooperation in the defence field must work because Europe has utterly failed to cooperate in the field of diplomacy and can hardly afford another failure.

In addition, there might also be a negative spillover. When soldiers' lives are at stake, the decisions are not easier but more difficult to make. If it was difficult to reach the required political consensus under the CFSP, why should it be easier to reach under the ESDP? And would such consensus arrive in time during a crisis? Politics aside, decisions about the use of force will probably require solid legal structures, and these tend to make the decision-making process less, rather than more, flexible (and also more time-consuming).

These last observations lead us to another problem. The Helsinki Declaration has produced different interpretations across Europe, creating a considerable degree of confusion in both Europe and the United States. Since we are dealing with issues of peace and security, such confusion cannot be taken lightly. Clearly the French justification of the project differs from the British, the Dutch or the Swedish one. British officials and commentators emphasised the opportunity for London to regain the initiative and assert leadership in the European Union.[13] However, they did their utmost to play down Europe's ambition to gain independence from American-dominated NATO, something cherished by the French.[14] The Dutch government, on the other hand, openly hostile to the idea of a common defence, reluctantly withdrew its veto at the last moment for the sake of the European unity needed for purposes other than defence.[15] The Dutch were especially worried about possible negative implications for NATO, a matter that was of lesser concern for the neutral members of the European Union. But the reaction of the neutrals has varied nevertheless. Finland supported the ESDP strongly, while Sweden's support has been much more ambivalent.

There is even greater confusion concerning the European Union's long- and medium-term policy aims in the defence field. The decision taken at the Helsinki European Council envisages only very limited capabilities: the Union's ambition is to have 50,000-60,000 soldiers able to perform the full range of Petersberg tasks by the year 2003, while the ambition to create a European army is specifically denied both in Helsinki and in Nice. Yet, many believe that the Helsinki Declaration represents the first symbolic step towards a genuine European common defence policy. But a genuine European common defence policy can hardly be confined to the peacekeeping tasks identified in the WEU's Petersberg Declaration of June 1992. Such defence policy must also include the defence of vital interests against direct attack envisaged by Article V of the Brussels Treaty. In addition, it must address the issue of a European nuclear defence capability. Are Britain and France prepared to extend their nuclear umbrellas to other European countries? Are EU citizens ready to undertake their defence on their own? Are they prepared to shoulder the financial costs of such defence? Does the European Union enjoy enough legitimacy to send soldiers into combat?[16]

Moreover, for a common defence policy to work smoothly, one envisages a need for serious institutional and procedural reforms within the Union. Some steps are already being openly discussed, such as coordination and the rationalisation of defence procurement and spending, or the simplification of the European institutional structure by merging the WEU with the EU. However, the most important priority is to find effective ways for formulating the Union's basic political and operational will. And all possible solutions for helping the Union to accomplish this task touch upon the difficult subjects of sovereignty, identity, legitimacy, the scope of commitments and membership rights. It is far from certain that the Union is ready to embark upon such a path.

Finally, it is not certain whether shifting from a "civilian" to a "military power" status will solve or create problems for the Union. Because the current Union's power is not military and hegemonic in nature, it does not drive other states out (through the balancing mechanism). Its civilian power attracts; it does not repel. Acquiring a military status may help the Union to cope with local violence, but it might also raise suspicion and induce balancing efforts. In other words, after Helsinki, both internal and external actors will watch the EU's policies as never before. To have a "gun at hand" not only widens opportunities for action, it also puts much greater responsibility for one's actions on one's shoulders. This is hardly ever mentioned by the proponents of the ESDP, although it should be, considering the EU's damaging performance in the Balkans.[17] In summary, the ESDP is still a very untested proposition and there are good reasons to doubt whether it is going to work any better than the CFSP. In fact, one can argue that a workable CFSP – a distant prospect at present – is a precondition for a workable ESDP.

The EU as an International Actor

U.S. officials have frequently complained about the CFSP's impotence. For instance, during the 1996 Turkish-Greek showdown in the Aegean, Richard Holbrook lamented: "Europe slept through the night".[18] Of course, a strong and coherent CFSP would make it much more difficult for Washington to assert its leadership in Europe. That said, it is difficult for Washington to make deals or share burdens with an incoherent European Union. The latter is an empirical problem; the former is only a theoretical one. However, the U.S. administration has never ceased to communicate and cooperate with Europeans through other channels such as NATO, G-7, UN Security Council, the (Balkan) Contact Group or bilateral negotiations. In fact, not only the Americans but also most Europeans see NATO as the most important pillar of transatlantic relations and security in Europe. The pattern of bilateral relations between Washington and individual European capitals shows that there is often competition between European governments for American attention, if not favours.

Furthermore, Americans seemed to understand well the limited role of the CFSP in the overall European structure. As Richard Rosecrance once put it:

The European Union's Common Foreign and Security Policy is a misnomer. Europe does not speak with one voice on either foreign policy or defence problems. CFSP is an acronym without empirical content.... Europe nonetheless has unique and unparalleled foreign policy strengths [and] these strengths are in the process of helping to reshape the contours of the wider international system.[19]

The argument is that with nearly 380 million people, combined GNP higher than that of the United States, the largest market in the world, a pivotal position in international trade, and the leading position in development assistance and humanitarian aid, the European Union cannot be dismissed from world affairs, regardless of all the CFSP's weaknesses. It is enough to look at the impressive list of applicants for EU membership to conclude that the Union has power of attraction – and substantial leverage. The creation of the European Monetary Union, with its arduous admission standards, further enhanced the EU's profile, not only in the world of economics but also in the world of politics. Even Europe's much criticised defence capabilities are not negligible by any standards.[20] In short, the European Union's international leverage cannot be judged by looking only at the CFSP and its apparent paralysis. In fact, most of the means at the EU's disposal are outside the CFSP framework. Table 6.1 illustrates the current division of the EU's internal budget related to foreign and security policy.

Not only is the CFSP one of many instruments for the EU's exercise of power, but it also has nothing to do with the running of the most important transatlantic issues. Economic issues have been at the top of the U.S.-EU agenda for years and they do not formally fall under the CFSP regime. The EU's enlargement is rapidly gaining in importance in transatlantic dialogue, but again the CFSP is only a small part of the enlargement package and not the other way around. And it is far from certain that defence issues will be handled through the CFSP channel in the future, especially when it comes to dealing with the Americans. But all this says more about constraints imposed on the CFSP, than about the real state of foreign relations between the EU and United States. To understand the latter, one has to analyse the three functional types of relations mentioned above in the fields of economics, defence and enlargement. This reveals important power discrepancies in individual fields and points to major conceptual problems in reshaping the transatlantic agenda in the post-Cold War period.

Of course, for those unfamiliar with the EU's institutional labyrinth, separating economics, enlargement and defence from the CFSP proper seems illogical and inefficient. But efficiency criteria and pure logic do not always count when it comes to constructing new forms of European cooperation amidst various political, bureaucratic, and cross-national conflicts and cultural differences.

European integration proceeded in an incremental and inconsistent manner without specifying its basic aims and without clear rules or structures. This also applied in the areas of diplomacy and defence.[21] European cooperation in these fields did not emerge overnight, rather it developed in an incremental and often disguised manner as of the 1950s. The result is not only a bizarre institutional "three pillar structure" governed by different decision-making procedures and with the artificial separation of economic external relations from foreign policy. There is a whole series of inconsistencies and paradoxes characterising Europe's foreign policy.[22] For instance, there is a striking gap between the Union's normative power of attraction and its weak empirical power to shape the international environment in any instrumental fashion.[23] The interplay between the Union's external and internal agendas is also quite unusual: The Union's policies towards the outside world are centred far more on maintaining an "amicable" relationship among a diverse set of EU members than on enhancing Europe's strategic interests, however defined.

There is a tendency, especially in America, to apply state-centric criteria when analysing and judging the Union's foreign policy. However the Union is anything but a traditional state: It has no proper government, no fixed territory, no army and no traditional diplomatic service – it even lacks a normal legal status. And it is not clear whether Europe aims at creating a kind of post-Westphalian super-state or something entirely novel. In fact, it was never spelled out whether European integration is only about economics or also about politics, let alone defence and diplomacy. We are faced with integration under disguise, based on vague and inconsistent political rhetoric and ambiguous legal arrangements.

The Union represents something different for everybody and there is no way to establish who is wrong and who is right. We do not know the answers to such seemingly basic questions as: Where will the borders of the Union be in ten years time? What division of power is likely to emerge from the current reform process of its government structures? Is the Union likely or not to become an all-round military power? In short, the Union is a very special type of international actor and it would be wrong to view it as a kind of United States of Europe dealing with America in a clear symmetrical fashion. In reality, transatlantic relations are by nature quite confusing and asymmetrical and, as such, manifest a strange mixture of cooperation and conflict.

It might be interesting to survey briefly this pattern of cooperation and conflict because it sheds light on the very nature of transatlantic relations.

Table 6.1: Means Available for External Policy Activities of the EU

External Policy Areas	Total of Available Means in 1998 in Million ECU (Commitments)	Percent of Budget for External Policy Areas
Food aid and supporting measures	579,038	9.71
Humanitarian aid	539,600	9.05
Cooperation with developing countries in Asia	396,150	6.64
Cooperation with developing countries in Latin America	274,500	4.60
Cooperation with developing countries in Southern Africa and South Africa	137,500	2.31
Cooperation with developing countries in the Mediterranean Region and in the Near and Middle East	1,142,000	19.15
Cooperation with the Central and Eastern European Countries (CEE)	1,126,340	18.89
European Bank for Reconstruction and Development	33,750	0.57
Cooperation with the newly independent states and Mongolia	465,250	7.80
Other supporting measures for CEE countries and the newly independent states	83,115	1.39
Cooperation with the former Yugoslavia	264,000	4.43
Other cooperative measures	410,211	6.88
European Initiative for the promotion of democracy and the protection of human rights	92,400	1.55
International Fisheries agreements	292,700	4.91
External aspects of certain EC policies	88,130	1.48
Common Foreign and Security Policy	38,000	0.64
Total	5,962,684	100

Source: General Report on the Activities of the European Union
1998, Luxembourg 1999.

Partnership Without Illusions

Looking only at press reports, one gets the impression that U.S.-EU relations are largely about conflict today. Trade disputes are mushrooming and transatlantic partners seem increasingly assertive. There is a dispute about matching the ESDP with NATO and about American plans to install an anti-missile defence system. And there is also an ongoing dispute about the scope and nature of the EU's responsibility for Eastern and Southern Europe. The frequently offered explanation is that the Alliance across the Atlantic was merely an artificial construct, bound to disappear without the presence of a life threatening, overtly hostile, "East".[24] This may well be true in the end, but so far, the evidence does not suggest any serious break in transatlantic links. Of course, both partners need to adjust to the messy post-Soviet and post-modern environment, but they both have vested interests in maintaining close cooperation in shaping this environment. The question is: How are they to go about shaping this environment? Will they try to do it by laying normative foundations for a new international order or will they indulge in unilateral policies? Will they exercise their leadership through international institutions or try to surpass them? And how much diversity on both sides are they able to accept?

In no other field are conflicts more apparent than in the field of transatlantic trade. Recent disputes concern such crucial areas as agriculture (beef hormones and subsidies), telecommunications, movie and television quotas, data protection standards, financial services, arms sales, merger controls, preferential trade agreements (e.g. the EC banana-regime for ACP countries) and the extension of U.S. legislation to cover extraterritorial companies (Helms-Burton and D'Amato Acts). However, all these disputes ought to be seen in the context of an otherwise highly successful, $1,400 billion relationship.[25] By far the largest economic relationship in the world! The problem is that the current disputes undermine confidence in the WTO system that was built with so much effort for the benefit of transatlantic partners and the broader trading community. Moreover, since the new disputes are increasingly about issues directly affecting citizens – health, environmental and safety regulations – they undermine public trust in the international community's ability to provide objective scientific evidence, construct workable regulatory agencies and strike a proper balance between commercial interests and environmental and social protection.

The EU is much more assertive in the field of economics than in others, largely because in no other field is the relationship so balanced in terms of power and leverage.[26] Moreover, in the economic field, the EU and its administrative body, the Commission, have special powers to handle relations with external actors, including the United States. (The Union does not posses similar powers in the CFSP field). This means, among other things, that Washington cannot easily get around the Union's institutions and negotiate separate deals with individual EU member states. It also means that the EU's representation in this field is more focused and structured than in other fields. There is no immediate prospect for any transatlantic balance of power and leverage in the defence field. But Europe's current ambition to set up its own independent defence capability may make the EU a more organised, effective and independent partner of America in this field.

While it is obvious that the United States wants Europeans to share the burden of its leadership in defence, it is less obvious whether it is also prepared to share with them the burden of leadership as such. This is why the successive administrations of Presidents Bush and Clinton had an ambiguous policy towards the ESDP effort.[27] On the one hand, the initiative was strongly endorsed as a step in the right direction of burden sharing, while on the other hand the United States repeatedly warned against creating a European caucus within NATO. The United States seems to fear that the ESDP will produce a decoupling of Europe's security from that of its other NATO allies, a duplication of effort or capabilities, and discrimination against those allies who are not European Union members. These fears have been confirmed in the first speech on the issue by the new American Secretary of Defence, Donald Rumsfeld. According to Rumsfeld: "...actions that could reduce NATO's effectiveness by confusing duplication or by perturbing the transatlantic link would not be positive. Indeed they run the risk of injecting instability into an enormously important Alliance".[28]

Europeans argue that the dangers are exaggerated, but do not deny that they are real. Nevertheless, they believe that appropriate institutional arrangements rather than political bullying represent the way to deal with these dangers. As François Heisbourg put it:

> The questions generated by the sudden and unexpected re-emergence of European defence are often difficult. But they can and should be addressed pragmatically, through setting up appropriate institutional interfaces, not least at the working level. The difficulties may be real but they are of practical, rather than of an existential nature. There is no "prima facie" incompatibility between the political and strategic principles contained in the relevant NATO decisions and those laid out in the fundamental European documents.[29]

The issues of decoupling and discrimination in the defence field bring us closer to the next difficult area of transatlantic relations: enlargement of Western institutions to Eastern and Southern Europe, and the EU's enlargement in particular. NATO is not just a collective defence organisation; it is also and foremost the major political instrument of American policy on the old continent. In fact, since the end of Cold War, U.S. officials have begun to present the institution as a guardian of not only peace, but also democracy and development. That is, a vehicle for European integration. In the words of Madeleine Albright:

> NATO's Cold War task was to contain the Soviet threat. But that is not all it did. It provided the confidence and security shattered economies needed to rebuild themselves. It helped France and Germany become reconciled, making European

integration possible. With other institutions, it brought Italy, then Germany and eventually Spain back into the family of European democracies. It denationalised defense policies. It has stabilized relations between Greece and Turkey. All without firing a shot. Now the new NATO can do for Europe's east what the old NATO did for Europe's west: Vanish old hatreds, promote integration, create a secure environment for prosperity, and deter violence in the region where two world wars and the Cold War began.[30]

In fact, unlike the European Union, NATO under the determined leadership of the United States was able to fully incorporate the first three members from Central and Eastern Europe within ten years of the fall of the Berlin Wall. And the American administrations pressed the European Union to take new members quickly too, especially those who were already members of NATO, such as Poland and Turkey. The American rationale is basically strategic: EU membership will provide economic foundations for the security architecture created by NATO.[31]

The European problem, however, was, and is, that EU membership is about many different, and more complex, issues than NATO membership. Including the unreformed economies of Poland and Turkey, for instance, might damage the EU's policies in the fields of agriculture, labour and welfare. And taking many new members from Eastern and Southern Europe, as suggested by the American partners, might totally paralyse EU institutions. Europeans complain that the Americans do not understand the real nature of the EU, but then they have never made it clear what its real nature is. Integration under disguise is now being followed by enlargement under disguise. After many years of protracted negotiations with candidate states, we still do not know who is going to join the Union, when and why.

This short review shows that the disputes and conflicts between the transatlantic partners are not of any fundamental nature; both partners promote a similar vision of peace and development in Europe and they certainly do not want to return to the old style of power politics, as some "realists" have argued.[32] Yet, they differ about the way leadership should be exercised in the modern world and have problems agreeing on sharing the costs and benefits of this leadership. If only because their global aims are more modest, Europeans are more relaxed in approaching global issues than are Americans. Moreover, Europeans prefer to rely on economic, cultural and political tools to meet their global or regional aims, while Americans often employ their enormous military leverage in pursuing its ambitions. Also, Europeans always prefer multilateralism, while Americans are ready to turn to unilateral solutions if the latter seem to suit their needs better. Europeans prefer to engage in a long-term diplomatic process, often with an unclear price and outcome, while Americans have a more instrumental or strategic approach to diplomacy. The fundamentally different natures of the United States and EU as international actors further complicate their relations.

Conclusions

Today there are few in Europe who would question American leadership. Europe, with its internal divisions and rather dubious legitimacy to act as an international actor, is unable to provide leadership of its own. However, leadership should not be confused with domination. The current U.S. tendency to apply a "my way or no way" approach towards its European partners is destined to produce more conflict than cooperation, let alone partnership.

The United States is right to point to the EU's many weaknesses. But some of these alleged weaknesses also have their virtues. For instance, the Union's most prominent features, such as diffusion of power, primacy of economic instruments and built-in multilateralism, make the Union ill-suited to cope with a pre-modern agenda of military competition, national interests, and ethnic pride and glory. At the same time, the same features represent the Union's greatest asset when coping with the post-modern agenda of cascading interdependence, mass communications, cross-cutting institutions and multiple cultural identities.

It is important to be accommodating and open in managing mutual relations across the Atlantic and the same applies when transatlantic partners deal with the outside world. Unilateralist is seldom cheap and legitimate, and it should therefore be abandoned. This does not mean that all kinds of multilateralism work. Most Europeans believe that a strong Atlantic partnership working within a frame of international institutions is the optimal solution. International institutions such as the United Nations, WTO or OSCE can hardly function effectively without a strong Atlantic partnership, and vice versa. If transatlantic leadership is exercised through such institutions, the CFSP might, in fact, prove useful. After all, the CFSP has provided Europeans with a crash course in hard multilateral bargaining over the last decade. But, in the years to come, relations between the EU and America will seldom be conducted within the CFSP framework.

Notes

1   This article is a revised version of a paper presented at the 7/8 July 2000 conference on "The New Transatlantic Agenda: Facing the Challenges of Global Governance", organized by the IAI and the Centro Studi di Politica Internazionale (CeSPI) at Palazzo Rondinini, Rome, and funded by the German Marshall Fund of the United States, the U.S. Embassy in Rome, the WEU Institute for Security Studies and the Rome Office of the Friedrich Ebert Foundation. The author would like to thank Hanna Ojanen, from the Finnish Institute of International Affairs for her constructive criticism of the paper at the conference and later in the process of its revision. The usual disclaimer applies.
2   European Commission, "Report on the Operation of the Treaty on European Union", SEC(95), Brussels, (10 May 1995), p. 5.
3   "The mood in expert circles is depressed", declared Elfriede Regelsberger and Wolfgang Wessels in 1996, "there is a common opinion that the first experiences with the CFSP are on

the whole negative. The handling of the Yugoslavian case is perceived, not as an exception to otherwise positive experiences, but as highlighting structural deficiencies". See E. Regelsberger and W. Wessels, "The CFSP Institutions and Procedures: A Third Way for the Second Pillar", *European Foreign Affairs Review*, Vol. 1, No. 1, 1996, p. 29.

4   For instance, the highly ambitious and comprehensive *Common Strategy of the European Union on Russia* was hardly applied during the war in Chechnya. See *Declaration on Chechnya. Presidency Conclusions*. Helsinki European Council (10-11 December 1999), Press Release: Brussels, Nr. 00300/99.

5   "CFSP and the Future of the European Union", Interim Report by the Bertelsmann Stiftung, prepared in collaboration with the Research Group on European Affairs (University of Munich) and the Planning Staff of the European Commission (DG1A), Gütersloh (July 1995) p. 12.

6   Most notably, the Treaty of Amsterdam created the office of the High Representative for the Common Foreign and Security Policy, which is meant to enhance continuity and order in the CFSP representations system and contribute to basic policy planning. Moreover, the Amsterdam treaty envisages that support of (only) a qualified majority is necessary when adopting joint actions, common positions, or taking any other decision on the basis of the so-called "common strategy". Recent reforms aimed at improving the defence component of the CFSP will be discussed later.

7   For a more detailed analysis of EU's successes and failures in South Africa, see M. Holland, *European Union Common Foreign Policy: From EPC to CFSP Joint Action and South Africa* (London: Macmillan, 1995) pp. 218-21.

8   K. E. Jørgensen, "The European Union's Performance in World Politics: How Should We Measure Success?" in Zielonka, J. (ed.) *Paradoxes of European Foreign Policy* (The Hague: Kluwer Law International, 1998) pp. 90-1.

9   See C. Hill, "The Capability-Expectations Gap, or Conceptualizing Europe's International Role", *Journal of Common Market Studies*, Vol. 31, No. 3, 1993, pp. 305-29.

10   For an impressive list of means at the EU's disposal, see K. E. Smith, "Instruments of European Union Foreign Policy", in *Paradoxes of European Foreign Policy*, pp. 67-85. However, as will be stressed later, many of these instruments are not formally at the CFSP's disposal.

11   For a more elaborate argument concerning divergent European and American perceptions, see W. Wallace and J. Zielonka, "Misundestanding Europe", *Foreign Affairs*, Vol. 77, No. 6, 1998.

12   See Presidency Report on the European Security and Defence Policy agreed at the European Council in Nice, December 2000. (Annex VI).

13   See, for example, G. Edwards, "Europe's Security and Defence Policy and Enlargement – A triumph of hope over experience?" *EUI Working Papers* 69 (Florence: European University Institute, 2000).

14   See Joylon Howorth, "Britain, France and the European Defense Initiative", *Survival*, Vol. 42, No. 2, 2000, pp. 33-55.

15   See, for example, E. Nysingh, "Nederland doet toch mee aan Euroleger", *De Volkskrant* (4 December 1999) p. 4.

16   For an in-depth analysis of some of these questions, see F. Heisbourg *et al.* "European Defense: Making it Work", *Chaillot Paper 42* (Paris: Institute for Security Studies of the Western European Union, September 2000). See also *The Common European Policy on Security and Defence* (London: The House of Lords Select Committee on the European Union, 25 July 2000).

17   It is worth recalling that creation of the CFSP a decade ago prompted European leaders to make promises in the Balkans upon which they were unable to deliver, wasting much valuable time before the United States decided to step in and become involved in the Balkans via NATO. See J. Gow, "Nervous Bunnies – The International Community and the Yugoslav War of Dissolution" in Freedman, L. (ed.) *Military Intervention in European Conflicts* (Oxford:

Blackwell, 1994) p. 33 and ff.

18   Richard Holbrook quoted in Bruce Clark, "No Escape from Destiny - Richard Holbrook explains to Bruce Clark why the U.S. must remain in Europe", *Financial Times*, 23 February 1996.

19   R. Rosecrance, "The European Union: A New Type of International Actor", in *Paradoxes of European Foreign Policy*, p. 15.

20   See, for example, data on defence expenditures of NATO countries between 1975 and 1999: *NATO Review*, Vol. 48, 2000, pp. D13-16.

21   Consider, for instance, the confusing language of the Maastricht Treaty: "The common foreign policy and security policy shall include all questions related to security of the Union, including the eventual framing of a common defence policy, which might in time lead to a common defence". But then one should also keep in mind that the European Defence Community project (EDC) of the 1950s failed because it was probably too straight-forward, too abrupt (i.e. not incremental) and too immodest. See E. Fursdon, *The European Defence Community: A History* (London: Macmillan, 1980) especially pp. 192-99.

22   For an analysis of inconsistencies and ambiguities in the ESDP project, see François Heisbourg, "Europe's Strategic Ambitions: The Limits of Ambiguity", *Survival*, Vol. 42, No. 2, 2000, pp. 6-10.

23   The Union has an enormous normative appeal because it represents an ever-growing club of rich, peaceful, socially sensitive and democratic countries. However, despite its enormous "power of attraction" the Union has serious problems transforming its normative strength into operational capability. In other words, the Union is quite ineffective in shaping the international environment in any instrumental fashion. As said earlier, the problem is not so much the lack of adequate instruments, but the inability to establish collective goals and set into motion any collective action in pursuit of these goals. As a consequence, the Union looks like a giant in normative terms but, in practice, is a dwarf. For a more elaborate analysis of these paradoxes, see J. Zielonka, "Constraints, Opportunities and Choices in European Foreign Policy", in *Paradoxes of European Foreign Policy*, pp. 10-12.

24   See, for example, O. Harris, "The Collapse of the West", *Foreign Affairs*, Vol. 72, No. 4 , 1993, p. 42.

25   Figures for 1998, counting two-way trade and investment.

26   Most recently, the EMU project has further consolidated EU's power position *vis-à-vis* the United States. This has not been ignored by the Americans: "With a successful move to EMU, and the integrating forces that EMU could unleash, many Europeans look forward to the day when Europe will fully punch its weight in international policy-making, not merely on economic issues but also in the broader global arena", declared Larry Summers in 1998. See L. Summers, "Transatlantic implications of the Euro", Speech delivered on 6 November 1998. See also D. Kunz, "The fall of the dollar order: the world the United States is losing", *Foreign Affairs*, Vol. 74, July-August 1995.

27   See, for example, S. R. Sloan, "The United States and European Defence", *Chaillot Paper 39* (Paris: Institute for Security Studies of the Western European Union, April 2000) pp. 3-19.

28   Remarks as Delivered by Secretary of Defense Donald H. Rumsfeld, Munich, Germany, February 3, 2001. Internet source: http://www.defenselink.mil/speeches/2001/s20010203-secdef.html. See also Alexander Nicoli, "U.S. cautions Europe over proposals for force outside NATO", *Financial Times*, 5 February 2001, p. 1.

29   F. Heisbourg, "European defence takes a leap forward", *NATO Review*, Vol. 48, Spring-Summer 2000, p. 11.

30   M. Albright, "Enlarging NATO: Why Bigger is Better", *The Economist*, 15 February 1997, p. 20.

31   See, for example, Z. Brzezinski, *The Grand Chessboard. American Primacy and its Geo-strategic Imperatives* (New York: Basic Books, 1997) pp. 30-56.

32   See, for example, J. Mearsheimer, "Back to the Future. Instability in Europe after the Cold War", *International Security*, Vol. 15, No. 1, 1990, pp. 5-56.

7 Balkan Clutter: American and European Handling of a Powder Keg

RADOSLAVA STEFANOVA

Introduction

The last decade of the twentieth century in temporal terms and the Balkans in geopolitical terms constitute probably the richest locus for the study of post-Cold War transatlantic relations. It is, in fact, overwhelming to note how many policy crossroads have been invoked in and provoked by the dramatic developments in the Balkans since 1991. The crises in Bosnia and Kosovo, have, in fact, often served as catalysts for the definition or the clearer articulation of a number of important issues on the transatlantic agenda in the post-Cold War period, such as U.S. national interests and the question of its global leadership and credibility, the search for a new *raison d'être* for NATO, as well as its military preparedness to conduct a non-nuclear war, the laborious formation of Europe's own security and defence policy, and European responsibilities in reconstructing the economically devastated areas in the "backyard" of the EU. A study of transatlantic behaviour during the conflicts in the former Yugoslavia will, therefore, have much broader implications, most of which go well beyond the Balkan region and its persistent problems of instability and underdevelopment.

The purpose of this chapter is to analyse Western involvement in the Balkan wars and crises in Bosnia-Herzegovina, Kosovo, Southern Serbia (Presevo Valley), and the Former Yugoslav Republic of Macedonia in order to identify and assess the changing nature of the transatlantic relationship, and the Allies' ability to adapt to the new challenges posed by the upsurge of geographically limited violent conflicts in the post-Cold War world. Specifically, it will be sought to compare and contrast the U.S. and the EU approaches in coining strategies when confronted with a particular crisis in the Balkans and overseeing the implementation of a stabilization plan. Based on the findings from the examination of the four cases outlined above, a trajectory of the new transatlantic relationship will be jot down, as well as some reflections on transatlantic crisis management and the Allies' capacity to influence the degree of security and stability in the crises-ridden Balkans.

Bosnia-Herzegovina

Bosnia and Herzegovina became the first Balkan crisis, which seriously challenged the unity and cohesion of the transatlantic relationship. The process of a U.S.-EC/U policy disjunction was if not predictable, completely natural, given the systemic shift ushered in by the collapse of the Soviet Union—it is just too unfortunate that it had to mature in the process of the peace search in the former Yugoslavia, and particularly in Bosnia-Herzegovina. Indeed, the early period of the Western involvement in the former Yugoslavia offers ample ground for analysis of some growing cleavages in the post-Cold War Atlantic Alliance.

Another important reason to study the case of Bosnia-Herzegovina is that after a torturous three-year period of inaction, during which the EC/U demonstrated its inability to conduct pacifying operations, it was there that the United States decided to take on the leadership role in bringing stability to the Balkans, whereby *de facto* upholding and strengthening its military engagement in Europe. However, the U.S. administration arrived at this Balkan *Pax Americana* almost unconsciously, as if pushed to do so not by a political decision of its own, but by some sort of fatal *force majore.*

At the outset of the war in 1991-2 it was immediately clear that the (then) Bush administration had no intention of spoiling its significant dividend from the Gulf War with a shadowy engagement in the Balkans seven months before Presidential elections were due in the United States. Also, the United States deemed inappropriate even humanitarian intervention in a conflict which leading Europeans, such as the British Foreign Secretary Douglas Hurd, had described as a "civil war".[1] Moreover, this almost natural U.S. policy choice was significantly facilitated by the European Union's decision to take care of the quelling of the Balkan conflict, proclaiming that "the hour of Europe" has dawned. UNPROFOR, the United Nations' Protection Force, was, in fact authorized by the UN Security Council through Resolution 743 from 21 February 1992 originally with the specific purpose of helping the warring parties in Croatia and Bosnia-Herzogovina reach a cease-fire and eventually an agreement under the European Community's Conference on Yugoslavia. However, the bulk of the force, composed of French and British peacekeepers came under fire from Serb forces as early as September 1993 during such complex operations as safeguarding of the arrival of humanitarian convoys at the Sarajevo airport, which the peacekeepers were not equipped to fend off. Such episodes which exposed EU's inability to handle the conflict in Bosnia in the absence of U.S. troops or NATO involvement—those were not to be deployed until early 1994—led to the assassination of EU soldiers by the Serb snipers and paramilitary attacks, in episodes which deeply scathed the relationship between the United States and the EU within the Alliance. In fact, the French still remember it as the United States idly observing the murder of European Blue Helmets operating within a UN framework.[2]

This event was further linked to another thorny issue that stood between the Europeans and the Americans, and that is the question of lifting the arms embargo on the Bosnian Muslims, which was imposed by the UN in 1991 on the whole of Yugoslavia, thus depriving the Bosnians form any legal means of defence against the Yugoslav army. That embargo, David Owen claims, "will go down in history as one of the most controversial of all those passed by the UN",[3] because it was imposed on Yugoslavia in 1992, and the UNSC persisted in upholding it well into 1994, in the meantime having recognized Bosnia as an independent state in 1992. The question of lifting the arms embargo also underlined the differences between the Americans and the Europeans, as well as the general lack of strategy in their involvement in the conflict. Europeans were against lifting the embargo for fear that such a move would contribute to the intensification of the fighting, and, consequently to even more casualties also for their Blue Helmets. The Americans had long talked of lifting the arms embargo, and allegedly, it would not have been difficult for them to convince the UNSC to support the withdrawal of UNPROFOR from Bosnia, while committing NATO troops to oversee the safety of the withdrawal[4] (as eventually happened in 1995). However, while they "were paralysed by indecision", their European Allies suspected they were only doing propaganda on the cheap.[5] This mutual suspicion evidenced again the growing flaws in the Alliance. Among other things, this EU inaction also scrapped any hope of pulling the CFSP out of the copious paperwork of the Maastricht Treaty that had just been signed.

Meanwhile, the presidential campaign in the United States was signalling an interesting possibility of a U.S. policy shift in the Balkans. Governor Bill Clinton, who was to become the new U.S. President as of January 1993, made Bosnia one of the central foreign policy pillars of his election campaign. In particular, he was advocating U.S. military engagement in Bosnia, by air attacks, by toughened naval control of the Mediterranean to ensure that sanctions against Yugoslavia were observed, and notably, by pushing the UN Security Council to authorize these measures.[6] In effect, Clinton's foreign policy proposals during the presidential campaign went far beyond what Bush was prepared or willing to do, and also far beyond what the EC/U was able to offer. However, as Fouad Ajami brilliantly explains, Clinton's humanitarian thrust was not to be taken seriously, quite in line with what he calls the "American imperium"[7] for it was not to be carried into the new President's foreign policy agenda. In a bitter emotive statement Ajami recapitulates the essence of the Clinton's approach towards Bosnia:

> We must see that American commitment as it really is: hedged, tentative, full of escape clauses, vulnerable to the twists of fortune, made in a highly political season by a U.S. President who seemed to be on the verge of losing the prerogatives of the presidency in the realm of foreign policy. The Congress was in rebellion against his stewardship of foreign affairs and against his policies in Bosnia, Haiti and Somalia. He rolled the dice in Bosnia as a matter of last resort.[8]

Most analyses of Clinton's early policies towards Bosnia are, in fact, very critical. Lord Owen, who is also convinced that Bill Clinton and his Secretary of State, Warren Christopher, were at the heart of the defeat of the January 1993 Vance-Owen Peace Plan, bluntly states that if former President Bush had been re-elected, the war in Bosnia-Herzegovina would have been put to an end by the Vance-Owen Peace Plan for a cantonised federal state (which was initially accepted by all sides), as early as February 1993 with minimal losses on all sides and with no U.S. engagement on the ground.[9] Ironically, direct troop engagement in Bosnia was what was seen as the most daunting prospect for the new administration. Clinton's key strategy advisors, such as Dick Morris, were convinced that Bosnia offered the prospect of another Vietnam.[10] This was also a thesis particularly advocated by the then Secretary of State, Warren Christopher, who, together with Clinton, was appalled at the prospects for the Presidency after the U.S. engagement in Somalia witnessed the return of 200 body bags in 1993. As a result, the U.S. policy not only lingered for over thirty months, while ethnic cleansing was escalating in all directions in Bosnia, but it was also responsible for contributing to the strong realization by the Europeans that they were not militarily self-sufficient, and consequently to their growing frustration with dependence on U.S. political initiative.

The Europeans were, in fact, struggling between "the hour of Europe" and their tendency to follow the United States. The EC/U was initially quite supportive of the Vance-Owen Peace Plan. It needs to be specified that while the plan did have some major conception problems (its implementation and enforcement part left a lot still to be desired), it did offer a realistic, and above all, acceptable to all parties, way to end the war, in its nature much more practicable than the mastodontic 1995 Dayton agreement. Since the Christopher crusade on the plan began as of early January 1993, even the British government, which had professed particular fondness of the Vance-Owen "Peace Process", had to abandon it in the Contact Group (consisting of the United States, Germany, France, Britain, and Russia, later joined by Italy). It is also possible that this EU-U.S. contrast on Bosnia's conflict management strategy led the Europeans, particularly the French, who had been openly interventionist at the beginning of the conflict, to resist the American idea of a strike-and-lift option, almost in retaliation to the U.S. bossiness in floundering the Plan.

Along those lines, in May 1993 the French advanced their own counter-proposal, which consisted in sending ground troops to protect the six safe areas designated by UN Security Council Resolution N° 824, while at the same time still lobbying, together with the Germans, in particular, for the Vance-Owen plan. Paradoxically, the Europeans were trying to outwit the Americans, counting on the fact that if they managed to get the Americans to accept it, eventually, it would be the Americans who would have to take care of protecting the six designated cities. However, after the UNSC finally approved the safe areas resolution in June 1993, it became clear that neither the Americans, nor the Europeans were seriously considering sending ground combat troops to Bosnia.[11]

The story of transatlantic relations in the early period of the Bosnian war clearly demonstrates an astounding adhocery and lack of foreign policy vision on both sides of the Atlantic. Most importantly, that lack of strategy and political will to settle on a common course of action in Bosnia inflicted a serious blow on European-American relations, and established a pattern of mutual suspicion in crisis management, as well as in general security and defence issues. It could, therefore, be claimed that the Balkan wars evidenced the unpreparedness and the incompetence of the transatlantic allies to cope with the challenges of the post-Cold War world, a fact that signalled the beginning of a process of corrosion of the successful five-decade North-Atlantic pact.

Richard Holbrooke revealed how Clinton persuaded himself that Bosnia required a more robust U.S. engagement. A month before the Serb massacre of Srebrenica the U.S. President learned that U.S. troops were committed in a "measure of automaticity" inscribed in a NATO-Pentagon plan (OpPlan 40-104) to support the UN withdrawal from Bosnia.[12] With re-elections the following year in his mind, Clinton decided that he could not afford any American casualties during such an operation. As early as the summer of 1995, the President thus began lobbying Congress for a more muscular approach in Bosnia with a view of a quick and stable peace agreement. In August 1995 Congress voted to lift the arms embargo on the Bosnian Muslims, the administration instituted an "arm-and train" program for the Bosnian Muslims, and NATO performed some "surgical" air strikes to protect the safe areas and humanitarian convoys directed there. U.S. envoys were dispatched to the Balkans to mediate a settlement and sell it to the Europeans too.

By the end of 1995 the Clinton administration shepherded the Serb, Croat and Muslim leaders to Dayton and locked them up in what resembled papal elections, until they agreed on a clumsy compromise, which became known as the Dayton agreement. It portrayed the U.S. impatience and un-willingness to be involved in crisis management even in areas strategically important to the stability of the European continent. The language of the Dayton agreement, indeed adopted little of the usual moralistic discourse the United States normally uses to describe its involvement in world affairs—it was practical and quite poorly adorned with nice phrases as "U.S. responsibility in promoting human rights observance". As Ajami puts it, it both in its style and execution, the Dayton agreement was "nearly un-American"[13] in that all moralistic rhetoric was put aside to ensure the primacy of a very limited U.S. engagement of one year (as it was thought in December 1995).

The Europeans remained rather secondary actors in both the conception and the *mise en scene* of the Dayton agreement. The United States did not even try to consult, or seriously negotiate with its Allies on the other side of the Atlantic in regard to the terms, nor even the implementation of Dayton, which *inter alia* envisioned a conspicuous European troop involvement under U.S. command in NATO's IFOR (Implementation Force) and then SFOR (Stabilization Force) missions.[14] Such an attitude, which practically left out the Europeans from the negotiations, confirmed and reinforced in Europe the worst apprehensions of the U.S. unilateral way of crisis management, which the Allies had already seen emerge in the pre-Dayton period over the discussion of the Vance-Owen Peace Plan. In fact, collaboration and commitment to the safeguarding of Bosnia's newly imposed peace on the part of the Europeans was slow and reluctant. Partly, that was because they were embittered to have been left out of a peace process they felt it was their duty to forge *in prima personae*, and partly because the pre-Dayton period had convinced practically all major EU countries that they cannot *de facto* provide the military support necessary to keep Bosnia under control without the Americans. The latter, on the other hand, continuously threatened to withdraw beginning the lapse of Dayton's first year, mainly due to pressures from the U.S. Congress, in particular, to avoid an "entrapment" of the U.S. troops in Bosnia, as well as to cut the costs entailed in that. As a result, the EU leaders, and particularly those of France and Britain, spent most of 1996, 1997, and 1998 admonishing the Americans to stay in the Balkans, and even threatening to leave (which would have resulted in the immediate floundering of the Dayton agreement), if the United States pulled out.[15] Needless to say, such an attitude considerably weakened any concrete developments on the front of the long-cherished ESDI (European Security and Defence Identity), for which the Bosnian peace maintenance was considered too complex.[16] Moreover, the European desire to persist with the ESDI, an effort viewed by increasingly influential circles in the United States as a potential threat to NATO's new role in the post-Cold war world,[17] may have conditioned the U.S. resolve in Bosnia, and even more so, in Kosovo in 1999.

The United States, for its part, while trying to reconcile its continued engagement in Bosnia with both its strong moralistic rhetoric, and an ever stronger push from Congress to withdraw troops, formulated a rather controversial policy of "no fixed end-date" for withdrawal, while specifying that presence was "not going to be open-ended" either.[18] What was meant by this ambivalent statement was probably that the United States was going to gradually reduce military presence, but by numbers so small, that the effective reduction would not provoke the Europeans to threaten in turn their own pull out, or in other words, the United States was going to creep out of Bosnia. In fact, a look at the statistics suggests a move in that direction. By the fifth anniversary of the Dayton accords, the United States had reduced the number of its troops to 5,700,[19] a little over three times less, as compared to the initial 18,000 deployed under IFOR.[20] In addition, the Bush administration recently announced that it will not replace some 750 soldiers in Bosnia, when their tour of duty runs out, specifying that this will also be accompanied by the withdrawal of ammunitions and equipment.[21] On the same line George Bush underscored on 13 March 2001 that: "We must tell our European Allies that over time we expect them to put the troops on the ground".[22]

These open contradictions in the conduct of the transatlantic policies in Bosnia undermine the legitimacy of the very conception of the Dayton accords. As a result, it is not hard to understand why, even if it physically stopped the war, the Dayton agreement does not enjoy a genuine support either on the part of the local population, or on the part of many opinion-makers in the West.[23] In fact, the three ethnic components of Bosnia-Herzegovina seem to be drawing farther apart, in many there have been attempts at an open defiance of the Dayton agreement; the ever growing powers of the High Representative that were designed to harness partition tendencies have, in many ways, exacerbated the situation.[24] Oddly enough, recurrent statements on both sides of the Atlantic to the effect that the West is tired of sustaining Bosnia, having already spent there over U.S. $5 billion,[25] with U.S. aid amounting to U.S. $958 million,[26] seem to be addressed to the Bosnians, but are, in reality, the biggest recognition of a transatlantic failure in Bosnia. Instead, the transatlantic allies should co-ordinate a peace strategy that takes due account of local needs (partition should not be excluded as an option) and renegotiate a genuine peace settlement, now that the U.S. administration is not faced with a re-election for another four years. Such an approach should also involve the Europeans on an equal footing as the Americans, an arrangement that would not only reinforce the legitimacy of the peace in Bosnia, but also mend growing divergences in the transatlantic alliance.

Besides indicating some serious frictions in the transatlantic alliance, which have emerged and consolidated over the last decade, the Bosnian crisis demonstrated also that the Allies are in pursuit of contradictory, and, often, self-defeating objectives, as they prepare to take on peacekeeping and crisis management responsibilities in the post-Cold war world. On the one hand, the new Bush administration, even more than the Clinton one, seems to be committed to a policy of zero casualties in crisis management operations, a difficult and unrealistic approach which had so markedly conditioned Clinton's policy choices in the first three years of the Bosnian war.[27] On the other hand, the United States does want to stay involved and lead the conduct of military operations launched in the framework of NATO. Consequently, it continues to see in a negative light the European desire for a creating an institutional niche for European-led initiatives within NATO, which would significantly hinder the realization of an autonomous Eureopan security and defence capability. This in turn will keep the Europeans as second-class partners in the transatlantic Alliance with the effect of eventually weakening the Alliance and its joint initiatives in the future.

Kosovo, the Rump Yugoslavia, and Macedonia

The U.S.-EU relations over the Kosovo crisis were even more characterized by U.S. predominance than they were in Bosnia. Overall, however, the allies on both sides of the Atlantic were caught up by the escalating tensions in a contemplating mode again, and allied reaction was generally too slow to keep up with the tragic events on the ground. While the forthcoming genocide in Kosovo was not difficult to predict,[28] as early as the beginning of the 1990s, and its omission from the Dayton accords was a gap many were aware of[29] (even if inevitable, since former Serbian President Milosevic was made one of the guarantors of the Dayton agreement), almost a year passed during which the Milosevic regime mounted a monstrous campaign against ethnic Albanians in Kosovo.

Probably encouraged by the scaling-down of U.S. troops in both Bosnia and Macedonia, where the UNPREDEP (UN Preventive Deployment) mission, which numbered 1049 troops (of who 362 Americans) was terminated on 28 February 1999,[30] and by the fact that it was clear that implementing the "Christmas warning" of the United States was going to encounter substantial problems in Congress,[31] Milosevic went on the offensive in Kosovo. He was also certainly considering the fact that the Europeans were still traumatized by the early experience of their troops in Bosnia under UNPROFOR, so he was not expecting to encounter any serious outside resistance. Mounting violence in the province prompted the radicalisation of the Kosovo political leaders, among who moderates, such as Ibrahim Rugova, became marginalized, paving the way for the growing mass support of the UCK, the so-called Kosovo Liberation Army. Albanian leaders in Kosovo also realized that it was only through escalation of the conflict that they could possibly summon enough international attention to warrant armed intervention against the Serbs.[32] As a result, for over a year, the world witnessed the Serbs expel hundreds of thousands of Albanians from their homes in Kosovo, killing and mutilating tens of thousands along the way with mesmerized United States and EU watching the massacres without managing to react.

The prolonged humanitarian tragedy in Kosovo, was, in fact, another serious challenge for the transatlantic alliance. However, as Daalder and O'Hanlon put it, Milosevic "so repulsed the Western publics with his barbaric actions that the alliance found a resolve it would almost certainly not have otherwise displayed".[33] Paradoxically, it was Milosevic's excessive violence and cruelty, which stirred the EU and the United States to get involved in what had become a grave human tragedy.

In October 1998 one of Dayton's prime actors, Richard Holbrooke, the U.S. envoy for the Balkans, felt he had to reiterate the Christmas warning personally to Milosevic, achieving a half-hearted deal, which provided for the Serbs' (temporary) withdrawal from some areas in Kosovo and for the introduction of some OSCE civil presence on the ground. It was highly probable that this accord was going to fail, as it did, but its negative consequences went beyond that—they allowed Milosevic to bluff and flirt with the West for months, thinking that, maybe, in his vest of a Dayton guarantor, he could "afford" the genocide in Kosovo, and hoping it was going to be "overlooked" in the West, very much in the Chechnya fashion.

After another wave of violence around the turn of the year, the Europeans also stepped in to get involved in the mediation of the conflict. In early February 1999 the French offered a nice compromise-conducive mansion in Rambouillet, where the Bosnia-time "Contact Group" (the United States, France, Britain, Germany, Italy, and, Russia) made another attempt to find a compromise between the Kosovars and Milosevic. A fundamental error characterized this diplomatic attempt at conflict resolution, which was to become the key to Western continued failure in its attempted peace brokerage in the Balkans. That was the *a priori* tacit agreement that the independence of Kosovo was never going to be put on the table. Many analysts argued that while Bosnia's independence could be secured from Milosevic, in Kosovo this was out of the question because Kosovo was "the cradle of Serbian civilization", and Milosevic would never renounce to it.[34] While the Western conviction of Milosevic's resolve to keep Kosovo under Serb control might have been correct, it is unacceptable that this argument precluded the use of all valid negotiation techniques, thus obviously giving Milosevic an edge in the negotiations. A serious doubt remains as to whether it was the West's excessive and openly manifested respect for Serbian territorial symbolism that persuaded Milosevic he should not give up on the status of Kosovo, as he had in Bosnia, or whether it was really that the Serbian cynical leader had concerns about the national identity feelings of his fellow countrymen, so he could not afford to discuss the question of Kosovo's independence.

The failure of the Rambouillet negotiations, after the Serbs refused to accept an American-driven clause that would have introduced NATO troops on Yugoslav territory, offer an interesting example of European-American divergence in crisis management. Like in the other diplomatic activities in the Balkans, the Americans architectured the structure and the nature of an accord, which was clearly unacceptable to both the Serbs and the Albanians—the former had to accept a NATO force on Yugoslav territory, and the latter received no assurance on independence prospects.[35] Naturally, the fact that some European diplomacies were openly criticizing the Americans for their "toughness" at Rambouillet certainly also did not contribute to the success of the negotiations.[36]

As a result, for over a month, Milosevic continued his assault on Kosovo Albanians, the Americans—their threats of the use of force, and the Europeans—their lingering doubts that diplomatic routes were not completely explored. Many Europeans, as well as some American analysts,[37] saw the dead end of Rambouillet as a U.S. negotiation failure (and particularly, a personal responsibility of Ms. Madeline Albright's impatience with Serb demands). In a bilateral meeting with President Clinton in early March the former Italian Premier

Massimo D'Alema expressed his concerns over the efficacy of an air campaign, suggesting, instead a stronger OSCE presence in the troubled province.[38] Other European leaders, notably the French, as well as high-profile politicians, such as Carl Bildt,[39] also stressed the use of diplomacy over the threat of force, and even tried to make a case where even force would not have worked without diplomacy (whose failure, paradoxically, provoked the use of force in the end).[40] However, the most important aspect of Rambouillet was that a week into the talks, the U.S. administration finally decided that if should back its use-of-force threats with a concrete vow for a limited ground deployment of about 4000 troops.[41] The UK had also made a pledge for ground involvement, making it conditional (and here it converged with the other Europeans) on U.S. continued involvement in stabilizing the situation once military activities had ceased.

On March 24 1999, a U.S.-led NATO bombing campaign finally began against a choir of grudging Europeans, without a UN mandate (due to the Russian and Chinese veto threat in the UN Security Council), and in the background of a public opinion in Europe, which was generally hostile to the war. The day after the bombing had begun, on March 25, the Italian Premier D'Alema called for its halt, claiming, contrary to all evidence, that the use of NATO force was on its way to achieving its objective—the withdrawal of Serbian troops from Kosovo—and demanding that diplomatic efforts should now take over.[42] Moreover, only the Italian Embassy in Belgrade remained open, in contrast to all other Western Contact Group members, in order, as Foreign Minister Dini put it, "to maintain an open channel of dialogue with the Yugoslav authorities, too".[43] Of the other allies, Greece also remained openly critical of the NATO attack on Belgrade, and refused to take part in the bombing campaign. Germany felt particularly embarrassed to find itself at war, even within the framework of the Alliance, having only recently removed the constitutional provision that prohibited deployment of its troops on foreign territories. It was also torn between its generally pro-American stance and its unease with the air campaign. Chancellor's Gerhard Schröder's hesitancy was demonstrated clearly in his failed *démarche* to support the Italian government's proposal for a cease-fire in mid-May 1999. In fact, the two were supposed to issue a common proposal to the alliance to abandon the bombing in favour of diplomatic efforts on May 18,[44] but it seems that in the end the Germans decided that such a policy would challenge NATO's legitimacy to act too flagrantly, so they decided not to sign the Italian proposal in the last minute. The two leaders issued a common declaration explaining why they did not proceed with the proposal. In France, President Jacques Chirac did not nurture any pro-Serb sentiments, unlike most of the leftist parties in that country, and unlike his predecessor, President François Mitterand.[45] The French, therefore, supported both the air strikes and the deployment of ground troops, but were, nonetheless, unhappy that the bombing campaign was left precariously at "the mercy of U.S. internal divergences", hesitantly caught, as they saw it, between the Presidency, Congress, the Pentagon, and SACEUR.[46] The British, on the other hand, criticized the United States for not being consistent enough with the military objectives of the air campaign and deploying ground troops, which, as already mentioned, Great Britain had proposed to do at an earlier stage. Frustrated with such initiatives, the Americans complained that European resistance led to imposing restrictions on the conduct of the military operations, which eventually worked against the rapid surrender of Milosevic.[47]

It is clear that the Kosovo war reaffirmed and expanded the range of negative patterns that had started to characterize the transatlantic relationship from the beginning of the 1990s. In Kosovo, the United States was leading a military campaign despite its reluctance to get involved, while the Europeans were following, despite their unease or dislike of doing so. Moreover, while following the United States, the EU member states could not even agree among themselves about the reasons they were unsatisfied with the conduct of the war, each member-state speaking with a different voice. It seemed that Italy and Germany were dragged into a war they did not want to conduct, but felt they had to, while France and Britain also felt dragged into a war they felt should have been conducted in a different way. Such lack of background consensus over the nature and the strategy of the military intervention against Milosevic was bound to not only lead to complications in the military conduct of the strikes, but also to problems that went far beyond the conflict, putting in question the new nature of NATO, the efficacy of air power in low-intensity conflicts, the place of Europe in the transatlantic alliance, and the evolution of the European Union's defence and foreign-policy related institutions. In the final count, all of the above were weakened, and lost some degree of legitimacy and credibility.

Most importantly, the conduct of the Kosovo war showed a complete lack of premeditated strategy designed to pursue the desired objective of stopping the Kosovo Albanians' genocide on the part of the U.S. administration, NATO, and the Europeans. As a result, it was difficult not only to exercise leverage on the Serbs, but also to sustain the war-making credibility of the Atlantic Alliance.[48] Moreover, besides the lack of strategy, some scholars also note the strictly military underestimate of the nature and the scope of the war.[49] As is already well known, at the start of the war the United States did not estimate to stay involved in hostilities except for a very short period, devoting, in fact, only a third of the air equipment it would ultimately end up using, a reason for which there was no clear sign of NATO military prevalence over the Serbs for six weeks. During those Milosevic intensified the ethnic cleansing of the Kosovars, bringing the toll to around 10,000.[50] Furthermore, strategy analysts claim that if it was not for the arming and strengthening of the UCK over that period, air power alone would not have sufficed to bring the war to an end by extracting the necessary concessions from Milosevic.[51] In that light it is striking to note that even after the end of the war when all details of its military conduct could have been carefully assessed for what they were worth, analyses of mainstream defence strategists still consider only a numbers estimation of the successfully neutralized moving targets on the ground as a criterion for measuring military success.[52] By contrast, analysts like Daalder and O'Hanlon point out that if it was not for the allied UCK force on the ground, many of the Serb tanks, armoured personnel carriers and artillery pieces would not have exposed themselves to air strikes conducted from over 15,000 feet above the sea level.

In a similar vein, NATO's operation "Allied Storm" in Kosovo also revealed another important divergence in the transatlantic alliance, and that is the U.S. marked military superiority as compared to its European allies, who supported the operation. NATO Secretary General George Robertson pointed out to the caveats of this "unfair" state of affairs.

> In Kosovo, we saw that some NATO members had to carry a disproportionate share of the burden when it came to the high-tech sophisticated missions. [European] allies simply did not have the capability to participate at all levels. This imposes an unfair and politically unsustainable division of labor within the alliance. ... . Quite simply, a "two-class NATO" will not work. [53]

A recent study of the NATO members' interoperability conducted by the RAND Corporation's *Project Air Force* found that not only does Europe lack key strategic capabilities on which the United States has come to rely in the conduct of high-intensity conflict, but there are also scarce possibilities that it would obtain any equitable capabilities in the future.[54] François Heisbourg underlines a significant and increasingly evident "divergence of perceptions" over defence spending and, above all, military research and development, between the Europeans and the Americans.[55] These are all significant problems that have existed beyond the NATO air campaign against the Milosevic regime, but which manifested themselves with an ever-growing gravity during, after, and because of the direct strategic comparison between the Americans and the Europeans in the course of the bombings of the Serbs during the Kosovo war.

The conclusion, which imposes itself after the analysis of transatlantic relations during the Kosovo conflict, is that there are fundamental strategic and ideological cleavages between the Europeans and their American allies, which have produced major changes both at the level of NATO and at that of bi-lateral relations. Moreover, the Kosovo war also exposed the fact that even when the Europeans and the Americans do converge (*volens o nolens*) on a given strategy, it is done in a reactive and non-premeditated way, which often prolongs and seriously complicates the problem the allies are trying to solve. This is also evident in the handling of the post-Kosovo war rump Yugoslavia.

What also emerged from the significant European defence inferiority, as evidenced by the Kosovo war, was a practice that has come to characterize the transatlantic alliance to the effect that if the Americans are capable of doing the fighting, it would be fair for the Europeans to assume the economic costs and the management of the new *de facto* NATO protectorate in the Balkans. The Europeans accepted this thesis grudgingly, because it points directly at their military inferiority, but took on the task as they realized that Balkan reconstruction responsibilities do lie with Western Europe, rather than with the United States. Over 1999 and 2000 the Europeans have thus been providing for 75% of Kosovo's consolidated budget, as opposed to 13% that came from the United States, while European troops currently bear the bulk of the international military burden in Kosovo.[56] In addition, the Europeans also established a Stability Pact for South-Eastern Europe aimed at generating corporate as well as governmental support for concrete development projects in the Balkans. The EU contributes by 65.7% of the Pact's total generated funds amounting to U.S. $ 2.09 billion. By contrast, the U.S. contribution to the Pact has been 3.3%.[57] However, the bureaucratic structure of the EU has tended to also spill over the management of funds generated under the Pact, whose German Coordinator, Bodo Hombach, is also a newcomer to Balkan politics.

A final consideration that shows the lack of transatlantic strategy in the former Yugoslavia, which has translated itself in an *ad hoc* and painful conflict management in the crises generated there, has to do with the premature, disproportionate, and unjustified support of the new administration in Serbia. While the democratic ousting of Milosevic in early October 2000 was a significant step towards democracy in Serbia, it was important for the West to make sure his successors were truly committed to the principles of democracy and showed due consideration for the thorny issue of the unresolved final status of Kosovo and its Albanian-populated adjacent areas, as well as for independence-minded Montenegro and autonomy-claiming Vojvodina. Instead, the new Serbian leaders have often demonstrated a significant degree of nationalism, and continue to defy important international institutions, notably the Hague-besed International War Crimes Tribunal.

The new Yugoslav administration shared between President Vojislav Kustinica and the Premier, Zoran Djindjic, continues to show no desire of settling the issue of Kosovo's final status in a sense that would lead the province to at least enjoy a loose autonomy status, and continues to refuse to hand Milosevic over to the International Crimes Tribunal.[58] Patrick Moore has referred to this precipitous U-turn of transatlantic policy towards Belgrade as "The 'End of History' in the Balkans",[59] warning against the unwarranted full-fledged and rapid readmission of Serbia into the international community without that country's having fulfilled some of the fundamental preconditions, such as human rights observance, cooperation with the War Crimes Tribunal, and market and institutional reforms—all difficult tasks required and expected of most of the other Yugoslav successor states. As Moore further suggests, it would be wiser for the West to pursue a policy of "hard-headed détente" instead, gradually releasing carrots (which would also boost transatlantic negotiation leverage) as it makes sure that the replacement of Milosevic on the top of Serbian political life has really ushered in a new era in Yugoslavia.[60]

Paradoxically, a fact, which most eloquently points to the flawed and premature transatlantic blessing of the "new" Serbia, is that instability and violence in the region have been exacerbated after the ousting of Milosevic. In fact, important ethnic groups, entities or regions that were previously opposed to the regime, and consequently cultivated and encouraged by the West in their opposition to Serbia, now feel left out on their own with the same problems. The most flagrant example in this respect is Montenegro, whose President Milo Djukanovic ran considerable risk of a Serb invasion for having opposed the regime of Milosevic since 1997. At the time, his government received considerable aid and attention from both the Americans and the Europeans, which viewed it as a natural ally against Milosevic, although at all times wary of encouraging independence.[61] The George W. Bush administration rebuffed the (former) ally during a visit to Washington, which Djukanovic undertook in view of the elections scheduled for 22 April, which had been expected to lead to a referendum on independence.[62] Despite the fact that his pro-independence coalition subsequently obtained only a slim majority, Djukanovic and his party still appear determined to pursue independence, even if there is a risk that it might produce increased instability for the region. It is unwise of the West to fall back in the pre-Bosnian status quo inertia and not recognize and support Montenegro's right and will to self-determination.

The Montenegrin case demonstrates again a lack of coherent and premeditated strategy on the part of the West, even if it offers at the same time a rare example of transatlantic concordance. Despite the fact that the country's incumbent government has been an exemplary partner contributing to stability in the difficult period before and after the Kosovo war, as well as by far the only government which has willingly and immediately offered its unconditional cooperation to the Hague International War Crimes Tribunal,[63] it is being continuously told that it should remain within a Yugoslavia, whose democracy credentials are yet to be proven. This transatlantic complacency with a flawed status quo, which is partially caused by a growing Balkan inertia in both Washington and Brussels, and partially by the Allies' inherent (but by no means justified) dislike for border change in the Balkans, has the real potential of encrypting the next Balkan bloodshed, as Montenegro becomes desperate over not being stocked together with an economically down-driven, and not yet particularly sensible to ethnic and identity divergence, dominant Serbia. The consequences of the same strategy (or, rather, the lack thereof) are already manifest in Kosovo itself, in the Albanian-populated Presevo Valley in Southern Serbia, as well as in the Former Yugoslav Republic of Macedonia, which are all hotspots of renewed sporadic and escalating violence.

In contrast to Montenegro, the situation in and around Kosovo has deteriorated, as the rush to uphold the new administration in Serbia on the part of the transatlantic allies, has made it increasingly clearer for the Kosovars that they are going to continue to be confined within a Serb-dominated Yugoslavia in an internationally sanctioned protectorate. It remains a mystery as to how, after winning the war, NATO and its members, essentially endorsed the Serb way in the end. It was entirely predictable that the desperation that brought the Kosovar Albanians to rise against the Serbs in 1999 was going to repeat itself, as it does, both inside Kosovo (although on a smaller scale due to the presence of the international troops), and outside of it in the Presevo Valley (where NATO blessed the return of the same Serb forces, which had performed the 1999 ethnic cleansing). Moreover, and, even more dramatically, Albanian dissatisfaction has flared up in Macedonia, which was for a long time considered to be the crown jewel of international preventive action.[64] It can be claimed that the rising violence in Macedonia is beyond any doubt linked to the Western lack of resolve and coherence in failing to deliver on the final status of Kosovo.[65]

Renewed violence in Southern Serbia and in Macedonia has, in fact begun to dominate regional politics. Almost immediately since the change of the administration in Belgrade in late 2000, the areas in and around Kosovo, the Presevo Valley, and along the Tetovo-Skopje line in Macedonia have been subject to escalating hostilities, which have again paved the way to refugee movements, civilian victims, and repeated cross-fire. Instead of taking due notice of this clear indication of policy failure, the transatlantic allies plunged back into their usual Balkan inertia, which had so tragically dragged them in unwanted wars in Bosnia and Kosovo. Instead of reconsidering the basic failures in the Western strategies in the Balkans, prime among these being the unresolved status of Kosovo, the Allies took a clumsy U-turn, as they fell back into their *peccatum originale*, and that is, their preposterous pretence of "De-Balkanising the Balkans"[66] by holding their potentially secessionist parts together at all costs. To be noted among other things is also the flip in transatlantic rhetoric: The Albanians, who were only two years ago referred to as the "freedom-fighters", have now been downgraded to "terrorists", "extremists", and "guerrillas" for pursuing essentially the same goals[67] under different circumstances—a new administration in Serbia.

Another explanation for the continued transatlantic inaction in the face of the current violence, besides Western reluctance of encouraging "Balkanisation", or fragmentation of states in the Balkans, has apparently been, the Allied fear that recognizing the independence of Kosovo, will pave the way for a Greater Albania.[68] Mathias Rueb has convincingly overthrown this eventuality in an article recently published in the *Frankfurter Allgemeine Zeitung*.[69] There is lack of any concrete evidence for such an Albanian aspiration in Albania proper, in Kosovo, or in Macedonia, and studies suggest that the three communities are generally too different to really aspire to live and govern in the same country.[70] The independence of Kosovo should be assessed when measured against the alternative of its remaining within a Serb-dominated state, an option that is clearly unacceptable to the Kosovo Albanians. In order to yield lasting results, among them reduced military presence and smaller and better spent development packages, transatlantic strategy should therefore concentrate on using its newly found leverage on the new regime in Belgrade to predispose the Serbs and the Kosovar Albanians towards a commonly acceptable accord in the direction of Kosovo independence. Such an approach will certainly contribute to the cessation of hostilities in Macedonia, too.

Conclusions

What inevitably emerges from this brief analysis of transatlantic relations in the Balkan crises-ridden areas is that the Atlantic Alliance, which oversaw the fall of the Berlin Wall and the demise of the Soviet empire, has entered a decade of re-definition. The differences—ideological, military, and economic—between the U.S. and the European member-states, on the one hand, and among the individual European states, on the other hand, cannot be underestimated. The wars in Bosnia and Herzegovina, as well as the challenges posed by the rump Yugoslavia and the increasingly unstable Macedonia, have indicated that the transatlantic allies lack a *modus operandi* to cope with geographically limited violence, which has the potential of posing a strategic dilemma to Europe and of questioning U.S. credibility. Moreover, the U.S. and European tortured involvement in the Balkans, also pointed out to the need to acknowledge a different conception of humanitarian intervention on the two sides of the Atlantic. Finally, the Balkan wars have also exposed a significant divergence between the U.S. and the EU military capabilities post-conflict implementation preparedness.

The case of Bosnia-Herzegovina was the first case, which revealed in particular an important normative constraint in the United States, which is not conceived in Europe quite in the same way, and that is the militarily outlandish pretence of conducting a war with zero casualties. While for most Europeans the UNPROFOR casualties were certainly not desirable, but were conceived as an inevitable by-product of peacekeeping, the U.S. administration was clearly under severe domestic pressure to avoid any casualties. That objective premise was at the core of a growing divergence between the Allies. The American zero-casualties strategy was also one of the major factors, that highlighted European military inferiority as compared to the United States, which only open warfare in Bosnia and Kosovo exposed to a realistic degree.

The case of Bosnia also emphasises the lack of unity and a growing dispute over leadership within the Alliance. While the Europeans are clearly not ready to lead a military operation in Bosnia on their own, and while they also criticized the U.S. failure to get involved early enough in the conflict to avoid the massacres of 1994, the Europeans demonstrated their disapproval of U.S. leadership style, when it finally took over to strike the Dayton agreement. This attitude is to an extent inherently contradictory, but also partly justified by the

American suspicions over the creation of a more tangible European Security and Defence Policy.

The case of Kosovo further exacerbated these trends. While in Bosnia, the Europeans were grudging about the American floundering of the Vance-Owen Peace Plan, and about the way in which the Dayton agreement was signed, in Kosovo many EU governments' open disagreement with the U.S.-led bombing campaign indicated that the difference from only four years earlier has been brought on a different level. In Kosovo the Europeans were those, who manifested moral unease with a campaign that included risks for a number of innocent civilians, as public debates in many countries indicated that the Europeans also have similar domestic constraints to those of the Americans. Last, but not least the fact that many Europeans governments or parties judged the air attack on Serbia unacceptable also confirmed the emergence of serious normative cleavages in transatlantic relations.

Another important and related transatlantic problem, which was brought to the fore particularly by the Kosovo conflict, is the burden-sharing between the EU and the United States. Both Bosnia and in particular, Kosovo established precedents whereby the United States took the lead in the military aspects, while the economic burden of development and reconstruction fell on the Europeans. This is clearly an asymmetrical distribution of different types of resources in the transatlantic alliance, which tend to underline European strategic inferiority, and is not healthy for the future of the EU-U.S. relations. A well-balanced distribution of crisis management tasks, which takes due account of both actual European and American potential to contribute to commonly pursued objectives is key to the preservation of a robust Alliance in the future.

In addition, the Balkan wars also triggered a long-warranted speculation related to the future of NATO, the institutional bastion of the transatlantic alliance. As it engaged in its first war, a fact which put one of its founding pillars—that of deterrence—in question, NATO took six weeks to gain strategic advantage over a militarily much weaker adversary. Moreover, recent violence in Macedonia continuously brings into question KFOR's actual ability to stand up to its mandate, i.e. perform an efficient border control on its border with Kosovo. These are all instances, which indicate that NATO needs a qualitatively new strategic concept, which takes due consideration of the tangible and intangible constraints of the member states.

Finally, turning to the region, the saga of the transatlantic relationship in the Balkans also pointed out to an alarming tendency towards inertia, improvisation, and adhocery on the part of both the Americans and Europeans. As long as the mega-question of whether or not upholding Balkan peace and stability is in their national interest has not received an unequivocal answer, transatlantic policy in the Balkans is bound to suffer the same trepidation, lack of direction, and impulsiveness as it did first in Bosnia, then in Kosovo, and now in Serbia and Macedonia. Even if many analysts have repeatedly pointed out the many reasons that make the region strategically important for the United States and for the EU, this realization does not seem to have convincingly pervaded the political spectrum of possible administrations in Europe and the United States. As a result, it is unlikely that this lack of conviction will lead to a well-thought out pre-emptive and synchronized transatlantic strategy for the Balkans. Most importantly, it is very unlikely that under such circumstances administrations in the transatlantic community will have the necessary stimulus and self-confidence to re-work the current half-hearted peace arrangements for the region into workable and durable solutions.

Notes

1   Noel Malcom, *Bosnia: A Short History* (London: Macmillan, 1994), p. 239.
2   André Dumoulin, "Les Ambitions de l'Europe: de l'Après-Kosovo aux Indicateurs de Cohérence", *Politique Étrangère*, Vol. 65, No. 2, Summer 2000, p. 487.
3   David Owen, *Balkan Odyssey* (London: Indigo, 1996), p. 47-48
4   Ibid., p. 309.
5   Ibid., pp. 309-10.
6   Ibid., p. 14.
7   Fouad Ajami, "Under Western Eyes: The Fate of Bosnia", *Survival*, Vol. 41, No. 2, Summer 1999, p. 44.
8   Ibid.,
9   Owen, p. 393.
10 Ajami, p. 45.
11 Ettore Greco, "I Dilemmi Della Comunità Internazionale di Fronte al Conflitto in Croazia e in Bosnia-Erzegovina", in Marco Carnovale (ed.) *La Guerra di Bosnia: Una Tragedia Annunciata* (Milan: Franco Angeli, 1994), p. 145.
12 Richard Holbrooke, *To End a War* (New York: Random House, 1998), as quoted by Ajami, p. 52
13 Ajami, p. 45.
14 Sophia Clément (ed.), "The Issues Raised By Bosnia and the Transatlantic Debate", *Chaillot Paper* No. 32, May 1998, WEU Institute for Strategic Studies, Paris, p. 4; Nicole Gnesotto, "Prospects for Bosnia After SFOR", in Clément, p. 25
15 Jane Sharp, "Prospects for Peace in Bosnia: The Role of Britain", in Clément, p. 33.
16 Gnesotto in Clément, p.25.
17 Charles Kupchan, "In Defense of European Defense: An American Prospective", *Survival*, Vol. 42, No. 2, Summer 2000, p. 18.
18 *Certification of U.S. Armed Forces Continued Presence in Bosnia and Herzegovina* (Washington D.C.: U.S. Government Printing Office, 1998), as quoted by Ajami, p. 49.
19 Michael O'Hanlon, "Come Partly Home, America: How to Downsize U.S. Deployments Abroad", *Foreign Affairs*, Vol. 80, No. 2, March/April 2001, p. 5.
20 *Unfinished Peace*, Report of the International Commission on the Balkans (Carnegie Endowment for International Peace: Washington, D. C., 1996), p. 8.
21 *RFE/RL Newsline*, Vol. 5, N. 52, 15 March 2001.
22 Ibid.
23 Tony Borden Versus Daniel Sewer, "Is it time to Review Dayton?", *NATO Review*, Winter 2000-2001. See Tony Borden's convincing case to rewrite the Dayton agreement.
24 The (former) Croatian member of the Bosnian presidency, Ante Jelavic vowed to lead the Croat community of Bosnia, including Croat participation in the army and the police towards

secession from the protectorate, declaring a separate state in Mostar on March 3, 2001. See *RFE/RL Newsline* vol. 5, No. 61, 28 March 2001, No. 52, 15 March 2001, No. 51, 14 March 2001, No. 49, 12 March 2001, No. 47, 8 March 2001, No. 26, 7 February 2001. Republica Srpska also seems to be taking a similar path, having recently signed an ambiguous cooperation agreement with the new administration in Belgrade, a fact which was bitterly disputed by the Croatian President Stipe Mesic. See *RFE/RL Newsline*, vol. 5, No. 46, 7 March, No. 45, 6 March.

25   Gerald Knaus and Marcus Cox, "Wither Bosnia?", *NATO Review*, Winter 2000-2001, p. 7.

26   "Future Directions for U.S. Assistance in South-Eastern Europe", The German Marshall Fund of the U.S., February 2001, p. 17.

27   Barbara Victor, "La Vigie du Président: Entretien avec Condoleeza Rice", *Politique Internationale*, No. 90, winter 2000-2001, p. 31.

28   As early as the Bush (father) Presidency, the U.S. administration issued to Milosevic the so-called Christmas warning, which consisted in a threat of U.S. intervention (troop deployment on the ground was not excluded) in case Milosevic was to engage in ethnic cleansing of Kosovo's Albanians. The pledge was also backed up by the presence of U.S. troops, which were sent to Macedonia as a UN-authorized (through Security Council Resolution N° 795 from December 11, 1992) preventive deployment. The Christmas warning was also reiterated by Clinton when he took office in early 1993. See also Tim Judah, "Kosovo's Road to War", *Survival*, Vol. 41, No. 2, Summer 1999, p. 5.

29   Ivo H. Daalder and Michael O'Hanlon, *Winning Ugly: NATOs War to Save Kosovo* (Washington D.C.: Brookings, 2000), p. 10.

30   UN Department of Peacekeeping Operations, UNPREDEP Mission Profile, http://www.un.org/Depts/DPKO/Missions/unpredep_p.htm.

31   Ivo Daalder and Michael O'Hanlon, "The United States in the Balkans: There To Stay", *The Washington Quarterly*, Vol., 23, No. 4, Autumn 2000, p. 164.

32   Daalder and O'Hanlon, "Winning Ugly", p. 10.

33   Ibid., p. 19.

34   Sophia Clément, "Conflict Prevention in the Balkans: Case Studies of Kosovo and the FYR of Macedonia", *Chaillot Paper* No. 30, December 1997, WEU Institute for Security Studies, Paris, p. 32.

35   The Rambouillet proposal practically recreated the protectorate concept of Bosnia, with a three-year UN interim administration. The Albanians unsuccessfully lobbied for a clause that would have committed the administration to conduct a referendum on independence before a decision on Kosovo's final status was to be taken at the expiration of the administration's mandate. The Serbs, on the other hand, were pressed to let NATO troops on Yugoslav territory, probably a good lesson from Bosnia, where the first UNPROFOR contingent lost soldiers under Serbian sniper attacks, but a negotiation tactic that offered little manoeuvring space, which finally resulted in their refusal to sign the accords.

36   Ettore Greco in "La Politica Italiana Durante il Conflitto del Kosovo", R. Aliboni, F. Bruni, A. Colombo, and E. Greco (eds.) *L'Italia e la Politica Internazionale* (Bologna: Il Mulino, 2000), notes that the Italian diplomacy was envisioning the possible failure of the negotiations because of the American threats of NATO air strikes against the Serbs, considered an unnecessarily "tough" technique. p. 145. Generally the personal attitude of Foreign Minister Lamberto Dini was also suspected to be mainly pro-Serb.

37   Jacqueline Albert Simon, "Entretien Avec Henry Kissinger: Ce Que Je Ferais...", *Politique Internationale*, No. 90, Winter 2000-2001, p. 17, p. 27n., Daalder and O'Hanlon, *Winning Ugly*, p. 14.

38   Greco in Aliboni et al., p. 145.

39   UN Secretary General's Special Envoy for the Balkans, Co-Chairman of the International Conference on the Former Yugoslavia, Co-Chairman of the Dayton Peace Talks, and High Representative in Bosnia-Herzegovina.

40   Carl Bildt, "Force and Diplomacy", *Survival*, Vol. 42, No. 1, Spring 2000, pp. 141-8.

41   Daalder and O'Hanlon, "The U.S. in the Balkans…", p. 166.
42   Greco in Aliboni et al. (eds.), p. 149.
43   Ibid.
44   Ibid., p. 152.
45   Steven Philip Kramer, "Les Relations Franco-Américaines à l'Épreuve de la Crise au Kosovo", *Politique Étrangère*, Vol. 65, No. 2, Summer 2000, p. 369.
46   Dumoulin, p. 488.
47   Greco in Aliboni, p. 146.
48   It is to be noted that the whole deterrence concept intrinsic in NATO's threat of the use of force was seriously shattered, when a militarily much weaker Serbia did not hesitate to defy the Alliance for 78 long days.
49   Daalder and O'Hanlon, *Winning Ugly*, pp. 2-4, p. 19.
50   Ibid., p. 13.
51   Ibid., p. 4.
52   Rebecca Grant, for example, examines NATO's "Kosovo Strike Assessment", according to which over the 78-day bombardment, the air strikes destroyed 26% of the Serb tanks, 34% of the armored personnel carriers, and 47% of the artillery pieces, noting, while acknowledging that the problem of target-finding does exist, that such a score alone is sufficient to conclude that "aerospace power is a very efficient tool". Rebecca Grant, "True Blue: Behind the Kosovo Numbers Game", *Air Force Magazine*, August 2000, pp. 77-78.
53   As quoted by Adam J. Hebert, "Why the Allies Can't Keep Up", *Air Force Magazine*, March 2001, p. 55.
54   Ibid., pp. 56-57.
55   François Heisbourg, "American Hegemony: Perceptions of the U.S. Abroad", *Survival*, Vol. 41, No. 4, Winter 1999-2000, pp. 5-19.
56   Daalder and O'Hanlon, "The U.S. in the Balkans", p. 166-7.
57   EU Presidency with the European Commission Delegation to the United States, www.eurunion.org, December 2000, quoted by the German Marshall Fund, February 2001.
58   Jane's Intelligence Review reported on 2 March 2000 that Serbia's new leaders have consolidated power by appeasing the Milosevic police and military establishment. *RFE/RL Newsline*, Vol. 5, No. 53, 16 March 2000. It would be unlikely, therefore, to expect any significant policy changes that challenge that establishment, which is a nest to a number of indicted war criminals. A flagrant example is general Nebojsa Pavkovic, who currently heads Serbia's General Staff, and who was the commander of the Third Yugoslav Army, which committed some of the most vicious ethnic cleansing in Kosovo in 1999. He now leads Serb forces engaged in the highly volatile Albanian-populated Presevo Valley in Southern Serbia. Paradoxically, NATO agreed to allow a phased return of Serb forces into the 5 km buffer zone, a fact that Belgrade interpreted as a first step towards an internationally blessed Serb repossessing of Kosovo. *RFE/RL Newsline*, Vol. 5, No. 47, 8 March 2001, No. 42, 1 March 2001. Kustunica and Djindjic have also repeatedly suggested the rewriting or outright cancellation of the 1999 Kumanovo accords, signed in the aftermath of the NATO bombing and establishing a 5 km safety zone around the province. Deputy Premier Nebojsa Covic also explicitly pointed out that "for the Federal Republic of Yugoslavia there will be no change of borders, no special status, no autonomy". *RFE/RL Newsline*, Vol. 5, No. 33, 16 February 2001. Moreover, despite the arrest on 2 April 2001 of Slobodan Milosevic, prompted by a U.S. promise for U.S. $100 million in exchange for his extradition to the Hague (although half would be disembursed immediately, regardless of collaboration with the Hague War Crimes Tribunal), the new Serb leadership has always stated that Milosevic's extradition to the Hague is "not a priority" for Belgrade. RFE/RL Newsline, End Note, Vol. 5, No. 24, 5 February 2001.
59   Patrick Moore, "The 'End of History' in the Balkans?" *RFE/RL Newsline*, End Note, Vol. 4, No. 233, 4 December 2000.
60   Patrick Moore, "Hard-Headed Détente", *RFE/RL Newsline*, End Note, Vol. 5, No. 3, 5 January 2001.

61 Jeffrey Gedmin, "Montenegro: The Next War?" *The Weekly Standard,* 22 November 1999, p. 18.

62 *RFE/RL Newsline,* Vol. 5, No. 24, 5 February 2001.

63 The Tribunal's Chief Prosecutor, Carla del Ponte, declared in Podgorica her appreciation for the Montenegrin government's "full and principles support of cooperation with the Tribunal, not only today, when it is much easier and safer, but also through the years of Milosevic's rule". *RFE/RL Newsline,* Vol. 5, No. 33, 16 February, 2001.

64 "Macedonia: Prevention Can Work", United States Institute of Peace Special Report, 27 March 2000; Radoslava Stefanova, "Preventing Violent Conflict in Europe: The Case of Macedonia", *The International Spectator,* Vol. 32, No. ¾, pp. 99-120; Alice Ackermann, "The Former Yugoslav Republic of Macedonia: A Relatively Successful Case of Conflict Prevention in Europe", *Security Dialogue,* Vol. 27, No. 4.

65 The Macedonian Premier, Ljubco Georgievski, attacked the U.S. and Germany for refusing to link the escalating violence in Macedonia to Kosovo's unstable peace, "for fear of exposing Western mistakes". *RFE/RL Newsline,* Vol. 5, No. 54, 19 March 2000.

66 This is the title of a Special Report issued by the U.S. Institute of Peace, 20 September 1999. The word "Balkanising" or "Balkanisation" was originally introduced around the turn of the century to mean fragmentation of larger states into smaller, and often hostile ones. For an excellent discussion on the origins and the use and misuse of this term see Maria Todorova, *Imagining the Balkans* (New York and Oxford: Oxford University Press, 1997), pp. 32-37.

67 Even if the Albanians in Macedonia claim that they are fighting for more rights in Macedonia, it is to be noted that, while far from perfect, their situation in Macedonia over the last decade cannot be convincingly compared to the persecution their ethnic brethren were subject to in Kosovo. In Macedonia, Albanians have regularly had parliamentary representation and the two major ethnic Albanian parties participated in governmental coalitions, often occupying key ministries. They are justified to want to improve their participation in Macedonian political life, but at no time have they remotely hinted or expressed interest in using violence to achieve goals the governments were willing to concede or at least negotiate. There is no convincing way of interpreting the current violence in Macedonia, expect by linking it to the severe disappointment with what must be seen by all Albanians as a Kosovo independence *débacle*, especially in the background of evidence that UCK has often used Macedonian territory for advancing its goals in Kosovo in the past. See Radoslava Stefanova in Luciano Bozzo e Carlo Simon Belli (eds.) *Macedonia: La Nazione Che Non C'è* (Milan: Franco Angeli, 2000), pp. 87-114.

68 Patrick Moore, "Responsibility and Democracy", *RFE/RL Newsline,* End Note, Vol. 5, No. 39, 26 February 2001.

69 As quoted by Moore in Ibid.

70 *Europa South-East Monitor,* Centre for European Policy Studies, Issue 21, March 2001, Brussels, p. 4.

8 The Advantages of Complementarity: The Middle East Peace Process

VOLKER PERTHES

Introduction

Since the Madrid conference of 1991, a transatlantic debate has evolved around the question of what role the European Union (EU) and its member states should play in the Middle East, particularly with regard to the Arab-Israeli peace process. There have been differences about what the U.S. did, or failed to do, with respect to that process; and U.S. policy-makers have often shown limited understanding for Europe's own concerns in the region.[1] Divergent opinions have been exacerbated by a measure of rivalry over regional influence. Generally, however, U.S.-European differences over the Middle East have to be characterised as differences of priorities and approach, rather than differences of purpose or vital interests. Needless to say that EU states are not always in full agreement with one another about their policies towards the region; the United States is not a unitary actor either.

Also, despite those differences, regional actors have scored little success in playing Europe and the United States off against each other. For Europe as well as for the U.S., relations with one another are much more important than either side's relations with the Middle East; and neither Washington nor Brussels (or Paris, London, or Berlin for that matter) would sacrifice transatlantic co-operation for its relations with any of its partners in the region. Moreover, since late 1998, efforts have been increased to improve the exchange of information and consultation on policies towards the Middle East; some differences have been overcome in practice; and both sides' perceptions of developments in the region have drawn closer – thanks to, as it were, the policies of the Netanyahu government (1996-99) and the way in which it frustrated U.S.-led efforts to advance the Arab-Israeli peace process as well as the serious crisis into which the peace process slid under the Barak government in the second half of 2000.

This chapter will first deal with the argument that has developed, since the start of the Madrid peace process, about Europe's "role" in the peace process. It will, secondly, examine the interests and diverging priorities of Europe and the United States in the region. Thirdly, the structural factors that account for different U.S. and European approaches will be analysed. This will be followed by a brief discussion of the specific relationship between the "Madrid" and the "Barcelona" processes. Finally, the possibilities of translating the comparative advantages of U.S. and European Middle East policies into practical co-operation will be explored.

The Question of a European Role in the Peace Process

Since the beginning of the recent phase of the Arab-Israeli peace process, i.e., the Madrid conference of 1991,[2] a transatlantic debate has been going on about how the Europeans could, and should, contribute to peace making in the Middle East. Arguments in this debate have become more pronounced in the second half of the decade. That Europe would have to play some role has never been in question between the United States and the EU. The issue was, rather, what kind of role that should be, how deeply Europe would become involved in political negotiation processes, and whether and how European activities might conflict with those of the United States.

Calls for a European role have been based on quite different theoretical and practical arguments.[3] From the U.S. side, European involvement in the peace process has been primarily regarded as a matter of burden sharing. Europe should have a supportive function, and it should concentrate on the economic dimension of regional peace building. This included financial support as well as Europe's role as "gavel-holder" in the multilateral Regional Economic Development Working Group (REDWG)[4] and its contribution to other regional and multilateral activities. Some American contributors to the debate went farther, demanding that Europe also share parts of the political burden – either to make up for failures or shortcomings of U.S. leadership in the Middle East,[5] or in a sort of trade-off whereby the United States would agree to share leadership in the Arab-Israeli fold, if Europe shared some of the military burden and risks in the Gulf.[6]

From the European side, two different lines of thinking have been behind the quest for a role in the peace process. The first line, featuring a realist world view, basically holds that after the end of bipolarity there is room for more actors, even in regions, such as the Middle East, that previously were theatres of superpower contest. Europe should not accept an American monopoly in the region. Rather, it should advance its own geopolitical and economic interests and naturally play a political part in the search for Arab-Israeli peace. This line of reasoning – which could be labelled "neo-Gaullist" – has not solely, but most assertively been professed by French policy-makers and commentators; and it is safe to assume that parts of France's political establishment view a European role in the Middle East basically as an extension of their own country's *"politique arabe"*.[7]

The second line of reasoning reflects what could be called the common denominator of EU policies, and it expresses the thinking of Brussels, i.e., the European bureaucracy and parliament. It focuses on the economic, cultural and, not least, the political and security interdependencies between the EU and the regional actors in the peace process, which are seen as part of a broader Mediterranean region. The European discourse alternatively emphasises Europe's common destiny with the peoples of the region and its responsibility for furthering peace, democracy, and development among its neighbours, or European security and economic interests which require both socio-economic development and political progress in the region, including, prominently, the peaceful regulation of the Arab-Israeli conflict. European commitment, accordingly, cannot be restricted to economic aid; rather, it has to include a political as well as a security dimension. The "Barcelona Process"[8] clearly reflects this linkage between the Middle East peace process and Europe's interest in building a safer Euro-Mediterranean regional environment.[9]

Europe has been in full support of the Madrid process, and it has never questioned U.S. (plus, formally, Soviet/Russian) sponsorship of the process. Neither has it ever suggested that Europe should try to *replace* the United States as the lead facilitator and mediator of Arab-Israeli talks. Some hard feelings remained, though, on the EU side, after not even having been invited to participate in the Madrid negotiations. There have been recurrent expressions of uneasiness about Europe's junior-partner position in the peace process. President Chirac's 1996 suggestion that Europe, or France for that matter, should become a co-sponsor of the peace talks clearly falls into this category. And there exists a feeling among European diplomats and experts that the U.S. would leave the less juicy but probably more financially costly issues in the Middle East to the Europeans and monopolise matters of high politics or even block or "torpedo" political initiatives which the EU or individual European states might come up with in regard to the peace process.[10] Given Europe's interests and strong relations with states and peoples throughout the region as well as its financial commitment to the process – Europe has in fact become the largest contributor of international aid to the Palestinian Administration (PA), as well as an important donor to Jordan, Syria, and Lebanon – the United States, so the argument goes, should accept that Europe should have a more significant political role in it.[11]

The stalemate of the peace process that ensued in the wake of Israel's 1996 war on Lebanon ("Grapes of Wrath") and Benjamin Netanyahu's election as prime minister of Israel provided added impetus to the European claim for a political role. This was particularly true as Europe had to realise that the blockade of the process had a strong negative impact on its own geopolitical initiative towards the countries on the southern and eastern shores of the Mediterranean, the so-called Barcelona process or Euro-Mediterranean Partnership, that had been launched in November 1995. European policy makers concluded that if they wanted "Barcelona" to succeed, they would also have to contribute to maintaining or regaining the momentum of the peace process.

As the most visible and practical step in that direction, the EU created the position of an EU Special Envoy to the Peace Process, to which Spanish Ambassador Miguel Angel Moratinos was appointed – a diplomat with ample experience in the region but not, as some more assertive European policymakers would have preferred, a high ranking elder statesman. At the same time, Europeans began to define the role they intended to play in that process as *complementary* to the American role. This concept, which is now regularly used, has a dual function: On the one hand, it is to underline the claim for a political role, to stress that Europe can be "a player as well as a payer";[12] on the other, it is meant to defuse American suspicions that Europe might actually want to compete with the United States or counterbalance U.S. policies in the region.[13]

European policy makers, officials and observers have not always been convinced of the wisdom of U.S. policies or positions towards the region and towards its main actors. The strong pro-Israel bias of U.S. policies in particular, expressed, among other things, in repeated U.S. vetoes against Security Council decisions that reprimand Israel for settlement building or other violations of international legality, has not been seen as helpful. The strong linkage of U.S. Middle East policies to domestic issues, particularly election campaigns, has disturbed Europeans. There have been fears, on the European side, that the United States would disregard the legitimate interests of core Arab players, such as the Palestinians or Syria, and eventually try to sponsor a form of settlement that would be neither just nor comprehensive.[14] And there have been disagreements about the wisdom of some regional initiatives, such as the projected establishment of a Middle East and North Africa Development Bank that the United States strongly supported while the EU considered it a duplication of existing institutions. In general, however, European criticism of U.S. policies in the Middle East was not so much about what the Americans did, as rather about what they failed to do – i.e., about an apparent lack of resolve with regard to the peace process.[15] The Clinton administration's more active intervention in the fall of 1998 that led to the signing of the Wye River Memorandum was therefore strongly welcomed, even though it was seen as belated and overdue. In the same vein, the EU and its member states appreciated President Clinton's effort to convene the U.S.-Israeli-Palestinian conclave at Camp David in July 2000. For many Europeans, however, Clinton's attempt to blame Yasser Arafat for the inability of Israeli and Palestinian leaders to reach an agreement during that meeting simply underlined a lack of understanding of legitimate Palestinian concerns and interests on the part of the U.S. administration.

Europeans, along with American critics of U.S. policies in the region, have also pointed out that U.S. influence on regional actors is limited, and U.S. efforts to settle the Arab-Israeli conflict have not been very successful in the first place.[16] One case in point, as stated by former U.S. Assistant Secretary of State Richard Murphy, was "(o)ur failure to persuade successive Israeli governments to refrain from building settlements on the West Bank and Gaza".[17] The failure of President Clinton attempt to clear the way for an Israeli-Syrian agreement through a summit meeting with his Syrian counterpart Hafiz al-Asad in March 2000 forms just one more recent example. This does not mean that Europe or individual

European leaders would do, or would have done, better. Europeans, as one French commentator has put it, sometimes tend to forget that: "Europe's means of action [in the Middle East] have not increased as a result of Washington's lack of breadth and imagination".[18]

The U.S. response to the European quest for a larger and more political role in the peace process, as well as to the concept of complementarity, was anything but enthusiastic. Americans do not deny that Europe has a stake in the region, but there exist serious doubts whether Europe would actually be capable of exercising a political or diplomatic function. In the eyes of many U.S. policy makers and advisors, Europe has neither the instruments for such a role, nor does it have the right constructive approach: The EU, it was argued, would never find a common position except in their criticism of U.S. policies.[19] Most of its members were unbalanced (i.e., pro-Arab or pro-Palestinian); they focused too much on specific outcomes of a settlement   (such as demanding Israel's withdrawal from the Golan); and their involvement into the actual negotiation process would complicate matters, rather than being helpful. European governments and the EU should therefore "forswear independent diplomatic initiatives unless asked by all the local parties directly involved". They should stick to what they can usefully do: Commit aid, participate in the multilateral talks, and develop their own Mediterranean co-operation schemes.[20]

In a sense, Israel's former prime minister Netanyahu helped to narrow the gulf between American and European Middle East policies – in the last six months of his premiership at least. His active frustration with then president Clinton's efforts to move the Oslo process forward (i.e., the failure of the Israeli government to implement more than a fraction of the Wye River Memorandum) paved the way for a new and positive bilateral relationship between the United States and the Palestinian Authority.[21] As the U.S. administration became more responsive to Palestinian grievances and demands, it also began to take positions that were closer to those of the Europeans. U.S. and European officials agreed, silently, in their wish for a change of government in Israel. They also both considered the possibility of a Palestinian declaration of statehood on 4 May 1999, a risk that could carry undesired results – both in terms of a possible outbreak of violence and of enhancing Netanyahu's electoral chances. U.S. and European officials effectively co-ordinated their positions on the issue; both sides worked on Arafat to dissuade him from a state proclamation before the Israeli elections. Consultations included the EU's March 1999 Berlin summit declaration, which, for the first time, endorsed the Palestinian right to declare a state, denied that any side have a veto against such a decision, and held out the prospect of recognising such a state "in due course". Washington, given its bilateral commitments to Israel not to acknowledge a Palestinian state against Israeli objections, could, and would, not use identical terms. U.S. officials, however, had signalled that they would not publicly object to the European declaration. The U.S. position was framed in more guarded words, such as president Clinton's repeated expression of support for, what he called, the Palestinian right of determining "their future as a free people on their land".

U.S. and European leaders unanimously welcomed the victory of Ehud Barak in Israel's elections of May 1999, and there were similar expressions of hope, on both sides of the Atlantic, that with a new Israeli government the peace process would come back on track. The EU appreciated the Clinton administration's stepping up of its efforts to move the Syrian and the Palestinian tracks forward; and individual EU states offered their good offices on occasion. France, for instance, played a significant role in having Syria accept the Israeli withdrawal from Southern Lebanon. The EU and its member states, initially at least, considered the Camp-David meeting an important step forward, not a failure,[22] and they went along with the United States, as well as with Russia and others, in encouraging Yasser Arafat to postpone the declaration of statehood another time, so as to give more time for further American mediation efforts. Europeans and Americans were similarly surprised by, and unprepared for, the crisis that broke out on the Israeli-Palestinian track in September 2000. In more closed circles, Europeans discuss whether the Clinton administration had actually contributed to the crisis by trying to rush Israelis and Palestinians into a final-status agreement they were not actually prepared for. EU declarations were more critical of Israel than those of the U.S. government: Rather than only condemning the "violence", the EU at times also pointed to the root causes of the events, namely Palestinian frustration with the lack of progress in the peace process and "the settlement issue".[23] It is noticeable, however, that there was little, if any, public criticism of the United States and its role on the part of EU policy-makers and institutions. Rather, the Europeans urged the Clinton administration to continue its efforts to reach a solution up to the last possible moment. Again, the main European fear was not that certain moves of the U.S. president might not help the cause of peace as, rather, that the U.S. administration might fall back into a hands-off approach, particularly in the presidential election and post-election period. The crisis, therefore, did not have any negative effect on U.S.-European exchanges over Middle East policies. Noticeably also, the United States refrained from any public criticism of President Chirac's failed efforts to reach an understanding between Prime Minister Barak and President Arafat in a meeting under his sponsorship in the beginning of October 2000. Israel voiced such criticism, and some Israeli voices argued that the failed Paris summit was proof for the inability of Europe to play any political role at all. Such voices were not seconded from Washington. Apparently, neither the United States nor the EU and its member states wanted to give Middle Eastern players the feeling that Europe and America could be played off against one another in the crisis.[24] This does not mean, however, that Washington and its European allies saw, or see, eye to eye on all Arab-Israeli matters.

U.S. and European Priorities

Europe and the United States have indeed different approaches to the Middle East and to the peace process. This is not so much a result of different, let alone, contradictory interests but rather of different priorities, and it is also a matter of geography and interdependencies, as well as polity structures and respective capabilities.

Both Americans and Europeans define their interests in the region with respect to a wider Middle Eastern or Middle Eastern-Mediterranean area, rather than just to Israel and its neighbours. The key U.S. interests have clearly and repeatedly been defined: They basically comprise the security and well-being of Israel, the free flow of oil, the security of friendly Arab states and regimes and, more recently, the non-proliferation of weapons of mass destruction. Europeans do not deny the importance of any of those U.S. interests. Their main concern, however, is regional stability – a central concept to European thinking in regard to the region, which is conspicuously absent from the U.S. list of priorities. Also, "peace in the Middle East" has been defined as a "vital" interest of the EU.[25] While oil security and the limitation of weapons proliferation are matters of interest, European policy makers are less concerned about these issues than their American counterparts. Given the strong economic interdependence between Europe and the states of the Middle East and North Africa, there is little fear that regional oil producers would try to withhold their product from European markets.

There also is a European consensus of sorts that there is no military threat from the region, while risks that emanate from local and regional instabilities, from inter-state conflict (Arab-Israeli or other), from social crises and political turbulences in individual countries of the region, as well as from economic imbalances between Europe and its Mediterranean neighbours, have to be taken seriously. Uncontrolled migration, the spread of religious or nationalistic extremist movements, and the export to Europe of regional conflicts via migrant communities or terrorist groups, are of particular concern.[26] Little wonder, therefore, that the EU, in its common strategy on the Mediterranean region, emphasises Europe's interest in the development of a "prosperous, democratic, stable and secure region, with an open perspective towards Europe".[27]

In regard to the Arab-Israeli conflict and peace process per se, Europe and the United States are in agreement both on the need to reach a peaceful settlement and on the legal principles that such a settlement should be based on, namely UN Security Council resolutions 242 and 338, i.e., the land-for-peace principle. A remarkable difference remains, however, between the American and the European positions: In the U.S. list of priorities, the security and well-being of Israel is featured as a prime interest, separate from, but consistent with, the interest in Arab-Israeli peace. European policy statements, in contrast, rather than focusing on the concerns of Israel, emphasise the need for comprehensive peace and security, including the legitimate rights of the Palestinians.[28] They regularly underline the "need to respect international law".[29] Such differences are more than linguistic. They reflect different leanings in respect to the regional parties that are due to geography and economic interest as well as domestic policy equations.

Geographic proximity and interdependence are major determinants of Europe's relation to Israel and the Arab states. Europe cannot ignore the fact that all southern and eastern Mediterranean states are its neighbours. It can entertain special relations with Israel, and probably always will, but in contrast to the United States, it could never afford to base its policies on "strategic relationships" with just one or two regional partner states. Any regional destabilisation is seen as a risk, even if it does not affect the security of Israel or the free flow of oil. There are strong social and economic relations between Europe and the entire Middle East, with European commercial interests being much stronger. The latter are also more diversified than those of the United States: Israel and its neighbours conduct more than 52 per cent, the Maghreb states about 72 per cent, and the Gulf states around 23 per cent of their foreign trade with EU states, compared to only 21, 7, and 11 per cent respectively with the United States.[30] As a result, Europe is generally more open to Arab demands and positions than is the United States – even though the EU, and basically all its member states, still have stronger, and normally also better, relations with Israel than with any Arab state.[31]

Generally, both European and U.S. policies towards the region, as well as their different leanings or biases, are based on national or respective European interests – not on the interests of particular groups or lobbies. This is not to deny that pro-Israeli groups possess considerable clout in the United States, certainly more than they have in European states. U.S. support for Israel has often been in conflict with other U.S. interests in the region, particularly with respect to the Gulf-Arab oil-producing states, and it is safe to say, as Michael Hudson has put it, that America's Israel lobby has been more powerful than the oil lobby.[32] All EU countries consider Israel a friend, some, particularly Germany and the Netherlands, have also strong emotional ties to Israel. In none of these states, however, is Israel, or support for Israel, as much an issue of domestic politics as in the United States. Questions such as to where one's embassy should be located in Israel (or whether, for that matter, one should give diplomatic recognition to the Palestinian entity) are very unlikely to be debated in an election campaign, be that any national election or the elections for the European parliament.

The Structural Backgrounds of Different Approaches

Different leanings do not necessarily form an obstacle to transatlantic consultation or even co-operation on Middle Eastern issues. They can be translated into comparative advantages, especially if seen in the context of different structures and capabilities.

To start with, the United States is one single state, and it is uniquely capable of projecting military power into the region and of threatening the use of force if deemed necessary. The EU, in contrast, is still a union of sovereign states that all have their own respective interests and biases and do not always act coherently. Common EU foreign policy approaches and actions – the Barcelona process represents a good example – contribute by themselves to the integration of Europe.[33] As yet, however, only Europe's commercial and economic policies towards the region have been effectively "communitised" under the auspices of the European Commission. The EU's common foreign and security policy (CFSP) is still in an infant stage; any meaningful common action needs inter-governmental consensus. With the adoption of the EU's Common Strategy on the Mediterranean, in June 2000, majority decisions on activities that pertain to this strategy are possible, in principle. Given that Arab-Israeli issues are contentious, however, sometimes even among the EU states, Germany and others have insisted that issues related to the conflict will not be subjected to the common strategy – and majority voting – before a comprehensive settlement has been reached.[34]

Apart from that, some of Europe's regional partners have been frustrated by the institutional complexity of Europe, by the constant change of interlocutors, or by the comparatively weak mandate of the EU presidency that must seek consensus among fifteen member states for any foreign policy position or action.[35] With the installation of a High Representative for the CFSP, Europe's foreign policy will at least get a "face" – the face of Javier Solana at the beginning. Solana's membership in the Mitchell committee, established by the U.S. president in the fall of 2000 to find and evaluate the facts that led to the outbreak of protracted Israeli-Palestinian violence, consequently gave a little more profile to the EU in the actual peace process and efforts at crisis management. The EU consensus problem, however, remains. Also, Europe's ability, as well as its willingness, to project military power is limited, and will likely remain so, despite the declared intention to develop a European security and defence and policy.

Other structural features that bear on U.S. and European capabilities and their respective ability to influence the course of events in the Middle East may favour the European side. Among these features is the dependence of U.S. foreign policies on electoral cycles and the four-year presidential term. U.S. policies towards the Middle East appear in the run-up to presidential elections – or, at least, are perceived as being paralysed – which eventually may have a similar effect. Accordingly, U.S. leaders tend to link the calendar of events in the Middle East to election dates in the United States.[36] Also, presidential idiosyncrasies play an important role in the approach each administration takes towards different problems and actors in the region.[37] Moreover, inter-agency differences tend to have a negative effect on the ability of the administration to follow through on its agenda. Congress, in particular, likes to interfere with Middle East policies, including special legislation that may complicate or even obstruct U.S. diplomatic efforts in the region: Consider the "Jerusalem Embassy Law" of 1995; congressional demands for sanctions against Syria in June 1997; the April 1998 letter to president Clinton from 81 senators, in which they warned him against putting pressure on Israel; or the so-called "Peace through Negotiations Act" of September 2000 which threatens to cut any U.S. aid to the Palestinians in case of a unilateral Palestinian declaration of independence.

In contrast, changes of government in EU member states, the semi-annual change of the EU presidency or even the appointment of a new EU Commission are hardly noticeable in terms of Europe's policies towards the region. The effect of individual leaders' idiosyncrasies is rather mild, as European Middle East policies are very much the brainchild of, and are implemented by, the bureaucracies in Brussels as well as in the national capitals – which tend to remain even when governments change and commissioners go. The European parliament and national parliaments in EU countries tend to accentuate these policies, with a particular concern for human rights issues, rather than counterbalance or obstruct them. As a result, European policies towards the Middle East mostly have a long-term perspective, rather than being connected to electoral cycles. The Barcelona process, with a 15-to-20 years time frame, is a telling example.

Compared to Europe, U.S. foreign-policy making is highly personalised, with the U.S. president being the prime mover and decision-maker. This also reflects on the way the United States and Europe conduct their policies towards the region. It is noticeable that U.S. Middle East policies tend to focus on regional leaders, and work with them, much more and much more effectively than the European Union and any single EU state. Presidential phone calls as well as invitations to White House summits are important instruments of U.S. diplomacy. A call by President Clinton to, say, President Asad or to Arafat was always taken seriously. It would almost certainly have some political impact, as well as become front-line news in the local media. The same will apply to calls by President George W. Bush, Jr. A phone call by the EU presidency, let alone the president of the European Commission, is unlikely to have any similar effects – perhaps, the regional leaders would not even know who is calling.

At the same time, it appears that U.S. officials and policymakers pay little attention to structural developments and socio-political dynamics in the region or to regional links between Middle Eastern states and societies. Europeans, in contrast, seem to have a better understanding of regional dynamics and of the sensitivities of local actors. Reflecting the institutional architecture of Europe, the EU, with all its complexities, also has an inbuilt tendency towards multilateralism. While individual European leaders do engage in high-level bilateral diplomacy with their regional counterparts, the EU approach is largely characterised by the establishment of multilateral or pluri-bilateral[38] dialogues on various levels, involving economic incentives, a focus on regional political institutions and infrastructure, and a considerable interest in the involvement of civil-society actors from partner countries. Europe also tries to play international politics to the rules, with a stronger emphasis on international legality and a certain disdain for a U.S.-type of power politics.

Given these differences of polity structure and comparative capabilities, Europe would never be able to forge on the regional parties anything like the Madrid peace conference – an undertaking that needed the intensive high-level diplomatic engagement of the United States and a certain degree of pressure on regional leaders. It would also be unthinkable for the EU presidency, the president of the European Commission, or for any national leader in the EU to succeed in summoning Israel's prime minister and the president of he Palestinian Authority to a Camp-David type of summit, let alone keeping them there for a fortnight. At the same time, it would be unthinkable for any U.S. administration to establish, support and maintain such a complex multilateral, multidimensional and multi-level process as the Euro-Mediterranean Partnership (EMP).

Madrid and Barcelona

Although European, as well as some Arab, leaders have tried to insulate the Barcelona process from the negative effects of the Arab-Israeli conflict, there exist strong inter-relations between the Barcelona and Madrid processes. In a sense, "Barcelona" has complemented "Madrid" without ever being designed for that purpose.

The Euro-Mediterranean Partnership (EMP), involving the 15 EU members and 12 Mediterranean partner states,[39] was launched at the Barcelona Conference of Foreign Ministers in November 1995 to build, as the so-called Barcelona-Declaration stated, a "common area of peace and stability" as well as "an area of shared prosperity".[40] In reality there is little doubt that "Barcelona" was not so much a common Euro-Mediterranean or Euro-Arab undertaking as rather a European initiative towards its southern neighbourhood. Europe, as mentioned, is primarily concerned with regional stability, and it has based its Mediterranean policies on, as one observer has put it, the "solid linkage between the EU need for more security with respect to instabilities coming from the South and the Middle East and North Africa (MENA) [and the] need for EU social and economic support in order to attain stability".[41] "Barcelona" therefore involved an upgrading of European financial aid to the Mediterranean partner countries; the perspective of establishing a Euro-Med free trade area by 2010 as well as bilateral arrangements to help these countries reform and open up their economies; enhanced exchanges in the cultural and, broadly speaking, civil-society fields; and – most importantly from the European viewpoint – the establishment of multi- and bilateral frameworks for enhanced political dialogue and security co-operation between the EU and the states of the southern and eastern Mediterranean.

The Barcelona conference would not have been possible had it not been for the Madrid and Oslo processes which had created an atmosphere conducive for the European initiative. Once the peace process stalled, however, Europe's Mediterranean project was also affected. This was particularly so for its security dimension: Starting with the second ministerial conference of the EMP in Malta in June 1997, the Arab states made it clear that they would not support Europe's ambitious ideas about institutionalised Mediterranean security co-operation as long as the issues of territorial occupation in the Middle East were far from a solution, nor would they agree on any list of confidence building measures as long as the basic regional confidence building exercise – the peace process – was blocked.[42] Again, in the fall of 2000, the Middle East crisis took its toll on the Barcelona process. Not only did Syria and Lebanon stay away from the fourth Euro-Mediterranean Conference of foreign ministers in Marseilles, but also, more ambitious plans, particularly those of the French EU presidency, to have this meeting adopt a draft Charter for Peace and Stability in the Mediterranean Region, had to be shelved.[43]

At the same time, the Barcelona process has contributed to maintaining a modest dynamic in the peace process. Most importantly, it has provided a forum, the only forum, in fact, where representatives of Israel, Syria, Lebanon, the Palestinian Authority and others met on a regular basis. This goes for the so-called Group of Senior Officials (high-ranking diplomats of all the twenty-seven states that participate in the process) which has been meeting regularly to dialogue about political and security issues, as well as for a multitude of meetings of government ministers and high officials concerned with economic, social, environmental or cultural issues. In a way, by sponsoring this process, Europe has managed to project a degree of multilateralism into the region that can, and most likely will, enhance structural peace building once peace agreements have been concluded between Israel and its neighbours.

Another important aspect of the Euro-Med partnership is that it helps individual Arab countries become fit for a new regional division of labour that will no longer be defined by the conflict with Israel. This is mainly so for a country like Syria, and to a lesser degree for Jordan, the Palestinian Authority, and Lebanon. Arguably, Syria's preparedness, in 1995, to overcome some of the domestic obstacles to peace and "normalisation" with Israel was linked to the launching of the Barcelona process and to the perspectives of Euro-Mediterranean co-operation: Basically, the European initiative promised the support which Syria needs to prepare its economy and society for the new and more intense forms of economic and political competition that regional peace will bring about.[44] It also offered the perspective of entering globalisation, as it were, through Europe, rather than through an Israeli dominated "New Middle East".

And the Palestinian quasi-state that has emerged from the Oslo agreements would probably not have survived at all without European financial and technical aid. A breakdown of the Palestinian Authority would almost certainly have triggered large-scale violence and terminated the Madrid process. In this sense, European economic support and support for Palestinian state building has been an active security policy.

Comparative Advantages: Prescriptions for a Division of Labour

The above record shows that U.S. and European efforts in the Middle East can indeed complement each other. Europe and the United States enjoy particular comparative advantages and weaknesses (that is, each side is better equipped for some activities than for others) that can and should be translated into a – rather informal – division of labour and responsibilities. Complementarity implies that U.S. capabilities cannot be the benchmark or standard against which the value, or the political importance, of European contributions is measured, and vice versa. There is no reason to assume that power projection is more important, or more conducive to promoting peace and stability in the region, than the projection of multilateralism. The former may have more short-term, the latter more long-term effects. Nor does complementarity and division of responsibilities mean that one party follow the other blindly, or that Americans and Europeans have to see eye-to-eye on every question that concerns their policies in the region. Rather, we may speak of a constructive competition of ideas and instruments whereby the comparative advantages of either side's approaches and capabilities are used to advance the peace process.

First, the United States will have to remain the main regional power broker. U.S. efforts should therefore concentrate on high-level diplomacy, especially in facilitating and mediating bilateral negotiations as well as giving regional leaders the final push they may need to make a deal. It is obvious that U.S. security assistance and guarantees to individual countries, particularly but not only to Israel, can reassure these countries' publics and compensate for certain territorial or political concessions they will have to make for an agreement with their neighbours. Europeans should not be deceived by Arab calls for a greater European role, or even for Europe as a counterweight to the United States: When it comes to forging a final deal, Israel as well as Syria, Lebanon or the Palestinian leadership will want to have the Americans at the table. The Arab states may have limited trust in the impartiality of the United States, but they certainly want its weight and power to be behind an agreement they will conclude with Washington's main ally in the region.[45]

Europe will generally have to concentrate on less visible, but no less politically important contributions to achieving and stabilising peace in the Middle East. First, the EU should be brought in charge of reviving the multilateral peace talks – it might be wise, for that purpose, to upgrade Europe's responsibility for the Multilaterals and make it the chair or co-chair of a renewed steering group that would co-ordinate and oversee the work of the negotiation process. The EU should of course continue to sponsor and support other – regional or subregional – multilateral activities, particularly in the fields of economic and security co-operation that are not necessarily linked to the peace process but have a positive bearing on it. Moreover, and aside from being a Western model for regional co-operation and integration, Europe can, as indicated, provide practical experience and get regional actors used to work in multilateral frameworks through its Mediterranean policy.

Second, regarding the bilateral Arab-Israeli tracks, U.S. leadership is not in question, and it will not be questioned by Europe provided that Washington does not abandon its responsibilities. European contributions will generally take place on the somewhat lesser diplomatic levels, and often with lower profile. This includes traditional diplomatic functions such as conveying messages between and developing ideas with regional leaders. It also includes more practical activities related to security-and- confidence building and to the implementation of existing agreements. Note in this respect Europe's support and training for the Palestinian anti-terrorism measures and other activities that can contribute to overcoming not merely technical obstacles to peace and co-operation in security-relevant fields. One example was the EU Special Envoy's efforts to work out, with Israeli and Palestinian officials, arrangements by which the Palestinian airport would become a fully operable and normal gateway for commodity exports and passengers.

Furthermore, in the context of peace negotiations or crisis containment, there will be a recurrent need to employ the special relations that Brussels, Paris, Berlin or others maintain with individual states in the Middle East, particularly with Syria and Lebanon or Iran, and to do so on different levels of diplomacy. France's efforts to make Teheran a silent partner in the so-called "April understanding" – the cease-fire agreement that ended Israel's 1996 "Operation Grapes of Wrath" and led to the establishment of the Israel-Lebanon Monitoring Group (ILMG) – wasn't at that time well received by the United States; it did, however, contribute to finding a format which, in the judgement of U.S., French, Syrian, Israeli and Lebanese observers, has worked considerably well. In May 2000, as mentioned, France again was central in conveying to Syria that it better accept Israel's unilateral withdrawal from Lebanon.

Third, and partly related to the latter point, Europe and European institutions should remain active organisers of second tracks – not only between Israelis and Palestinians. The "Oslo" process, and the invaluable contribution of Norway's (which is not, of course, a member of the EU) diplomacy to that process, certainly represents a case in point. Given Europe's strong interdependence and more diversified relations with the region as well as the predilection of European policies for the creation of multilateral networks and their focus on societal actors, Europe will, in general, be the better interlocutor for such low-level diplomatic or semi-diplomatic activities.

Fourth, Europe has an important role in institution building. This applies to regional frameworks, such as, among other things, the establishment of REDWG (the working group of the Multilaterals concerned with economic development) as a regional institution with a permanent secretariat in Amman, or the development of institutions that have emanated from the Barcelona process (and may work in such different fields as diplomatic training, research networks, local water management, preservation of cultural heritage, or statistics). Such regional links will become even more necessary in a post peace-process era. It also applies, no less importantly, to institution building in the Palestinian territories. In practice, this means to lay, or help lay, the groundwork for a viable and reliable Palestinian state. While Europe should have a leading role in this field, the issue is not only a European concern. Neither should it exclude U.S. involvement, nor Euro-American or Euro-American-Middle Eastern co-operation.[46]

Finally, there could be a limited European military peacekeeping role, if and where, the regional parties so wish. This will most likely apply to Israel and Syria. Israel will not agree to UN peacekeepers on the Golan, but an international military presence modelled on the Multinational Forces and Observers (MFO) in the Sinai could be acceptable to both countries. We should therefore envisage a joint peacekeeping force of U.S., French and other European units. Also, the ILMG, with U.S. and French co-operative involvement, could be reinvented so as to stabilise the situation at the Israeli-Lebanese border before an eventual peace agreement comes into force.

Generally, rather than only demanding a political role in the peace process, Europe will have to perform, and earn it. European policy-makers will have to accept, with a bit more self-confidence perhaps, that most of Europe's less highly visible contributions to the process are nevertheless highly political. This includes, but it is not restricted to, mid- to long-term financial commitments. Above that, the EU will have to give a convincing answer as to whether it really has a common foreign and security policy (CFSP) with regard to the Middle East. It has not been lost on the regional actors that European states have not always spoken with one voice, and that it is often difficult for the EU Special Envoy or the EU presidency to generate consensus on important policy matters.

U.S. policy makers will have to acknowledge that the European contribution is essential enough to necessitate regular consultations and co-ordination – rather than only information or briefing sessions by the Americans for their European colleagues. Under the New Transatlantic Agenda, the EU and the U.S. have endorsed continued co-operation of the Special Envoys to the peace process.[47] In some cases, joint U.S.-European approaches and actions will be needed. This applies, for instance, for peacekeeping operations or an extension of the ILMG. In many other cases, such as organising material support for Palestinian state building, consultation and co-ordination is sufficient.

Both Europeans and Americans have to be aware that their influence on events in the Middle East is limited. Eventually, the regional actors are in charge: External actors can assist in peace efforts, they can help stabilise the region and grant political and economic support, but they cannot make peace on behalf of Israelis and Arabs.

Notes

1   "Europe", here and in the following, is used as shorthand for the EU and its member states.

2   Speaking of the Middle East or Arab-Israeli peace process, it should not be forgotten that this term has been in use since at least 1973 when, in the wake of the October- or the Yom Kippur war- a first Middle East peace conference was held in Geneva. Of course, even before the recent phase of the peace process, there had been differences between Europeans and Americans over the appropriate policy towards the Middle East. Among other things, there was strong disagreement about the European Communities' Venice declaration of 1980 that endorsed, for the first time, the Palestinian right of self-determination, or about Washington's tacit support for Israel's 1982 invasion of Lebanon. The main competitor of the United States with regard to the Middle East, however, was not Europe but, until its disintegration in 1991, the Soviet Union.

3   For a more detailed discussion, see V. Perthes, "Europe, the United States and the Middle East Peace Process", in *Allies Divided. Transatlantic Policies for the Greater Middle East,* eds. R. D. Blackwill and M. Stürmer (Cambridge: The MIT Press, 1997), pp. 79-100 (85-87), on which this article partly draws.

4   Following the Madrid Conference, five multilateral working groups have been established to parallel the bilateral talks between Israel and its neighbours, each chaired by an extra-regional gavel-holder: Economic development (EU), environment (Japan), water (U.S.), refugees (Canada), and arms control and regional security (U.S. and Russia co-chairs). A steering group to the Multilaterals was also co-chaired by the United States and Russia. For a discussion see D. D. Kaye, "Madrid's Forgotten Forum: The Middle East Multilaterals", *The Washington Quarterly,* Vol. 20, No. 1, 1997, pp. 167-186; Joel Peters, "Can the Multilateral Peace Talks be Revived?" MERIA Journal, Vol. 3 (December 1999), No. 4 (http://www.biu.ac.il/soe/meria/index.html).

5   See, e.g., W. Pfaff, "EU should Weigh in on Mid-east Peace Process", in *International Herald Tribune,* 26 October 1996. H. Siegmann (Project Coordinator), U.S. Middle East Policy and the Peace Process. Report of an Independent Task Force Sponsored by the Council of Foreign Relations (New York: Council on Foreign Relations, 1997).

6   See D. C. Gompert, J. Green, F. S. Larrabee "Common Interests, Common Responsibilities: How an Atlantic Partnership Could Stabilize the Middle East", Rand Review, Vol. 23, No. 1, 1999, (www.rand.org/publications/RRR/spring 99).

7   See P. C. Wood, "Chirac's 'New Arab Policy' and Middle East Challenges: The Arab-Israeli Conflict, Iraq and Iran", *Middle East Journal,* Vol. 52, No. 4, 1998, pp. 563-580. M. Bonnefous, "Réflexions sur une politique arabe", in *défense nationale,* Vol. 54, 1998, pp. 44-67. Bonnefous explains that France, given its long involvement in the region, has a legitimate "title" to a role in the peace process (p. 56).

8   See below.

9   See, e.g., Commission of the European Communities *The role of the European Union in the Middle East and its future assistance,* Communication from the European Commission, COM(97) 715 fin., January 16, 1998; European Council Amsterdam, 16-17 June 1997, *European Union Call for Peace in the Middle East* (Presidency Conclusions, Doc. SN 150/97); and analytically: E. Rhein, "Europe and the Mediterranean: A Newly Emerging Geopolitical

Area", *European Foreign Affairs Review*, No. 1, 1996, pp. 79-86; V. Perthes, "Der Mittelmeerraum, der nahöstliche Friedensprozeß und die Europäische Union", *Internationale Politik und Gesellschaft*, No. 2, 1999, pp. 143-149.

10 See, e.g., U. Steinbach and C. Hacke, "Auf ewig der Juniorpartner Amerikas?", *Frankfurter Allgemeine Zeitung*, 15 May 1999.

11 See, e.g., R. Hollis, "Europe and the Middle East: Power by Stealth?" *International Affairs*, Vol. 73, No. 1, 1996, pp. 15-29.

12 M. A. Moratinos, "Give Peace a Hand", *The Financial Times*, 3 June 1999.

13 See M. Rifkind, "Blueprint for a region at peace", *The Times*, 5 November 1996; Commission of the European Communities, *The Role of the European Union in the Middle East*.

14 See V. Perthes, "Points of Difference, Cases for Cooperation: European Critiques of U.S. Middle East Policy", *Middle East Report*, Vol. 28, No. 3, 1998, pp. 30-32.

15 See, e.g., D. Moïsi, "Europe's backyard: The EU should be more active in Middle East Peace Talks", *The Financial Times*, 13 October 1997: "Seen from Europe", he writes, "Washington's strategy could be summarised – unfairly, of course – as: 'The situation is extremely dangerous and explosive: It is imperative that we do as little as possible'."

16 See, e.g., M. Kaim, *Macht oder Ohnmacht der U.S.A im Nahen Osten? Die Politik der Clinton-Administration im israelisch-palästinensichen Konflikt*, HSFK-Report 3/1999 (Frankfurt/Main: Hessische Stiftung Friedens- und Konfliktforschung, 1999); from an American perspective see, among others, W. Pfaff, "U.S. Imperium is Impotent in the Middle East", *International Herald Tribune*, 6 September 1997.

17 R. W. Murphy, "Mideast on Hold", *Washington Post*, 1 December 2000.

18 Moïsi, "Europe's backyard".

19 See S. Serfaty, "Bridging the Gulf Across the Atlantic: Europe and the United States in the Persian Gulf", *Middle East Journal*, Vol. 52, No. 2, 1998, pp. 337-350.

20 R. N. Haas, "The United States, Europe, and the Middle East Peace Process" in *Allies Divided*, pp. 61-77; see also R. Satloff, "America, Europe, and the Middle East in the 1990s: Interests and Policies" in *Allies Divided*, pp. 7-39.

21 See A. D. Miller, "There's no Turning Back", *Middle East Insight*, July 1999 (http://www.mideastinsight.org). Miller is the deputy U.S. Special Envoy to the peace process.

22 See: Déclaration de la présidence du Conseil sur la situation au Proche-Orient, Intervention de M. Pierre Moscovici, ministre délégué des Affaires européennes, devant le Parlement européen réuni en session plénière (Strasbourg, le 5 septembre 2000) (http://www.presidence-europe).

23 "Situation in the Middle East. Declaration of the European Union", *Euromed Report*, 21 November 2000.

24 Philip Gordon has noted that progress in the peace process – as was the case in the wake of Oslo – usually makes it easier for Americans and Europeans to advocate similar policies towards the region. See his *The Transatlantic Allies and the Changing Middle East*, IISS Adelphi Paper 322 (London: IISS, 1998). The experience of the Netanyahu government and the crisis of fall 2000 suggest that substantial risks to the process may eventually also spur the U.S. and Europe to seek a more co-ordinated approach.

25 See "Declaration by the Presidency on behalf of the European Union on the Middle East Peace Process", 1 October 1996.

26 See, among others, R. Aliboni, "Re-Setting the Euro-Mediterranean Security Agenda", *The International Spectator*, Vol. 33, No. 4, 1998, pp. 11-15; E. Rhein, "Europe and the Greater Middle East" in *Allies Divided*, pp. 41-59 (49 f.).

27 "Common Strategy of the European Union on the Mediterranean Region", adopted at the European Council at Santa Maria da Feira, 19-20 June 2000.

28 In this sense, the "European Union Call for Peace in the Middle East" (European Council Amsterdam, 1997) stresses "the right of all States and peoples in the region to live in peace within safe, recognized borders". In the special part dealing with Israeli-Palestinian negotiations, both Israeli and Palestinian concerns are addressed: The EU calls on "the people of Israel to recognize the right of the Palestinians to exercise self-determination, without

excluding the option of a State", and its calls "upon the Palestinian people to reaffirm their commitment to the legitimate right of Israel to live within safe, recognized borders".

29　See, e.g., the above-quoted "Déclaration de la présidence du Conseil sur la situation au Proche-Orient" of 5 September 2000.

30　Figures are for 1997: International Monetary Fund (IMF) *Directions of Trade Statistics Yearbook* (Washington D.C.: IMF, 1998).

31　Note that Israel alone among Europe's Mediterranean partners has become a member to the EU's Research and Technology Framework Programme, the EU's main institutional instrument to sponsor R&D.

32　M. Hudson, "To Play the Hegemon: Fifty Years of U.S. Policy Towards the Middle East", *Middle East Journal*, Vol. 50, No. 3, 1996, pp. 329-43. In the Arab world in particular, U.S. strategic interests in the region and their overlap with Israeli interests are often underestimated while the influence of the pro-Israel lobby on U.S. foreign-policy making is exaggerated. For a recent analysis of the nature of pro-Israeli lobbies in the U.S., see P. Bennis and K. Mansour, "'Praise God and Pass the Ammunition!': The Changing Nature of Israel's U.S. Backers", *Middle East Report*, Vol. 28, No. 3, 1998, pp. 16-18/43.

33　See G. E. and E. Philippart, "The EU Mediterranean Policy: Virtue Unrewarded or...?" *Cambridge Review of International Affairs*, Vol. XI, No. 1, 1997, pp. 185-207.

34　See the "Common Strategy of the European Union on the Mediterranean Region" (Part 1, No. 6): "... this Common Strategy will cover the EU's contribution to the consolidation of peace in the Middle East once a comprehensive peace settlement has been achieved".

35　See J. Monar, "Institutional Constraints of the European Union's Mediterranean Policy", *Mediterranean Policy*, Vol. 3, No. 2, 1998, pp. 39-60.

36　This is not to say that they shouldn't do so. The difference of perspective and perception, however, between U.S. and European leaders is sometimes striking: While President Clinton, in his speech to the United Nations Millenium Summit (i.e., two months before the U.S. presidential elections), told the world that time was running out for Israelis and Palestinians to reach an accord (See, *International Herald Tribune*, 7 September 2000), Europeans, around the same time, were more relaxed: The EU appreciated that after Camp David and given President Clinton's being "more determined than ever to use his ... influence to promote, before the end of his presidency, a positive outcome to the negotiations" there was an "exceptional window of opportunity" which might not be open too long ("Déclaration de la présidence du Conseil sur la situation au Proche-Orient" of 5 September 2000). But the Europeans did not subscribe to the notion of a last chance, which Clinton's speech implied.

37　See W. B. Quandt, *Peace Process: American Diplomacy and the Arab-Israeli Conflict Since 1967* (Washington, D.C.: Brookings, 1993) p. 9.

38　The concept is borrowed from R. Aliboni, "The Charter for Peace and Stability in the Mediterranean", *EuroMeSCo News*, No. 5, 1999, pp. 4-6. It refers to relations between the European Union, on one hand, and individual partner countries, on the other.

39　Algeria, Cyprus, Egypt, Israel, Jordan, Lebanon, Malta, Morocco, Palestinian Authority, Syria, Tunisia, Turkey. Libya was invited as an observer to the Euro-Mediterranean Conference of Foreign Ministers in Stuttgart (April 1999) and is set to become a full member of the process once the UN Security Council sanctions have been lifted (in 1999, they were only suspended) and Libya accepts the "Barcelona *acquis*" (which includes, i.e., an endorsement of the Middle East peace process).

40　There are three dimensions of co-operation under the EMP; the "political and security partnership", the "economic and financial partnership", and the "partnership in social, cultural and human affairs". See European Commission DG 1B - External Relations, *Euro-Mediterranean Partnership: Barcelona-Declaration, Work Programme*, Brussels (n.d.). For a general discussion of the process and its problems, see: A. Vasconcelos and G. Joffé (editors), *The Barcelona Process: Building a Euro-Mediterranean Regional Community*, London and Portland, OR (Frank Cass), 2000.

41 R. Aliboni, "Change and Continuity in Western Policies toward the Middle East", in Guazzone, L. (ed.), *The Middle East in Global* Change (London: Macmillan, 1997), pp. 216-36. On the security background of the Barcelona initiative, see also G. Joffé, "The Euro-Mediterranean Partnership: Two Years after Barcelona", *RIIA Briefing Paper*, No. 44, 1998; Claire Spencer, "Security Implications of the EMPI for Europe", *The Journal of North African Studies*, Vol. 3, No. 2, 1998, pp. 202-11.

42 See in more detail: F. Tanner, "The Euro-Med Partnership: Prospects for Arms Limitations and Confidence Building after Malta", *The International Spectator*, Vol. 32, No. 2, 1997, pp. 3-25.

43 See "Presidency's formal conclusions. Fourth Euro-Mediterranean Conference of Foreign Ministers, Marseilles 15 and 16 November 2000", *Euromed Report*, 22 November 2000. In its diplomatic language, the declaration explained that the ministers had "agreed ... to defer adoption of the Charter owing to the political context".

44 See V. Perthes (ed.), *Scenarios for Syria: Socio-economic and Political Choices* (Baden-Baden: Nomos Publishers, 1998).

45 Contrary to conventional wisdom, this is not the result of the end of the Cold War and the disappearance of the Soviet Union. Even at earlier stages, the Arab states wanted the United States to be the main mediator of deals with Israel. Remember Egypt's embrace of the Rogers Plan (1969), it's insistence of having the U.S. mediate what became the Camp David accord, or Syria's acceptance (in the absence of U.S.-Syrian diplomatic relations) to have U.S. Secretary of State Henry Kissinger negotiate a disengagement agreement with Israel after the October war of 1973.

46 See M. Asseburg and V. Perthes, *Surviving the Stalemate: Approaches to Strengthening the Palestinian Entity* (Baden-Baden: Nomos Publishers, 1998); *Strengthening Palestinian Public Institutions. Report of an Independent Task Force*, Sponsored by the Council of Foreign Relations (Michel Rocard, Chairman, Henry Siegman, Project Director), Executive Summary (New York, NY: The Council, 1999). Both studies reflect strong concern with Palestinian institution building. The first was originally a report to the European Commission; the second is a co-operative European-American exercise that was funded by the European Commission and by the government of Norway.

47 See "New Transatlantic Agenda Senior Level Group Report (Released at the U.S.-EU Summit Dec. 5)", U.S. Information and Texts, 12 December 1997.

9 Russia and China: The Risks of Uncoordinated Transatlantic Strategies

HALL GARDNER

Introduction

In March 2000, the chief diplomats of the United States, Russia, and the European Union (EU) held a joint meeting in Lisbon for the first time in post-Cold War history. The event was depicted as a "troika" or "world politburo" in the Russian press, and viewed positively in that it appeared to promise that Russia would, from now on, be treated as an "equal" of the Americans and Europeans.[1] The U.S. and European press, however, largely ignored the significance of the reunion, and generally focused on the negative, the brutal Russian military intervention in Chechnya.

In his 2 June 2000 Aachen address (after receiving Germany's prestigious Charlemagne Prize), then President Bill Clinton proposed a long-range plan for an expanded Euro-Atlantic community that would incorporate Russia as a member of both NATO and the EU; he also proposed that Turkey become a member of the latter.[2] That same week in his historic 5 June speech in the Russian Duma, he urged Russia to continue its reforms to enter the World Trade Organization (WTO). Needless to say, Clinton's Aachen speech rankled the Europeans. Most members remain extremely reluctant to accept Turkey—or Russia for that matter.[3] NATO itself has sustained an "open door" policy but has thus far kept Russia at a distance, not even at the door step. In the meanwhile, Russian membership in the WTO remains an uphill battle.

The question of Russia and Turkey rankles the transatlantic relationship to the west; the additional question of a militarily powerful, yet politically and economically unstable, China looms to the east. Almost a decade after the Tiananmen Square crackdown, the United States, in part in economic rivalry with the EU, opted for a new path of "constructive engagement"; the EU in turn sought a more far-reaching "Comprehensive Partnership" with China. Both the United States and EU have supported China's bid to enter the WTO whose 140 members account for roughly nine-tenths of international trade. At the same time, Beijing itself has attempted, in part by threatening a closer "strategic partnership" with Russia, to play U.S., EU (and Japanese) interests against each other in its efforts to assert its regional hegemony, if not ultimately to reunify with Taiwan.

In January 2001, the administration of George W. Bush began a fundamental internal review of American policy. While it initially sought to distance itself from Clinton administration policies discussed above, it will be argued that the Bush administration will still need to address the issues of Russian membership in a still "open" NATO and the EU, at the same time that it deals with the Turkish question. In effect, the Bush administration began to change the Clinton administration's tone in regard to both Russia and China, but then began to backtrack, more in regard to Russia than to China, however. At first, it publicly labelled Russia as a "threat", and took a standoffish approach to proposals for an early U.S.-Russian summit, but then retracted its previous views and reached out for a summit held in Slovenia in June 2001.

In regard to China, the Bush administration appeared to reverse President Clinton's "engagement policy" by dubbing Beijing a "strategic rival". U.S.-Chinese relations literally crashed to their lowest point (following NATO's "accidental" bombing of the Chinese embassy in Belgrade in 1999) when a Chinese fighter jet collided with a U.S. EP-3E surveillance aircraft in April 2001—shades of the U-2 spy plane! The Bush administration was thus confronted with its first major international crisis (outside that with Iraq) in which Beijing attempted to impel Washington to "apologize." Secretary of State Colin Powell stated: "China is a competitor and a regional rival but also a trading partner willing to cooperate in areas, such as Korea, where our strategic interests overlap. China is all these things, but China is not an enemy, and our challenge is to keep it that way."[4]

The Bush administration also began to play a game of "high stakes poker" with its initial emphasis on developing *national* ballistic missile defences (BMD). Yet once again it backtracked by effectively dropping the term "national" in response to both Allied and Russian criticism. Despite statements in favour of breaking out of the constraints imposed by the 1967 ABM treaty (preferably, but not necessarily, with Russian agreement), the Bush administration has not entirely ruled out "compromise" in regard to the possible development of joint American-EU-Russian *non-strategic* or *theatre* BMD defences—which, if truly implemented, could effectively bring Russia into a new form of NATO-EU membership. At the same time, however, the deployment of *any* form of BMD system could alienate Beijing, if such systems are used to defend Taiwan.

This chapter will first discuss the global ramifications of the war "over" Kosovo; it will then examine EU relations with Russia, with a focus on the Baltic region and Kaliningrad, and the issues raised by the Schengen Information System, in particular, as well as Russia and the WTO. This section will be followed by an examination of U.S.-EU-Russian rivalry for China's political-economic and military allegiance, and the question of China's membership in the WTO, as well as a possible formation of a Sino-Russian alliance. And finally, the chapter will conclude with an analysis of the problematic issues raised by the NATO-EU "double enlargement" (NATO-EU-Russian-Turkish relations) as well as those posed by BMD. It shall be argued that the United States and EU need to forge a coordinated strategy in regard to China and Russia. In essence, transatlantic strategy should soon shift more decisively toward Russia (but without fundamentally alienating China)—in an effort to split the burgeoning ties between Russia and an increasingly assertive, if not militant, China.

Global Ramifications of the War "over" Kosovo

The belated (and ineffective) effort of the Clinton administration in March-June 2000 to forge closer NATO-EU relations with Russia stemmed, in part, from an effort to patch up the international "collateral" damage caused by NATO's war "over" Kosovo. Although NATO regarded the latter as an "exceptional" humanitarian intervention, the war nonetheless bruised U.S. relations with Russia, China, as well as with the EU, and raised issues crucial to the maintenance of global peace in the long term. The war "over" Kosovo:

- Raised the concern of Europeans, following the 1999 Rambouillet Summit, that the EU was cut out of the American-led decision-making process, and that the EU lacked the capability to *threaten* force through power-based bargaining to make its own diplomatic initiatives credible and, if necessary, engage forces in peacekeeping or combat.
- Posed questions in regard to the credibility of NATO-Russian Founding Act that was intended to give Russia "a voice but not a veto" in the NATO decision-making process.
- Caused Beijing (particularly following the "accidental" bombing of the Chinese embassy in Belgrade) to think in terms of worst-case scenarios. Not only did the action augment Chinese demand for Russian military capabilities, Chinese war planning has now assumed that Washington would come to the assistance of Taipei should the latter attempt to "secede" from the People's Republic.
- Denigrated the role of the UN Security Council (and hence the role of both Russia and China) and raised the prospects that NATO could intervene unilaterally to defend the interests of even non-NATO member states and peoples (thus moving away from "collective defence of territory" and toward "collective defence of interests," however the latter may be defined).[5]

EU: Slow Steps toward Integrating Russia

On the one hand, the war "over" Kosovo embittered Moscow who believed that its proposals to deal with pan-Serb ethnic cleansing had been brushed aside by Washington without a fair hearing; on the other, the "second war" in Chechnya likewise upset U.S.-EU relations with Russia. In January 2000, the EU suspended approximately 180 million Euros in technical assistance to the CIS states, largely as punishment for Russian actions in Chechnya. Yet the EU did not go so far as to engage in sanctions or else expel Moscow from international organizations. Much tougher policies had been demanded in Paris by a number of human rights activists ("les Intellos Français [IF]", so-called "French Intellectuals") who, not at all unjustly, accused Russia of "disproportionate use of force" and of "crimes against humanity" in continuing to wage its brutal war. In response, Moscow countered that life in the region was "returning to normal".

In many ways, Russian acquiescence in NATO's war "over" Kosovo could, in part, be interpreted as a trade-off or *quid pro quo* for Russian intervention in Chechnya. Russian Foreign Minister Ivanov claimed that Russia was: "...defending Europe's common borders from a barbarian invasion of international terrorism, which is ... working to create an axis of influence: Afghanistan, Central Asia, the Caucasus, the Balkans".[6] The Putin leadership claimed that its troops should have never left the region after the first Chechen war that had been mediated by former Russian Security Council Secretary Alexander Lebed in 1996. In effect, in seeking closer relations with Moscow, the EU argued that it was better to compromise with Russia in the hope that Russian policy would ultimately moderate its actions in Chechnya, rather than try to criticize Moscow from the outside—without having any real *linkage* over Russia's intervention. At the same time, however, neither the EU (nor the United States) attempted to *engage* with Russia to supply significant political and economic supports for the entire Caucasus region in order to more thoroughly address the socio-economic roots of the conflict.[7]

German-Russian disputes over aid and finance likewise slowed the process of EU-Russian rapprochement. When the EU began to thaw relations with Russia, Germany strongly criticized the war in Chechnya. On the one hand, Berlin publicly supported the NATO bombing campaign "over" ex-Yugoslavia; on the other, it more quietly whispered its dissent within NATO in regard to the nature of the bombing campaign, a fact which angered Moscow. From an economic standpoint, Russia's default on more than $140 billion in public and private eastern debts—half of which are held by Germany, its biggest creditor—had disillusioned German banks and investors. One option considered was that Germany could convert a large share of Russia's $14 billion debt to Germany into equity stakes in Russian companies (including a bigger German share in Gazprom); Germany could then become a major shareholder in Russian industry. Russia already supplies about 35% of Germany's gas needs.[8]

The Chechen factor had accordingly delayed more positive EU-Russian accords, but concord over a EU-Russian "energy-bridge" appeared to speed the new détente.[9] On the one hand, the EU has sought to diversify its energy and fuel sources as it has been confronted with rising prices and instability in the Middle East/Persian Gulf and the diminishing North Sea oil supplies. On the other hand, the EU has sought to stabilize relations with Russia over a twenty-year period (but some EU states fear too great a reliance or dependence on Russian energy).

Russia has sought billions in Western assistance (involving EU incentives and subsidies to transcend the reluctance of private transnational firms to invest) to revitalize its dilapidated oil industry. Russia's Gazprom, plus a consortium of German, French and Italian firms have plans to build a 600km pipeline that will transverse Belarus, Poland and Slovakia. The fact that the pipeline route bypasses Ukraine, coupled with Russian accusations that Ukraine had not paid its debts and siphoned off Russian gas destined for European customers, has been seen as an act of intimidation by Kiev. Warsaw has likewise been concerned that the chosen route could alienate Kiev, as Polish-Ukrainian relations have already been strained by the implications of Schengen for cross border trade and immigration. (See discussion below.) On other hand, additional pipelines have been proposed, which could possibly pass through Ukraine.[10]

At this time, American opposition to forge an "energy bridge" between Europe and Russia involving oil, natural gas, and electricity appeared to have been overcome. Supported by President Clinton, the United States appeared to have reversed its strong Cold War opposition to a Soviet oil pipeline in the 1980s (see Bernhard May, this book) that Washington feared would "Finlandize" western Europe and drain hard currency reserves (at a time when the U.S. farmers were permitted to trade with Moscow on the grounds that Soviet purchases of American grain drained "hard currency" from Moscow). Russia could soon play a role in resolving European energy crisis, not only in regard to natural gas and petroleum, but also electricity and nuclear power (the latter problematically!). At the same time, Washington still retains fears that Russia and the EU could begin to cooperate in technological research in rivalry with the United States and Japan, or else the EU could become too dependent upon Russian oil.

In October 2000, the EU Council of Ministers had approved an outline of six-month co-operation with Russia, endorsing the Common Strategy on Russia designed at the June 2000 Feira European Council summit. The latter initiated "the opening of an open-ended dialogue" in the areas of energy, fiscal and legal reforms, regulatory reliability, transparency, in an effort to help make the Russian climate "more investor-friendly" and to review co-operation on economic matters, justice and home affairs (especially the battle against organized crime), the environment and nuclear safety.[11]

Principle elements of the plan attempted to define new guidelines that would make it possible to develop the "strategic partnership" and provide "new foundations" for co-operation with an emphasis on rule of law, institutional structures, and a judicial framework that matches the needs of a modern economy and society. The focus included the consolidation of democracy, rule of law and public institutions, integrating Russia into a common European economic and social area. It envisaged more political dialogue on defence, disarmament, and nuclear non-proliferation, as well as on EU enlargement and on "regional questions of common interest" (in reference to Chechnya, the Caucasus, Central Asia, and the Balkans; the report, under the French presidency, appeared, however, to overlook the Baltic region). The mechanisms foreseen included: Incentives for restructuring the Russian banking system, building a legal framework covering real estate, business operations, taxation, bankruptcy, and money laundering. The mechanisms also included action targeted on assisting Russia's accession to the WTO (including assistance on intellectual property rights), high level economic dialogue, promoting a Customs Code and approximation of standards, in an effort to strengthen Russian relations with the EU, its member states and international financial institutions.[12] (Russia has sought to join the WTO since 1993, but its accession target has been stretched out from 2001 to mid-2002. Another intermediate option, prior to WTO membership, would be to forge a CIS "payments union," see below.)

The problem, however, in regard to attracting foreign investment (in Russia, Ukraine, and other post-Soviet states) is that of the "damaging links between the old political structures—the *nomenklatura*—and the new economic structures". The latter issue is seen as a "danger to foreign direct investment". Moreover, present economic weaknesses make it questionable whether Russian and CIS businesses. Finally, continued political-economic instability could "jeopardize economic and political reform".[13]

The Schengen Information System: A "Micro-Electronic" Curtain?

EU enlargement has begun to raise fears of isolating the Russian enclave of Kaliningrad—raising Russian fears of both a geostrategic and "economic blockade". EU enlargement, combined with steps toward a CESDP, has raised transfrontier questions in regard to visas and immigration, as well as in regard to a potentially trade diverting, as opposed to trade creating, relationship; it could ultimately raise security and defence questions for the EU as well. The danger is that EU and Schengen rules in regard to trade and immigration could raise a new "micro-electronic curtain" around EU members.

The EU has engaged in a number of positive initiatives designed to bring Russia closer to WTO and EU membership; yet it is not yet clear whether these efforts will ultimately prove successful. The European Union's "Northern Dimension" project has sought to increase cooperation between the enlarging EU and Russia. The project includes countries that are not EU members, such as Poland and the Baltic states, as well as Russia. Lithuania and Russia, for example, are planning projects in infrastructure, energy, environment, trade and social contracts, supported by the EU PHARE and TACIS programs. Projects include modernization of the Kaliningrad-Kaunas road corridor, construction of a gas pipeline to Kaliningrad, setting up a joint business centre, in addition to strengthening border controls to minimize contraband smuggling and illegal migration.[14] Another aspect of the Northern Dimension project is the idea of creating a "Karelian Euroregion" with the participation of various eastern Finnish communities. The idea is to create "gateways" for transborder cooperation between Finland, and the Republic of Karelia (seized by Russia during the Russo-Finnish war), Saint Petersburg and the Leningrad oblast. Projects, involving timber processing and paper manufacturing, may obtain TACIS financing.[15] Likewise, the United States has sponsored the Northern European Initiative to train local officials and businessmen; in the year 2000, the U.S. and Swedish governments planned to initiate training programs in regard to managing former military bases and assist the conversion of military industry, as well as disposal of waste armaments and chemical materials.[16]

The problem is the following: As the EU enlarges, new members must accept the implementation the *acquis communitaire*; EU rules, if not significantly modified in accord with EU concepts of greater "differentiation" and "variable geometry," could seriously heighten tensions between new EU members and their neighbours. At present, it is up to current EU member states to decide whether the accession of new members will result in an immediate lifting of border controls between the current and new member states. Abolishing internal border controls thus depends upon a unanimous European Council decision that all member states have enough confidence in external frontier controls of CEE state members. In general, borders with the Schengen countries became more porous once CEE countries became part of the common frontier zone. But any concessions made by the present EU members in regard to the western borders of the CEE will be only implemented if CEE states begin to apply tougher controls on their eastern borders. As Heather Grabbe has put it: "Extending Schengen eastwards thus implies a bargain: Freer movement westwards at the price of not allowing free movement from the east".[17] In effect, the CEE "are becoming a new form of buffer zone for the EU: one for immigration".[18] This fact (along with NATO enlargement discussed below) could upset the carefully negotiated political-economic and social relations with Russian Kaliningrad, as well as in regard to relations with the Baltic states, Belarus and Ukraine.

Countries preparing for EU membership have been preparing visa requirements for citizens of the Commonwealth of Independent States (CIS). The Baltic states introduced visa requirements first: Estonia in 1991; Latvia and Lithuania in 1993; Lithuania (so far) has made an exception only for Russian citizens of Kaliningrad. Yet, according to the updated EU Accession Partnership for Lithuania, no exception for Kaliningrad has been granted. On the contrary, Lithuania is to "adopt new laws on National Border Control and complete border demarcation with Belarus; start border demarcation with Kaliningrad" in addition to "implement(ing) border and migration legislation to prevent illegal immigration and to enable full participation in the Schengen Information System".[19]

Concurrently, Lithuania's special relations with Kaliningrad, for reasons of local trade and relations, have complicated its EU accession negotiations. The EU Nida Initiative has, however, sought to sustain a special cooperative relationship in order to deal with the incomplete settlement of contractual relations between Russia and the Baltic states as regards customs control between Kaliningrad and Lithuania if the latter enters the EU.[20] On the one hand, as argued by political groups such as the Liberal Union of Lithuania, good relations with Russia and investment in Kaliningrad have kept open additional corridors to the Russian market. On the other hand, Kaliningrad firms owe Lithuanian businesses around twenty-five million dollars in bad debts. Lithuanian demands to obtain compensation for damages resulting from Soviet occupation have angered Russian officials but (so far) have not threatened Lithuanian relations with the Kaliningrad oblast.

Following the 1991 Polish-Schengen multilateral readmission agreement, and the 1993 Polish-German bilateral readmission agreement, Germany has been able to block migration from Poland (making the latter a country of settlement rather than transit).[21] Poland further restricted Russian citizen entry in 1998 and subsequently instituted visa requirements.[22] These policies (which have been accompanied by tighter border controls and laws on aliens causing some popular protest in Moscow, and an official protest in Minsk) appear to contradict stated Polish efforts to maintain a positive *Ostpolitik* with Belarus and Russia as well as Ukraine. (Poland has attempted to sustain a "special partnership" with the latter in particular. By advocating stronger NATO and EU links with Kiev *over* those with Moscow and Minsk, Poland has sought to counter-balance Russian pressures.)

In the near term, Moscow is more immediately concerned that, when Poland and Lithuania become EU members, Schengen borders will restrict the freedom of the movement of Russian citizens, and transit rights to Kaliningrad. The same holds true for free access to Poland that citizens of Kaliningrad presently maintain. Russia has negotiated transit rights across Lithuania "in perpetuity" for military personnel and equipment by rail; it has sustained a significant military garrison there.[23] Lithuania argues that the Transit Agreement does not impede its bid for NATO membership since Lithuania has no military co-operation pact with Russia. The Transit Agreement, however, could affect Lithuania's relations with NATO and its bid for NATO membership since NATO could attempt to supervise Russian military access to Kaliningrad. (See discussion later in chapter.)

The double, largely uncoordinated, enlargement of the EU and NATO thus threatens to increasingly isolate Kaliningrad, leading to two conflicting domestic responses. Some local leaders argue that these special circumstances mean that Kaliningrad should increase its "autonomy". It has been argued that Kaliningrad could serve as an "off-shore" zone to attract foreign investments. Kaliningrad could use the expansion of European institutions as a means to bargain greater legislative self-sufficiency from the Kremlin and seek the status as a special financial-economic zone. It should demilitarise rather than militarise in response to NATO enlargement.[24] In effect, Kaliningrad, with its high degree of pollution, drug abuse, AIDS, and organized crime (not unlike the Chinese triads) would become a peculiarly Russian version of Hong Kong.

Thus one option would be to grant Kaliningrad Oblast an associate membership in the EU (particularly as it appears unlikely that Russia will enter the EU as a "full" member because of its size and effort to retain its status as a major power). Vygaudas Usackas, Deputy Minister of Foreign Affairs of Lithuania, has argued that the: "Kaliningrad region should not be seen as a problem but rather as an opportunity for introducing new forms of regional cooperation. In light of the ongoing political changes in Russia, Kaliningrad presents itself as an interesting test of Russia's 'Europeanisation' vis-à-vis the processes of Euro-Atlantic integration".[25]

Pro-Kremlin groups, however, are suspicious of foreign involvement in Kaliningrad (and in other special regional zones such as Primoryi and Krasnodar); they argue that NATO and EU expansion means that the Kremlin should exert greater centralized controls. These groups have been concerned that, over the long term, the increasingly powerful political-economic influence of the EU and of the "Euro" will tend to draw Kaliningrad away from Russian controls, much as the Soviet Union feared the powerful influence of the German Mark over Czechoslovakia and over other "east bloc" states during the Cold War. It accordingly fears that Kaliningrad could consequently seek independence as did the three Baltic states (or be "bought out" by Germany as rumours have it!). On 1 March 2000, three Kaliningrad politicians set up a political grouping called Russia's Frontier (Rubezh Rossii); the latter argued that the Russian President should appoint the governor of Kaliningrad, due to "threat" of NATO expansion, the political conflicts between local and regional leaders, and the region's poor social and economic development, as well as its inability to attract investment.[26]

The dilemma is that the EU and NATO have not yet developed a common policy toward Kaliningrad, a situation that has been exacerbated by the Baltic state efforts to enter both the EU and NATO. Whether Kaliningrad becomes a problem, or part of the solution will largely depend upon ability of NATO, the EU, and Russia to forge a full concert so that the parties do not continue to work at cross-purposes. A constructive first step would be to establish a joint EU-CEE border and customs service along the external border of the current EU membership and to seek the advice of Poland and other applicant states as to the management of borders.[27] The EU needs to initiate greater interaction between the PHARE and TACIS programs for more effective implementation of joint projects on the Lithuanian-Kaliningrad border. EU Commissioner Chris Patten has proposed that the EU open a centre in Kaliningrad.[28] In January 2001, the new Swedish presidency sought to make the region a priority. After internal EU discussion, the EU opted to seek out the views of Lithuania and Poland; it quietly discussed the issue at the EU-Russia summit in May 2001.[29] Yet EU discussions alone with Russia will not suffice: Greater policy coordination between NATO, the EU, and Russia in regard to the CEE *as a regional bloc* is necessary due to the potentially *exclusive* nature of the NATO-EU double enlargement and potential Russian counter-reaction.

Russia and the WTO

In his historic 5 June speech before the Russian Duma, and in the same week as he proposed Russian membership in NATO and the EU, President Clinton stated that Russia should "make an all-out effort to take the needed steps to join the WTO.... and finish putting in place the institutions of a modern economy, with laws that protect property, that ensure openness and accountability, that establish an efficient, equitable tax code".[30] The EU has likewise underlined the importance of early Russian acceptance into the WTO.[31] This is crucial as European Union rules require that its members trade with only WTO members.

The dilemma is that both the EU countries and the United States have been reluctant to open their markets to Russian products, largely in fear of dumping highly subsidized goods, such as steel (while Russia seeks to block EU eggs and alcohol!). As it struggles to become a market-oriented economy, and unless it can make the reforms necessary to enter the WTO, Russia could thus find its access to international markets increasingly closed.[32] Russia, however, has thus far been unable to stick to the reform process; and its proposals to enter the WTO constantly flip-flop. An intermediate step before WTO membership, would be to forge a "payments union" of the Commonwealth of Independent States (CIS). This proposal would make sense as most Russian trade is regional, among the former Soviet bloc states, and not global.[33] Russia could then enter the WTO at a later date.

Ironically, steps to bring Russia into the WTO have additionally encouraged uniform economic rules and practices, working to undermine Kaliningrad's position as a "special economic zone". WTO membership requires a unified legal system throughout the country, a factor that could prove "disastrous" for regions such as Kaliningrad, which possess special economic status, and for those regions bordering Poland and Lithuania, and which use Kaliningrad as a centre of transit for their imports.[34] Accordingly, supported by federal politicians, Russian membership in the WTO inadvertently tends to support Russian centralization as opposed to decentralization and differentiation. The administration of Vladimir Putin has, in the meantime, begun to put tighter controls over the Kaliningrad oblast as part of a general policy of placing tighter central government controls on all regions in the Russian Federation.[35]

Moreover, the potential membership of Latvia, Estonia, Kyrgyzstan and Georgia, as well as other former Soviet bloc states, in addition to China, in the WTO may provide these countries with greater global political and economic opportunities relative to Moscow. WTO membership may also provide former Soviet bloc states with greater strategic leverage to assert their interests against

Russian political-economic pressures, as they could now potentially block Russia's own bid for membership in the WTO.[36] The fact that China has been progressing faster on meeting WTO regulations than Russia could be regarded by Moscow as an attempt to play China *against* Russian interests—unless Moscow and Beijing could be brought into the WTO at the same time. Bringing the Russian Federation into a larger Euro-Atlantic space ultimately requires drawing Russia (as well as former Soviet bloc states) closer to the new regional geo-economic interrelationships now being forged, NAFTA, the WTO, the OECD, the EU, if not an Asian Free trade area, *but with special qualifications in each case*.

U.S.-EU Rivalry over China

The United States and EU have engaged in an unspoken rivalry for the China's political and economic allegiance that began to intensify just following the Tiananmen Square repression in 1989. Both the United States and EU began to take a path of "constructive engagement" in regard to China; both have sought to bring the latter into the WTO (despite China's often questionable trade practices and pressures on Taiwan). Toward the end of the Clinton presidency, both the EU and U.S. began to downplay—but not entirely ignore—geopolitical disputes, such as the question of the forced unification with Taiwan, and the question of Tibet, China's threatened support for North Korea, as well as ecological concerns and significant human rights abuses, including a sustained government crackdown on the religious group, Falun Gong, whose leader lives in the United States.

NATO's "accidental" bombing of the Chinese embassy in Belgrade in 1999, and the collision of a Chinese fighter jet with a U.S. EP-3E surveillance aircraft in April 2001, have, however, tended to exacerbate Sino-American tensions (but could also open the door to closer Sino-EU ties). Following the January 2001 U.S.-UK bombing of military installations in southern Baghdad, the Bush administration asked a reluctant Beijing to investigate Chinese companies that had been violating the UN trade embargo on Iraq. The air raids had been timed to prevent them from striking Chinese workers who had been installing underground fibre optics cables so as to improve Iraq's air defences. Having killed Chinese embassy personnel in Belgrade during the war "over" Kosovo, Washington did not want to make the same mistake in Baghdad!

Following the events in China in 1989, Washington became involved in a trade war over intellectual property rights, textiles, as well as U.S. corporate access to the China market. Concurrently, the United States accused China of supplying arms, missiles, or nuclear technology to Iran, Saudi Arabia and Pakistan in the period 1988-89 (actions that took place *prior* to Tiananmen Square in 1989). Moreover, Chinese seizure of some of the oil rich Spratly island group in 1988 had raised questions as to Chinese intentions in the region. By

1992, France and Germany (following Japan), however, then sought to improve political-economic ties. By that time, Russian Su-27s fighter sales to China led France to justify a major arms contract for Mirage 2000-S fighter jets and six Lafayette naval frigates. (The latter "Frigate affair" resulted in a bribery scandal involving then Foreign Minister Roland Dumas that has since plagued French domestic politics). Washington likewise justified a major arms sale of F-16s and anti-submarine helicopters to Taiwan in 1992, a contract that Beijing regarded as breaking the Second Shanghai Communiqué of 1982 which had pledged that U.S. military sales to Taiwan would not exceed the 1979 level in either qualitative or quantitative terms.

In January 1994, however, France reversed itself and formally promised not to sell arms to Taiwan, in exchange for Chinese commercial contracts. That same year, Washington delinked China's Most-Favoured Nation status with the human rights question. Tensions, however, exploded once again between Washington and Beijing in 1996 when China fired unarmed missiles into Taiwanese harbours (in an effort to intimidate Taiwan's pro-independence movement and elections) during military exercises. Washington interposed the 7th fleet, sending two aircraft-carrier battle groups into the region. That year, China rejected Boeing or McDonnell-Douglas and ordered Europe's Airbus instead.

The first-ever annual EU-Chinese summit, which sought to implement "a comprehensive Partnership with China",[37] was held in 1998 (nine years after the events of Tiananmen). The EU-Chinese summit was then followed by U.S. steps to enhance trade with China through the November 1999 Sino-US Agreement (in the same year that Congress accused China of significant espionage activities and of stealing of American nuclear secrets). The EU engaged in discussions on arms control, non-proliferation (the Comprehensive Test Ban Treaty), the Missile Technology Control Regime, biological weaponry, landmines, dual-use exports and "security developments in Asia" (Taiwan and the Korean peninsula, primarily), among other issues. In regard to Taiwan, the EU Presidency issued a declaration in July 1999 supporting the "one China" principle, but emphasized the importance of resolving the question peacefully. The EU noted some improvement in "economic and social rights, but a deterioration in the area of civil and political rights, in regard to Tibet and religious freedom, rights of association and free speech".

The 19 May 2000 Sino-EU summit, which was intended to "vastly" improve Chinese access to EU markets, was also intended to pave the way for China's accession into the WTO. EU efforts to bring China into the WTO not so inadvertently worked to pressure Washington into taking steps to drop its annual review of China's trade status. The U.S. House of Representatives consequently then voted to support Permanent Normal Trading (PNT) status for China on 24 May 2000; the U.S. Senate then followed up in September 2000, but significantly, the passage of Permanent Normal Trading status was linked to the eventual acceptance of Beijing into the WTO.

Also in September 2000, fourteen-year old talks on China's accession to the WTO broke down over both U.S. and EU insistence that China, which is the EU's fourth largest trading partner after the United States, Switzerland and Japan, end its dual set of rules for domestic and foreign enterprises, and that it clarify its "opaque or unpredictable" legal codes. In October 2000, however, the EU then came close to finalizing accords involving insurance licensing and retail distribution (hypermarkets, department stores, warehouses, even car distribution) in the (failed) effort to bring the PRC into the WTO by 1 January 2001. Other issues to resolve included the gradual deregulation of banking services, piracy and counterfeiting operations, illegal immigration, and to ratify UN Conventions it signed in 1997 and 1998. (The Chinese National People's Congress [NPC] ratified the International Covenant on Economic, Social and Cultural Rights in February 2001 but sought to amend clauses on free labour unions; the NPC, however had not yet ratified the International Covenant on Civil and Political Rights.) For the first time in a top EU-China dialogue, the EU handed Beijing a list of individual Chinese dissidents to be freed from detention.

In addition to EU arms sales, Beijing protested a French commercial satellite sale to Taiwan, which Beijing claimed could have military applications. Chinese officials were furthermore outraged by EU Commissioner Chris Patten's suggestion that unification with the Republic of Taiwan was unthinkable: "There is no example I can think of where a community which is already democratic and free has chosen to be less democratic and less free".[38] (Here, Beijing sees its "just" demands to unify with Taiwan as analogous to German unification.) From the Taiwanese side, Taipei is concerned that Beijing has added "new elements" to the "rules of the game" concerning the WTO accession for the two sides: "Mainland China intends to reiterate its 'one China' principle in its entry protocol, and also attempts to apply Article 33 of the WTO Charter to downgrade the Republic of China's status" (by applying for WTO membership in the name of Taiwan, Penghu, Kinmen [Quemoy] and Matsu Customs Territory).[39] Taiwan has proposed that all EU members establish liaison offices on Taiwan after both Beijing and Taipei are admitted *as equals* to the WTO.

WTO talks once again broke down, however, in January-February 2001, exactly when China was expected to enter! China's membership bid ostensibly stalled over questions of subsidies for China's agricultural products and over questions regarding the extent that it will open its protected insurance sector, in addition to a number of political factors mentioned above that played in the background. As the U.S. Congress had linked passage of Permanent Normal Trading status to membership in the WTO, President George W. Bush then asked Congress to renew China's Normal Trade Relations (NTR) once again on 1 June 2001 for one year.

The issues raised by China's potential membership in the WTO are complex, and it is dubious that its membership in the WTO will restrain its demands for unification with Taiwan. China's eventual membership in the WTO may well bring significant economic benefits, but it could also exacerbate domestic and international instability (if protected non-competitive state industries lay off millions of workers without providing social security or options for retraining). At the same time, as is the case for both China and Russia, new profits brought by the WTO could be used for military purposes and to assert regional claims—if WTO rules are not strictly obeyed or enforced, and if Russia and then China are not brought into a new concert.

China and Russia: From "Partnership" to "Alliance"?

In a nutshell, perceived efforts by the U.S. and EU to play China and Russia against each other have led the latter to take counter-steps and to play upon U.S.-EU fears of a Sino-Russian alliance for their own mutual benefit. At the same time, however, Beijing and Moscow still remain suspicious of each other's intentions. Moscow remains wary of China's rising population and potential claims to the Russian Far East; China opposes a NATO-Russian entente or alliance. China appears to be relishing its game of playing "barbarian" versus "barbarian" and probably does a better job than does Russia (particularly as Beijing has been able to lobby the American Congress—unlike Moscow!). China has thus sought to play the United States and EU (and Japan) against each other at the same time that it plays Russia against all three. From this perspective, Russia and China have each been playing their own game vis-à-vis the Americans: Sino-Russian efforts to woo the Europeans, *threats* to forge a strategic partnership, high tech arms sales, combined with calls for the establishment of a "multipolar" world, represent efforts to counter American "unipolarity".

The May 2000 EU-China Bilateral Accord, for example, was followed on 4 July 2000 by a number of Sino-Russian accords, including a reportedly $2-3 billion accord to assemble up to 200 Russian-designed Su-27s in China. China could also obtain new Russian-made destroyers, anti-ship missiles, plus air defence systems, and ultimately Su-30s. During the years 2000-05, China is expected to purchase an estimated $15 billion in manufactured items, or production licenses from Russia. A second phase from 2005-15 represents plans for the joint development and manufacture of munitions and weapons, including joint research and development of next generation aircraft, missiles, laser-based and high tech weapons systems.

Closer Sino-Russian ties were evident in the 17-18 July 2000 official summit where Vladimir Putin and Jiang Zemin signed the Joint Statement on Anti-Ballistic Missile treaty and the Beijing Declaration. The former statement opposed the U.S. support for BMD (but overlooked Putin's proposal for a more limited *non-strategic* Theatre Missile Defence (TMD) system. The latter Beijing Declaration provided Russian support for China's quest to unify with Taiwan (and without direct reference to Chechnya). Russian president Putin purportedly stated that Russia "firmly supports China's grand course of national unification with Taiwan".[40] (Taiwan's President Chen Shui-bian stated that he was ready for peace talks with Beijing but would not concede to Beijing's demand of the recognition of the "one-China" principle.[41])

With stronger Russian backing, Beijing has consequently warned against U.S.-EU efforts to provide Taiwan with advanced weapons systems such as the Aegis missile cruiser; it has reserved the right to use force against Taiwan in case the latter attempts to seek independence. After a policy review, the Bush administration opted to sell Taiwan a significant number of arms including 8 diesel submarines, 12 anti-submarine patrol aircraft and weaponry, and 4 Kidd-class destroyers that could serve as the precursors of the Aegis anti-missile defense system.[42] Despite its own efforts to develop coastal missile defences with Russian SA-300s, Beijing has thus far perceived Bush administration plans to deploy either BMD or TMD systems as aimed primarily at China. It has consequently warned that it will increase its nuclear arsenal ten times from 16-20 Inter-Continental Ballistic Missiles (ICBMs) to 200-250 ICBMs if the United States does opt to proceed with missile defences aimed at Chinese interests and if it continues to enhance Taiwanese military capabilities.[43]

The NATO and the EU: An Uncoordinated "Double Enlargement"

The double, yet uncoordinated, enlargement of NATO and the EU has been perceived as creating a "double buffer zone" by Russian observers. The primary concern is that of the essentially *exclusive* nature of NATO membership. There has been an effort to mitigate this exclusivity through the Partnership for Peace (PfP); yet the fact that NATO enlargement (without Russian inputs) is best characterized as a stratagem of *strategic denial* with primarily defensive, but also potentially offensive, capabilities indicates that states that are not "full" NATO members can be excluded from decisions and military actions that affect their perceived vital interests.

The enlargement of the EU likewise poses questions, but largely due to the political-economic ramifications of Schengen and EU membership, which could potentially result in "trade diversion" as opposed to "trade creation" and make mutually beneficial transborder transactions, travel, and trade more difficult (in addition to checking potential waves of immigration into the EU). At the same time, the "militarisation" of the EU (see Anne Deighton, this book), and creation of a 60,000-man rapid deployment force (designed to provide a European alternative to American political influence and to provide the EU a capability to engage in diplomacy that requires a credible *threat* to use of force) raises new questions as to the exact nature of the strategic relationship between NATO, the EU and Russia—and within the EU itself!

Without substantially repeating the critiques of Anne Deighton, Jan Zielonka, or the more positive views of Karsten Voigt, the first salient point is that the EU has yet to clearly define the appropriate role for the High Representative (presently held by former NATO Secretary-General Javier Solana) and that of the EU Commissioner for External Relations (presently held by Chris Patten) in regard to foreign policy. This fact represents an internal institutional cleavage within the EU in addition to its distinct national policy differences. One option is for the Commissioner to handle intra-EU affairs, the economics of defence reorganization, and to strengthen the civilian aspects of crisis management and crisis prevention; the role of the High Representative could be elevated in regard to foreign and defence policy.[44] (In response to Henry Kissinger's now clichéd concern, discussed by Calleo and Boyer in this book, American officials already appear to prefer to call the mobile number of the High Representative and not that of the Commissioner!)

An additional question concerns the nature of EU security guarantees. If the WEU is to be adapted and changed into an all-EU force, the question of whether security guarantees should be extended to all EU members has not yet been resolved.[45] As Article 5 of the Brussels treaty represents a stronger security guarantee than that provided by the North Atlantic Treaty, an attack on one EU member necessitates action by all EU members. The latter issue is further complicated by the fact that the Common Foreign and Security Policy (CFSP), according to Article 11.2 of the EU treaty, guarantees the frontiers of Member States as external borders of the EU.[46] The EU will accordingly be responsible for the defence and security of *all* its members: Many EU applicants may have not completely resolved actual and potential disputes that may involve historically contested borders and irredentist claims with a number of EU, non-EU, non-NATO members—and not just with Russia alone.[47] And finally, related to this question is the need to clarify the principles and legal basis for EU decisions to intervene on the territory of a third country, an issue that has evidently proved problematic for NATO itself following its "exceptional humanitarian intervention" in Kosovo.[48]

Despite the fact that NATO generals publicly warned that a European "caucus" within NATO would represent a "red line," the Clinton administration (unlike that of George Bush, Sr.) generally supported the concept of ESDI as long as the decision-making process of the latter remained coordinated *with* NATO. Yet the implementation of a more "autonomous" CESDP (coupled with ideology in support of a "multipolar" world to counterbalance the American *"hyperpuissance"*) has accordingly raised American fears of a worst-case scenario in which the EU could act without the explicit advice and consent of Washington and other non-EU states, as the UK and France did in the 1956 Suez crisis. One worst-case scenario envisions Article 5 of the Brussels Treaty going into effect without the EU having developed the necessary defence capabilities; Article V of the North Atlantic Treaty might then remain legally non-applicable, at the same time that conflicting partisan pressures call for NATO to either act or stay out. On the other hand, should NATO ultimately opt for enlargement to the Baltic states, the latter action could not only prove dangerously provocative to Russia, but also highly problematic from a defence standpoint, if NATO and EU member Sweden cannot coordinate defence strategy in the region. (NATO is not in a strong position to defend all three Baltic states from Poland.)

A less dramatic, but nonetheless problematic, scenario might be that an "autonomous" EU could cut the interests of non-EU member interests, such as Turkey or Norway, out of the decision-making process. The EU could also opt to utilize NATO assets of non-EU members in addition to common pools—a prospect most opposed by Ankara. From this perspective, should a significant crisis erupt within, or contiguous to, a EU state that is not a NATO member or in other regions (such as civil strife in Bulgaria, Romania, Belarus or Ukraine, for example), the results could pit American, European, and Russian, interests against each other. At the same time, it is probable that the interests of NATO and EU members could also diverge—with some states urging intervention and others restraint.

The Turkish Question

In regard to NATO-EU relations, Turkey, as one of the six European non-EU members, is perhaps the most concerned that CESDP could exclude Turkish interests should EU members opt for "autonomous" actions outside the NATO framework or use common NATO assets without Turkish consent. Turkey has accordingly threatened to veto EU access to NATO assets should it not participate in EU decision-making.[49] Washington has accordingly pressured the EU to accept the Turkish application to join the EU while Turkey has threatened to veto any "autonomous" European actions in which Turkey has not been properly consulted. (American pressure to bring Turkey into EU membership, combined with Turkish threats to veto any "autonomous" European actions, has led Turkey to be depicted by Europeans as an American surrogate; a charge denied by Ankara.) Concurrently, however, NATO itself has been unable to settle tensions between its two disgruntled members, Greece and Turkey, which resurfaced in a quarrel over airspace in NATO exercises in 2000.

Most EU members remain extremely reluctant to accept Turkey (or Russia) as members. This reluctance is largely due to Ankara's failure to address and protect the legal rights of minorities and human rights violations, geopolitical and economic tensions with EU member Greece, its largely unspoken military predominance in civil relations, and lack of a common European "culture" or "civilisation" (despite historical Ottoman interaction with Europe and membership in the Concert of Europe following the Crimean war). The EU has consequently demanded that Ankara engage in constitutional reforms on freedom of expression in accord with Article 10 of the European Convention on Human Rights; that it guarantee fundamental human and cultural rights (permitting broadcasts in Kurdish for example); that it abolish the death penalty (now linked to the imprisonment of PKK leader Abdullah Ocalan); that it reform its prisons in accord with UN standards; that it formulate a clear separation of military and civilian institutions; that it continue the process of privatisation of its public industries; and that it begin to apply EU regulations on the protection of information for its integration into Europol and Schengen. The EU has likewise been concerned with Turkish immigration (as there are roughly three million Turkish workers now in Germany).

Yet the Turkish question is not only problematic for the EU, but for Russia as well. It is often overlooked that NATO-member Turkey has newfound interests in the Caucasus and Central Asia, following Soviet collapse, which may clash with those of Iran and Russia. Turkey has been at war (from at least 1984 until 1999) with Kurdish independence movements who have been regarded by Ankara as being supported by Syria, Iraq, Iran, and possibly Moscow. The latter has accused Ankara of unofficially seeking to re-establish a Turkic Commonwealth, linking Azerbaijan, Kazakhstan, Uzbekistan, Kyrgyzstan, and Turkmenistan (potentially linked to Slavic Ukraine and Iran in Russian eyes).[50] Moscow has likewise claimed that a "Caucasus conspiracy" has been forming between NATO–member Turkey, Azerbaijan, and Georgia against Russia, Iran, and Armenia. Russia has also appeared highly suspicious of U.S. and Turkish intent in regard to oil routes from the Caspian Sea. (Here, the still simmering dispute between Armenia and Azerbaijan could draw Russia and Turkey onto opposing sides, although both Ankara and Teheran have tried to mediate that unresolved conflict.)

For its part, Turkey has claimed that its policies are intended to counter pan-Islamic movements and Uighur separatism that the "Shanghai Five" of Russia, China, Kazakhstan, Kyrgyzstan, and Tajikistan have been unable to contain. (In August 1999, the Shanghai Five pledged to cooperate in fighting terrorism, drugs, arms smuggling, illegal migration, national separation and religious extremism.) NATO-member Turkey has also stated its intent to contain pan-Islamic movements stemming from the Afghan Taliban, Iran, and the Islamic Movement of Uzbekistan. In this regard, Ankara has signed an "anti-terrorist" agreement with Moscow in regard to Chechnya.[51] Turkey has signed military-cooperation agreements with Kyrgyzstan and the Uzbek leadership. (The latter has thus far refused Russian supports against the Islamic Movement of Uzbekistan, which has launched incursions into Uzbekistan, Kazakhstan, and Kyrgyzstan). At the same time, however, the continuing conflict in Afghanistan may ironically provide an opportunity for NATO-Russian cooperation through the PFP (although there are some fears that NATO may be drawn unwillingly into burgeoning conflict).[52] It is also possible that Beijing may cooperate with Washington and Moscow against movements in Afghanistan that support the secession of Uighurs from China.[53]

In advocating both Russian and Turkish membership in the EU in his June 2000 Aachen address, President Clinton's intent was, in part, to help bring Russia and Turkey into cooperation in Eurasia, but he was primarily concerned with EU-Turkish relations within Europe itself. Clinton applauded European efforts "to treat Turkey as a real candidate for membership" so as to help reconcile Greece and Turkey and to find a compromise over Cyprus (which is also an applicant for EU membership).[54] The issue of Cyprus has remained a "hot spot" of contention between Greece (which has threatened to block EU enlargement if Cyprus does not soon enter) and Turkey. The issue has likewise threatened to postpone Turkish membership in the EU, following the break down of the December 2000 "proximity talks" over Cyprus. Turkey, however, has refused to accept any link between resolution of Cyprus question and Turkey's accession to the EU. Ankara argues that Cypriot membership in the EU will exacerbate the economic gap between the Greek and Turkish Cypriot communities, resulting in renewed conflict; moreover, once in the EU, Greek Cypriots could reclaim territory taken by Turkey.[55] Ankara also regards the December 1995 EU-Turkish Customs Agreement as disadvantageous without "full" EU membership and believes that its threats to leave the 1995 Custom Union led the EU to reassess its application for membership (coupled with U.S. pressures).

Although Greek-Turkish tensions appeared to be winding down somewhat following "earthquake diplomacy" in 2000, followed by the EU decision to accept the Turkish application for membership in 1999, Turkey was, in February 2001, confronted with a major financial crisis and political infighting between its pro-reform President Ahmet Necdet Sezer and its Prime Minister, Bulent Ecevit. On the one hand, its political-economic crisis could force Ankara to work closer with the EU to contain the potential for hyperinflation; on the other hand, it could also send Turkey toward radical pan-Islam or really pan-Turanianism (movements enflamed, in varying degrees, by tight military controls over civil society, Turkish secularism, repression of the pan-Kurdish movement, the break-up of oil routes and economic relations with Iraq, and Turkish defence links to the United States and Israel). The crisis could also lead Turkey toward disaggregation.

Russia, the EU—and NATO

Moscow, at least initially, appeared prefer EU enlargement to that of NATO (and denies the attempt to play a unified Europe versus the United States). Although some Russian analysts did raise early concerns over the creation of a "double buffer zone," the precise nature of the emerging EU defence policy and that of the

CESDP have begun to raise more concrete questions in the aftermath of the December 2000 Nice summit. The first problem is that there has been no clear EU response as to the precise nature of the processes that the EU will take to link Russia to crisis management operations, for example. The second issue is that the EU has not yet explicated the exact nature of the links that the EU will maintain with NATO; the third is the question of what kind of force posture that the EU ultimately intends to create. Moscow and Washington appear to possess somewhat similar concerns!

Russian spokespersons have stated that Moscow does not oppose the formation of CESDP as long as the latter does "not create new dividing lines in Europe".[56] Yet they have still feared that EU and NATO enlargement will deepen the trenches between Europe and Russia. Moscow has also questioned the future of EU policy preferences in regard to the OSCE, not to overlook existing UN peacekeeping and regional security commitments that have been made by Russia, France, and Germany. (One can also wonder how the Contact Group might function if its EU members are restricted by a common CESDP?) According to French Foreign Minister Hubert Vedrine, Russian defence and military-technological cooperation with the new EU defence "identity" was possible "on the condition that transparency was guaranteed and that it would not modify the equilibrium of forces in Europe"; yet the EU is still in the process of "inventing" these relations at present.[57]

On the one hand, the EU has promised to enlarge its membership at the same time that it begins the process of developing a CESDP with still undefined features. Concurrently, having expanded into central Europe, NATO is expected to debate a second wave of enlargement, and to possibly announce which states should join by the year 2002. Here, U.S. and European elites are split as to whether to enlarge at this time and, if they do enlarge, which states should enter, and whether Russia, in particular, should be included or excluded. At the same time, NATO may have a hard time balancing its resources in regard to its newfound interests in "peacekeeping" and its more original mission of "collective defence". Moreover, following the 1998 St. Malo summit, it is still not clear to what extent the UK (as member of NATO's integrated nuclear command) and France (whose nuclear forces are outside of NATO's integrated command) can, if necessary, coordinate their nuclear capabilities against potential conventional or missile threats that confront any new (or old) member of the EU, if only to coordinate *threats* in the process of diplomatic bargaining.

NATO and the EU have, up to the end of 2000, focused their attention primarily upon the continuing conflict in Bosnia and Kosovo (a conflict that began to spread to Macedonia in early 2001 with the rise of Albanian secessionist movements). At the same time, underlying tensions in the Baltic region have been building; this is in part due to Swedish and Danish support for Baltic state membership in NATO (despite the historically "neutral" position of Sweden). Efforts of the "Vilnius Nine" [Lithuania, Latvia, Estonia, Slovenia, Slovakia,

Romania, Bulgaria, Macedonia, and Albania] to enter NATO through a "big bang" in the year 2002 have also raised Russian concerns.[58] Warsaw has likewise supported Lithuanian membership in NATO as a "buffer" to be in a better position to defend itself against a potential Russian seizure of Lithuania, as Poland would find itself "caught in an iron ring between (the Lithuanian port of) Klaipeda and (the Polish city of) Gdansk".[59] Just following the presidential victory of George Bush Jr., there has been a renewed push by Senator Jesse Helms in support of NATO membership for Lithuania and Estonia.[60] Yet, Slovenia, and possibly Slovakia, possess the best chance to enter NATO on the next round as both states link Hungary to the rest of NATO members.

Russia has warned that the full integration of the Baltic states into NATO's integrated command would represent a *casus belli*. The perceived "threat" of NATO enlargement, among other issues, has consequently led Moscow to *threaten* to tighten its alliance with Belarus[61] and to forge a counter-alliance with eastern European states not entering NATO, as well as with Iran, China and India. The latter, despite their regional suspicions, have likewise begun to oppose American "unilateralism". Moscow has also begun to pressure states, such as Georgia, the Baltic states, and Ukraine, to accept "neutrality" (or alignment with Russia) rather than become NATO members.

By December 2000-January 2001, the *Washington Times* alleged (based upon "anonymous" official sources) that Russia had, since 1998, begun to deploy nuclear capable tactical missiles in the Kaliningrad enclave—an action categorically denied by Moscow. Russian analysts regard this as an act of disinformation designed to speed the decision to enlarge NATO to the Baltic states by magnifying the Russian "threat" and/or to gain popular support for the Bush administration's plan to develop BMD. Other analysts argued that the public disclosure of the purported deployment is part of a secret U.S.-Russian deal to reveal the inability of Europe's CESDP to protect against such a threat![62]

In response to American BMD proposals, Russia, China and France have all launched a verbal assault against American unipolarity and have lent support to the concept of a "multipolar" world. The French have attacked America as a "hyperpuissance" in Foreign Minister Vedrine's terms. The Europeans, the Canadians, the Chinese, the Koreans (South and North), and the Russians have all protested American proposals to renounce the ABM treaty based upon the concept of Mutual Assured Destruction (MAD). At the same time, however, the Russians, unlike the Chinese, have thus far remained open to *a jointly operated, non-strategic,* system of BMD. From the EU perspective, the implementation of a nation-wide American BMD system has been regarded as potentially decoupling the United States from European security. The promise of a *joint theatre* or *non-strategic* BMD system, however, may temper EU and Russian criticism.[63] (On the other hand, President Reagan's Star Wars proposal had promised contracts for European military-industries and for Russia, but these never materialized.)

If Russia and the EU were able to jointly participate in the development of limited regional BMD system as *equal* partners with the United States, then a closer NATO-EU-Russian relationship could be established. The latter option has been proposed by Russian President Vladimir Putin, but has thus far been rejected by Washington on the grounds that BMD technological breakthroughs (to be shared by Russia) might be leaked to hostile third parties.[64] Yet as argued by Alexei Arbatov, Vladimir Putin's proposals for a joint non-strategic ABM system represent a very significant offer that should not automatically be turned down. In effect, it represents a proposition for a NATO-Russian alliance and would mean closing down Russian relations with those "rogue" states with ballistic missile programs that Russia is presently supporting, and of "cutting back on her relations with China".[65] He thus argues that Washington has been too passive in pursuing an entente or alliance with Moscow, and of drawing the latter away from its present support for Beijing. The issue raised here is that even without a formal Sino-Russian alliance, Moscow could counter NATO enlargement in the west by continuing its efforts to deflect China's interests toward the Asian littoral in the east and away from Russian Siberia, while China itself continues to threaten Taiwan and assert regional hegemony versus Japan.

While the Nixon Center (specifically mentioned by Arbatov) argues that "too visible American concern over a Russian-Chinese entente might only further tempt the parties to exaggerate their leverage"[66] is essentially correct in this regard, it is also true that the so-called pragmatic "balance of power" approach (tilting back and forth and perpetually playing China against Russia) has failed to recognize that American policy, *since the Nixon-Kissinger administration itself*, has generally tilted *toward* the People's Republic of China.[67] From a geohistorical perspective, the so-called "balance of power" approach has largely served to exacerbate tensions rather than work to *prevent* major power conflict in that such an approach does not emphasize the necessity to engage in *thorough* irenic negotiations with the primary antagonists. The Nixon Center's priority is to prevent Russia from becoming a "spoiler" and then from using its relations with states like China, India, Iran, and former Soviet allies such as Iraq and North Korea to disrupt American and European interests; yet to effectively prevent Russia from becoming a "spoiler" state will require a *deeper* entente or alliance relationship with Moscow, meaning a more *decisive* tilt toward the latter.

Toward a Concert or Confrontation?

From a superficial perspective, the EU recognized that the 2000 Nice summit only established the rudiments of a CESDP; the EU still does not have the means to plan its own army; NATO still represents the basis of the collective defence of its members. But a number of significant dilemmas remain: 1) Contrary to the above pessimistic scenarios, it is dubious that the CESDP will stray too far from American interests since at least eleven of the present EU members are also NATO members; at the same time, it is still unclear exactly when the EU can act independently of NATO and with what assets. 2) The EU does not plan its own European army, but it may still end up duplicating a significant number of American conventional and C⁴I assets so as to reduce its political-military dependency upon the United States. 3) The U.S./NATO still represents the basis of the collective defence of its "double-hatted" NATO/EU members—but the significant problem has developed that U.S./NATO may indirectly provide the basis for the security guarantees of the entire, and expanding, EU as well—unless the EU *does* develop a more significant defence capability.

As long as both international regimes, NATO and the EU, possess strong ambitions in the area of crisis management, it is essential that the two increasingly engage in mutual cooperation. Obviously the three dilemmas described above can only be resolved by closer EU-NATO policy coordination, but also coordination with Russia. From the European perspective, the question of whether the EU can ultimately formulate a CESDP is fundamental to the question as to the ability of the EU to coordinate strategy on a basis of "parity" with both Washington and Moscow (and likewise *threaten* to use force to achieve its diplomatic goals). Overall, the formation of a CESDP should, in principle, permit the Europeans to play in the world of diplomacy on more equal ground with the Americans and the Russians, but without being able to supersede the United States or Russia militarily for that matter (at least for the time being!). At the same time, there are areas in the Petersberg peacekeeping tasks that the expanding EU can develop in coordination with both NATO and Russia.

Rather than digging the trenches between Russia and Europe even deeper, by developing an American-controlled BMD system, an alternative option is feasible. First, NATO, the EU and Russia can strengthen the inspection capabilities of the Missile Technology Control Regime (MTCR). This, coupled with a U.S. decision to ratify the Comprehensive Nuclear Test Ban Treaty (after the U.S. Senate had previously failed to ratify it), could at least help to mitigate the apparent need to deploy a *national* BMD system. Second, NATO, the EU and Russia could begin to develop more limited non-strategic theatre systems in the near term.[68] Thirdly, and more immediately, NATO, the EU, and Russia could begin to implement a concerted policy that applies *overlapping* or *conjoint* NATO-EU-Russian security guarantees to the Baltic states and Kaliningrad.[69]

In this approach, NATO would coordinate strategy with the EU and Russia in support of Baltic state security and independence; yet it would largely remain in the background by providing logistical support for the deployment of multi-national Euro-Atlantic Partnership for Peace forces in the Baltic region under the command of the Military Committee of the Euro-Atlantic Partnership Council, which includes Russia and other non-NATO states, as members. An internationalised EAPC command structure would be integrated in such a way as to surpass the problems of the UN-NATO "dual-key" system that had plagued operations in Bosnia.

The implementation of overlapping security NATO-EU-Russian guarantees in regard to the Baltic States and Kaliningrad would go a step further than proposals made by the Nixon Center, for example. The latter has suggested that an interim step could be considered: "A declaration of NATO's stake in Baltic independence, on the model of NATO's Charter with Ukraine—short of an Article V commitment, but a security guarantee nonetheless".[70] Moreover, Kaliningrad should not only become a special economic zone of trans-frontier EU-Russian cooperation, as suggested by Zbigniew Brzezinski;[71] Kaliningrad should *also* become a headquarters for the NATO Euro-Atlantic Partnership Council. Setting up a NATO-EU-Russian headquarters for PfP operations in Kaliningrad would ease Russia's transition into the Euro-Atlantic community.[72] The point here is to make the black hole of Kaliningrad a special economic zone, a peculiar kind of Russian Hong Kong. Establishing a EAPC headquarters, as well as an EU center in Kaliningrad, would thus work to accept Russia as a new form of "full" member of both NATO and the EU, as the definitions of "full" or "associate" membership continue to change.

The deployment of Euro-Atlantic Partnership war-preventive forces in the Baltic states would represent a first step toward the creation of a Central and Eastern European Economic and Security Community *as a regional bloc*. Such a community could be strengthened by the development of joint NATO-EU-Russian theatre non-strategic ballistic missile defences, for example. It could be further strengthened by the eventual membership of EU members Sweden and Austria in NATO, if these states, as producers, and not consumers, of security would accept NATO membership. Or, alternatively, Sweden and Austria could opt for closer cooperation with NATO and the EU in order to develop a stronger system of overlapping NATO, EU, Russian security guarantees throughout the Baltic region as well as central and southeastern Europe.

On the one hand, there is a real risk of a backlash by Russia, and by those states that do not join the EU or NATO, if Washington *overplays* its cards; on the other hand, there is also a risk of backlash if the EU *underplays* its hand and does not fully engage its "multilateral" diplomatic and economic capabilities. In July 2000, European Enlargement Commissioner Günter Verheugen stated: "If enlargement fails, you risk getting a dozen Belarus' and twenty-four Kosovos".[73] To a large an extent an exaggeration (just one more Kosovo could prove devastating to EU and NATO solidarity!), the comment still indicates the necessity for the EU to become fully engaged in preventing the isolation of those states that possess difficulties in achieving the *acquis communitaire*.

States that cannot obtain WTO status, or whose regional socio-economic relations are disrupted by Schengen arrangements, may be alienated. This argues for the necessity to "customize" the EU's customs procedures. The purpose is to develop an individualized approach to the specific needs of different applicants in accord with EU principles of variable geometry and thus apply greater degrees of differentiation of norms, permitting some exceptions to each of the chapters and to accept periods of transition, where appropriate, for applicant countries. Moreover, if the EU is to take the call to prevent future Kosovos seriously, it will require greater focus, not just on the capabilities and needs of individual states, but "constitutional regions" as well. Here the EU has been reluctant to deal with the latter issue within its present membership; yet a number of such regions in the CEE (if not in the EU itself) could cause a major crisis after an enlargement—if not before!

Preventing regional tensions following EU enlargement to selected states thus may ultimately require bringing eastern European states into the EU overtime as a more politically and integrated group, as a Central and Eastern European Economic and Security Community. Concurrently both NATO and the EU will need to re-assess their relationship with both Russia and Turkey, in the effort to develop new, more flexible mechanisms, and through the establishment of new forms of "associate" or "full" membership. The restructuring of NATO, coupled with defence coordination in regard to non-strategic BMD systems, and other forms of strategic cooperation, could possibly permit Russia to enter NATO as a new form of "full" member.

The uproar raised over allegations of Russian tactical nuclear weapons deployment in Kaliningrad points to the need to address the security needs of the entire region, a problem recognized by the new Swedish Presidency of the EU in January 2001. Somewhat ironically, just following the December 2000 Nice summit which announced a new rapid reaction force for crisis management operations, the new Swedish presidency of the EU appeared to order an "about face". Swedish Foreign Affairs Minister Anna Lindh chaired a public debate on 22 January, and along with Javier Solana, stated that conflict prevention is at the heart of the European Union, and must be made a priority in its external relations (with a particular emphasis on the Baltic region).[74] The Swedish position appeared to take a step back from the concept of CESDP with its emphasis on *crisis management*, and represented an effort to strengthen the Petersberg concepts of *crisis prevention* and *preventive diplomacy*. Perhaps unintentionally, the step also appeared to represent a tacit recognition that it would be more reasonable, and less provocative (to both Washington and Moscow), for the EU to emphasize its *crisis prevention* skills *in the near term* that could better complement actual NATO *crisis management* and *collective defence* capabilities. Ultimately, however, the EU would need to develop more autonomous CESDP *crisis management* capabilities.

Ideally, if an alternative irenic strategy can ultimately be pursued, it would be best to bring both Russia and China into the WTO at the same time—if possible. Concurrently, steps toward WTO membership for Russia (following the establishment of a CIS payments Union) and China should take place as part of a proactive irenic diplomacy that seeks preventive diplomatic solutions to salient geopolitical disputes, first in regard to Kaliningrad, and then Taiwan, once Russia is brought into a NATO-EU entente or alliance as a first step in breaking an apparently tightening Sino-Russian alliance. A regional settlement (backed by the United States, EU, and ultimately Russia) that seeks a confederal, "one nation, two states, several systems," approach to the PRC-Taiwan dispute could help ameliorate tensions in the long term by bringing the two China's closer together on the basis of parity.

On the one hand, as long as the EU cannot, by itself, guarantee security for its new members, it will continue to require NATO support; on the other hand, NATO alone is not sufficient: The EU needs to enhance its own defence capabilities if only to augment its bargaining and diplomatic leverage so as to engage in *credible* and *effective* preventive diplomacy and crisis prevention for its enlarging area, and to deal effectively with Russia in particular. At the same time, neither NATO, nor the EU, can afford to ostracize Russia, and all three powers need to coordinate strategy in regard to China. Post-Cold War Euro-Atlantic security concerns, plus disputes or conflicts in other regions of the world, may instigate a significant number of crises that may or may not be provoked by Russia, and that will, in most cases, require bringing Russia into more positive cooperation with the United States and EU—going beyond the accords established by the 1997 NATO-Russian Founding Act.

Let us hope that the process can move fast enough and far enough.

Notes

1   See, for example, Gennady Sysoyev, *Kommersant* 4 March 2000 cited in *Current Digest of the Post-Soviet Press*, Vol. 52, No. 10 (2000), 22.

2   President Clinton, Aachen address, 2 June 2000. "Because the stakes are so high, we must do everything we can to encourage a Russia that is fully democratic and united its diversity... That means no doors can be sealed shut to Russia - not NATO's and not the EU's. The alternative would be a future of harmful competition between Russia and the rest, and the end of our vision of an undivided continent". On the other hand, "If (Russia decides that it has no interest in formally joining European or transatlantic institutions), we must make sure that, as the EU and NATO expand, their eastern borders become gateways to Russia, not barriers to trade, travel, and security cooperation".

3   See Martin Walker, "Analysis: German Groups Dismiss Clinton's Plan for Russia in NATO" (Atlanta: United Press International, 25 September 2000). One unnamed German official who participated in an Atlantic Bridge meeting in September 2000 opposed Russian membership in either body; "Russia's size and geographical spread into Asia, let alone the state of its economy and of its political culture, make this a nonsensical proposition". The German participants were also criticized Clinton administration efforts to formally accept Turkey as a candidate for EU membership. In essence, the Germans argued that Europe and NATO cannot be "ever-open doors". For an argument to let Russia into the EU, but not Turkey, see Alexandre del Valle, "Les Relations Union européene-Russie" GéoStratégiques No. 2, Fevrier 2001. http://www.strategicsinterna tional.com.

4   Hearing of the East Asia and Pacific Subcommittee of the House International Relations Committee, (Washington, DC: Federal News Service, 12 June 2001).

5　See Hall Gardner, "The Genesis of NATO Enlargement and of War "over" Kosovo," in *Central and Southeastern Europe in Transition*, ed. Hall Gardner (Westport, CT: Praeger, 2000).

6　*Current Digest of the Post-Soviet Press*, Vol. 52, No. 4 (2000), 21.

7　Alexander Yanov, "Open Letter to the West" in *Bridging the Gap*, Club Russia, ed. Mischa Gabowitsch http://www.clubrussia.org/_eur/bridging/yanov. See also my reply: http://www.clubrussia.org/_eur/ briding/gardner/

8　"Russia's Bid for WTO Accession", *Stratfor.com* December 2000.

9　Russian Foreign Minister Ivan Ivanov argued the EU-Russian strategic partnership was put on hold for more than a year due to pro-Chechen rhetoric. *Le Figaro*, 1 November 2000, 15.

10　*International Herald Tribune*, 21-22 October 2000, 1; 21.

11　*European Report*, No. 2539, 28 October 2000. The nuclear power question is not technically an EU concern, but has upset EU relations with the Czech Republic in regard to the Temelin plant, and nuclear plants in the Baltic states, for example. Dangerous plants include Kozloduy in Bulgaria and Bohunice in Slovakia. Safety conditions at the plants will need to be addressed, as was the case for Chernobyl in Ukraine.

12　"EU/Russia: Ministers Approve Action Plan for EU Common Strategy" *European Report*, Europe Information Service, No. 2521, 29 July 2000.

13　European Enlargement Commissioner, Günter Verheugen, cited in "EU Enlargement: Verheugen Warns on Political Intrusion into Economics" *European Report,* Europe Information Service, No. 2520, July 26, 2000.

14　"Northern Dimension to Build Russian links to Lithuania?" *Euro-East*, No. 85, February 29, 2000.

15　See East-West Institute, Russian Regional Investor, Vol. 2, No. 32, 7 September 2000.

16　"Solutions Sought for Kaliningrad" Euro-East Europe Information Service, No. 88, 23 May 2000.

17　Heather Grabbe, "The Sharp Edges of Europe: Extending Schengen Eastwards," *International Affairs*, Vol. 76, No. 3 (2000), 527.

18　Ibid.

19　"The Accession Partnership- The February 2000 Update, "The Euro-East Europe Information Service, No. 86 March 30 2000.

20　"Solutions Sought for Kaliningrad" op. cit. See also Baltic News Service: *Problem in incorporating Kaliningrad in Baltic Transit Customs Agreement*, September 27, 2000.

21　Ibid, 529.

22　Slovenia restricted entry in December 1999 for citizens of RF and CIS; the Czech republic announced visa requirements for citizens of Russia, Ukraine and Belarus. *Current Digest of Post-Soviet Press*, Vol. 52 No. 6 (2000). The Schengen accords could also disrupt relations between Hungary and the Hungarian Diaspora; it could also upset the EU's own sponsored regional cooperation project in the Carpathian Euro-region (covering the borders of Hungary, Moldova, Romania, Slovakia and Ukraine).

23　"Solutions Sought for Kaliningrad" op.cit.

24　See for example, statements of Andrei Nikolaev, of the Union of Popular Power and Labour, "Nikolaev: Expansion of NATO, EU Benefits Kaliningrad," East-West Institute, Russian Regional Report, Vol. 5, No. 9, 9 March 2000.

25　"Solutions Sought for Kaliningrad" *Euro-East*, Europe Information Service, No. 88, 23 May 2000. Igor Leshukov put it this way: Integration (with the EU) will not be possible if Russia keeps full sovereignty over Kaliningrad... the expansion of the EU to Poland and the Baltic region without a resolution of Kaliningrad's status is not possible. Kaliningrad would then remain an abscess that hampers normal development. Sophie Lambroschini, "Russia: New Study Sees NATO, EU Threat" *RFE/RL Newsline*, 15 September 2000.

26　"New Group Seeks Appointment of Kaliningrad Governor," East-West Institute, Russian Regional Report, Vol. 5, No. 9, 9 March 2000. The Liberal Democratic Party of Mr. Zhirinovsky has opposed letting Kaliningrad become a free trade zone.

27   Heather Grabbe, "The sharp edges of Europe: extending Schengen eastwards" *International Affairs* Vol. 76, No. 3 (2000), 535.

28   "EU focuses on Kaliningrad, While Moscow Looks Away" EastWest Institute, Russia Regional Report Vol. 6, No. 3, 24 January 2001. On January 18-19, 2001, Chris Patten outlined the EU's plans for building cooperation with Russia, Lithuania and Poland. He presented ideas on demarcating borders, financing transportation projects, and providing energy to the region. TACIS is to resume 15 million Euros assistance focusing on modernizing border checkpoints and the Kaliningrad port; yet "despite the increased outside attention, Kaliningrad continues to face severe problems at home. Thanks to the new tax code, Kaliningrad lost many of the benefits it had gained from the establishment of a free economic zone. Prices of imported goods have gone up 20% in the region and locally produced goods are losing their competitiveness on the Russian market". Concurrently, Latvia is planning to force Kaliningrad residents to obtain visas to travel to the rest of Russia.

29   "EU/Russia: Kaliningrad Gets Attention At Last" European Report, No. 2561, 20 January 2001. By April 2001, Lithunania and Russia sought to forge accords over transit rights to Kaliningrad. How the EU and NATO might regard those accords remains to be seen.

30   RFE/RL Newsline 5 June 2000.

31   European Report, No. 2540, 1 November 2000.

32   Michael Lelyvld, "Russia: Moscow Agrees to Reduce Steel Exports to U.S". Radio Free Europe/ Radio Liberty http://www.rferl.org/nca/features/1999/07/f.ru.990715124852 .html. In July 1999, the U.S. compared Russian prices with those of Turkey, which could set a "standard in future trade disputes over a host of Russian exports that U.S. industry sees unfairly competitive or cheap.... Russia may find that the principle of comparing its costs with those of Turkey may affect its exports for years to come. As the country struggles to become a market economy, it may face more markets that are closed".

33   Jacques Sapir, Lecture (Paris: American Embassy, 21 June 2001).

34   EastWest Institute, Russian Regional Report, Vol. 5 No. 35, 27 September 2000.

35   For a critique of Putin's policy, and governor's desires to be appointed rather than elected, see Leonid Smirnyagin, former presidential advisor, "Putin Brain Trust Seeks to Improve Federal Agencies in Regions" *Russian Regional Report*, Vol. 5, No. 11, 22 March 2000. On 1 January 2001, Kaliningrad lost its "special economic status" within Russia.

36   Global Intelligence Update, "As a WTO member, Georgia Gains the Upper Hand" (Stratfor.com: 16 June 2000). (Both new and old NATO members could, likewise, potentially block Russian membership in NATO).

37   See Report on the Implementation of the Communication "Building a Comprehensive Partnership with China COM (1998) 181 Brussels, COM (00) 552. http://europa.eu.int/comm/external_relations/ china/report_2000_a.htm

38   *European Report* No. 2538, 25 October 2000; European Report No. 2539, 28 October 2000.

39   Taiwan Minister of Foreign Affairs, Tien Hung-mao, cited by Sofia Wu in "Foreign Minister Describes Europe Visit as 'Fruitful' in Central News Agency," Taipei, 25 September 2000.

40   See Yu Bin, "Putin's Ostpolitik and Sino-Russian Relations," Comparative Connections, Pacific Forum CSIS, 3rd Quarter 2000. http://www.csis.org/pacfor/cc/003Qchina-rus.html

41   *BBC Summary of World Broadcasts*, 12 February 2001.

42   *International Herald Tribune*, 7 March 2001; 26 April 2001. German and Dutch officials protested the proposed sale of diesel submarines, stating that the U.S. could not use their designs and technology to build the ships.

43   China's October 2000 white paper on defence provides greater transparency than before (stating that its nuclear missiles are under the direct command of its Central Military Commission), but it continues to regard the U.S. as a potential threat that could use "human rights" as a pretext for military action. The NATO attack on Yugoslavia, BMD defences; the U.S. military presence in Asia and stronger U.S. military ties to Japan, and to other states are criticized. China would threaten to use force if Taiwan indefinitely delays reunification.

44   On the declining role of the Commission (and the subsequent need to become democratically

accountable if it is to gain greater legitimacy), see Ben Hall "European governance and the Future of the Commission" (London: Centre for European Reform, 2000), 7-8. www.cer.org.uk.

45   See Mr. Marshall, "The Implementation of the Common European Security and Defence Policy and WEU's future role- reply to the annual report of the Council," Assembly of West European Union Document C/ 1720 WEU 47th Session, 15 November 2000. Paris: 16 October 2000, p. 19. "It is hoped that all signatories share the view of the French presidency . . . that the collective commitment under Article V is maintained in full.... The importance of Article V should also be seen against a new background of international risk". At the same time, the report states "the prospect of transferring the substance of this commitment into an EU protocol would not be realistic for some time to come".

46   *European Report*, No. 2538, 25 October 2000. The EU concedes (albeit with contradictory statements emanating from different capitols) that it has no intention to compete with NATO, but has yet to clarify question of territorial defence or problematic question of Article V of the Brussels Treaty. See also Deighton, this book.

47   For discussion, see Hall Gardner, *Dangerous Crossroads: Europe, Russia and the Future of NATO* (Westport, CT: Praeger, 1997), Chapter 3.

48   On EU parliamentary debates on this issue, see "Defence: European Parliament Starts to Debate the EU's Nascent Policy," *European Report*, No. 2538, 25October 2000.

49   Çinar Özen, "The Consequences of the European Security and Defence Policy for the European Non-EU NATO members," Lecture, the Cicero Foundation, 14 December 2000. http://www.cicerofoundation.org.

50   See reports, *Current Digest of the Post-Soviet Press*, Vol. 52, No. 3 (2000), 18.

51   *The Economist*, 25 November 2000, 46.

52   By November 2000, the United States, Russia and India (and possibly China) looked as if they were forging a common policy toward the Taliban. As the latter ostensibly continues to harbour the alleged terrorist, Ben Laden, the United States has threatened "cruise missile diplomacy" to bomb positions in the south of the country as it did in August 1998 after the bombing of U.S. embassies in East Africa. *International Herald Tribune*, 2 November 2000. On dilemmas of NATO cooperation with Russia and other states in Central Asia, see Robin Bhatty and Rachel Bronson, "NATO's Mixed Signals in the Caucasus and Central Asia" *Survival* Vol. 42, No. 3, Autumn 2000.

53   Ahmed Rashid, "The Hard Road to Revenge", *Far Eastern Economic Review*, 7 December 2000.

54   *European Report*, No 2542, 11 November 2000. The EU had signed the Turkish Association Partnership Document (APD) after the 1999 Helsinki Summit (at the same time that the EU took a more decisive step toward a CESDP). By 8 November 2000 the European Commission then proposed to inject a "new momentum" into the enlargement process to complete negotiations with leading countries during 2002 and proposed an "Accession Partnership for Turkey".

55   *The Economist* 24 February- 2 March 2001. Turkish Cypriots earn roughly one-fifth of their Greek Cypriot counterparts. The vast majority of Turkish Cypriots (90%) favour EU membership; 32% would support a loose confederation; 23%.

56   Russian Ambassador Vassily Likhachev cited in "EU/Russia: Where are the Next Steps" *European Report*, No. 2541, 4 November 2000.

57   *Interfax Russian News*, 30 September 2000.

58   "Leader of U.S. Poles Initiates Bloc in Support of Lithuania's NATO Entry" *Baltic News Service*, 18 May 2000.

59   Ibid. Mr. Jan Nowak-Jezioranski cited in "Leader of U.S. Poles Initiates Bloc in Support of Lithuania's NATO Entry"

60   Senator Jesse Helms "Towards a Compassionate Conservative Foreign Policy," (Washington, D.C.; The American Enterprise Institute, 11 January 2001).

61   Alexei Arbatov, cited in "Russian MP warns Latvia over NATO Membership Plans" *Baltic*

News Service, 5 June 2000. (The 9 December 1999 Russian-Belarus Treaty of Union had called for a creation of a Higher Council, comprising the presidents, prime ministers and speakers of the legislatures of both countries, to coordinate policy; it also sought the creation of a single currency and tax policy by 2005, and a joint military doctrine by the year 2000).

62   For comments on a secret U.S. deal against the EU, see "Kaliningrad Neighbors Calmly Assessing US Press report of Nukes Redeployed," *Baltic News Service*, 3 January 2001.

63   In February 2001, Congressman Weldon brought a proposal to jointly develop a TMD system as a personal message from President Bush to President Putin. President Bush, however, has proposed one TMD system involving joint research and development and ultimately a joint system for command and control of anti-missile defences; President Putin has proposed another system that would only be set up if Russia and the Europeans first agreed there was a threat and after talks aimed at dealing with the threat by political or peaceful means. The three sides need to continue to talk!

64   "It would be foolish in the extreme to share defences with Moscow if it leaks or deliberately transfers weapons technologies to the very states against which America is defending". Condoleezza Rice, Op-Ed "Exercising Power without Arrogance," *Washington File*, 3 January 2001.

65   Press Conference, State Duma Committee for Defence Vice Chairman Alexei Arbatov on Vladimir Putin's Foreign Policy, Press Development Institute, 5 March 2001. http://www.fednews.rus) Here, Arbatov adds a number of countries to the list of potential "rogue" states: In addition to North Korea and Iran [overlooking Iraq], he argues that Pakistan, Algeria, Egypt, and perhaps NATO-member Turkey and U.S. ally Saudi Arabia, could turn toward "Islamic Fundamentalism;" moreover, the Taliban could use drug profits to buy missiles in the next 10-15 years.

66   See "What Is to be Undone? A Russia Policy Agenda for the New Administration" http://www.nixoncenter.org

67   See my thesis, Hall Gardner, *Surviving the Millennium: American Global Strategy, the* Collapse of the Soviet Empire, and the Question of Peace (Westport, CT: Praeger, 1994)

68   General John M. Shalikashvili has made several recommendations as to how to strengthen the CTBT and gain Senate support for its ratification. http://state.gov./www/global/arms/ctbtpage/ctbt_report.html

69   Hall Gardner, *Dangerous Crossroads: Europe, Russia, and the Future of NATO* (Westport, CT: Praeger, 1997). See also "L'OTAN et l'Union European: Les risqués de "double èlargissement" *Geostrategiques*, No. 1 Janvier 2001. http://www.strategicsinter national.com.

70   See "What Is to be Undone? A Russia Policy Agenda for the New Administration", www.nixoncenter.org. The same article states, "The deployment of Russian nuclear weapons in Kaliningrad, if confirmed... would affect not only Baltic security but also arms limitation arrangement in Europe, including the premises of the reassurances given by NATO at the time of its enlargement". In order words, NATO could review its unilateral decision not to deploy nuclear weapons in the region, or could deploy TMD *against* Russia.

71   Zbigniew Brzezinski, "Living with Russia" *The National Interest* (Washington, DC: Fall 2000).

72   See Hall Gardner, *Dangerous Crossroads*, op. cit.

73   "EU Enlargement: Verheugen Warns on Political Intrusion into Economics" *European Report*, Europe Information Service, No. 2520, July 26, 2000.

74   Dr. Javier Solana Brussels, "Open Debate on Conflict Prevention," General Affairs Council, 22 January 2001. Stating that "[t]he European Union came into existence as an exercise in conflict prevention," Dr. Solana outlined three points: "First, we must take steps to develop more coherent strategies towards regions at risk of conflict.... Second, we must continue to develop our own capabilities for effective conflict prevention.... Third, we must continue to build and sustain effective partnerships at all levels".

10 Uneasy Triangle: Transatlantic Partnership and UN Governance

DANA H. ALLIN

Introduction

It has been a decade since the recognised strategic purpose of the Atlantic Alliance disappeared. Hard-nosed realists have been at a loss to explain why the Alliance itself has survived. Its survival is somewhat less surprising, however, to those who recall that from the outset the Western Alliance had more than one rationale. The emergence of a Soviet threat certainly endowed the project with a sense of urgency. But the project itself was a more complex creation. In Europe, it was a necessary compliment to the dream of European unity, embraced by European Socialists, Christian Democrats and Gaullists – members of a coalition that had resisted Hitler, spent time together in concentration camps, and shared a conviction, that after the suffering and struggle of Europe's 30-year civil war, a more just and peaceful European and international order had to be created.[1] In the United States, the Atlantic Alliance was the project of a New Deal generation of Democrats, whose scorn for Republican isolationism was coupled with contempt for the political ineptitude of Democrat Woodrow Wilson's first attempt at structuring a permanent American engagement with the rest of the world. To be sure, in the idea of a United Nations, Franklin D. Roosevelt did resurrect Wilson's League of Nations. But the Wilsonian surface covered a Bismarkian core.[2] The new Wilsonianism would be more robust and more realistic. At its inception, then, the post-World War II project concerned much more than a Soviet threat. Indeed, as Robert Kagan has noted:

> It is too easily forgotten that the plans for world order devised by American policymakers in the early 1940s were not aimed at containing the Soviet Union, which many of them still viewed as a potential partner. Rather, those policymakers were looking backward to the circumstances that had led to the catastrophe of global war. Their purpose was to construct a more stable international order than the one that collapsed in the 1930s: an economic system that furthered the aim of international stability by promoting growth and free trade; and a framework for international security that, although it placed some faith in the ability of the great powers to work together, rested ultimately on the keystone of American power.[3]

The East-West confrontation, emerging in stages over the early post-war years, helped to mobilise American resources and to concentrate transatlantic minds. As the "original post-war goal of promoting and defending a decent world order became conflated with the goal of meeting the challenge of Soviet power",[4] the Alliance benefited from a useful confusion, or at least a misleading clarity. Differences and ambiguities about the desired shape of world order were papered over. Now that usefully false clarity is missing, the differences and ambiguities have re-emerged. For American conservatives such as Kagan, the goal should be to maintain a global order based on benign American hegemony.[5] For liberal internationalists – American, but especially Europeans – the goal should be even more ambitious: To resume the construction of a UN-based system for regulating, legitimising and judging the necessity for the use of force, and for cooperative efforts to address international emergencies such as global warming.

The goals of a benign U.S. hegemony, on the one hand, and a UN-based multilateral order, on the other, do not necessarily or inevitably contradict one another. There is, to be sure, some logical tension between them. Yet it is also easy to see how the underpinnings of American power, even hegemony, would be needed to sustain the transition to a genuinely multilateral order. Indeed, one could imagine American military power remaining so preponderant, for so long into the future, that it would constitute a *de facto* monopoly of force for enforcing the rule of international law.

However, such a future would require at least a tacit international consensus – and especially a transatlantic consensus – about the rules of global governance. And confidence in such a consensus is undermined by increasing anxiety about the gap between U.S. and European views of such governance. The return to power of a Republican administration has heightened the anxiety, and liberal critics worry that U.S. hegemony, which for most of the post-World War II era clearly supported the international system, is now more likely to subvert it.[6] In this critique, the prevailing U.S. attitude toward the United Nations is starting to constitute one of the more serious obstacles to improved global governance. Lack of support for UN peacekeeping makes it very difficult for UN peacekeeping to reform itself in ways that U.S. officials say it should reform itself. Inconsistent but in the end quite hostile attitudes toward the International Criminal Court culminate in the rather preposterous (but nonetheless sinister) efforts of Senate Foreign Relations Committee Chairman Jesse Helms to sanction any country that supports the Court. And urgent forms of global co-operation in the UN framework – notably co-operation against global warming – are stymied by a lack of U.S. leadership, not to mention irresponsible selfishness. Worried friends and indignant critics see all of this as part of a "new unilateralism" – the flip side of the coin of traditional U.S. isolationism. Or perhaps it is not so new; rather, it is a particular source of transatlantic tensions at the moment, because aspirations – particularly European aspirations – for improved global governance based on the UN system are greater after the Cold War than they were before.

These critics are right: The U.S. attitude is deplorable and even dangerous. But it is also unlikely to change. On the whole, greater support for the United Nations may have to come from a more coherent and capable Europe (if such can be created), rather than from an increasingly fractious and insular United States. But to affect U.S. attitudes at the margin, and to appreciate what needs to be done without the United States, it helps to understand the sources of American UN-bashing. Some of those sources are mystifying, not to say primitive. Some of them are more understandable, and deserve a hearing.

The American Predicament

To begin with, there is a difficulty inherent to the American role in the world. The U.S. position is complicated: A traditional legalist and promoter of multilateral institutions to underpin global security; but also the guarantor of last resort that must, to a certain extent, work outside the framework of international law.

America's multiple roles and multiple personalities in international politics have been laid out with some nuance by Yale law professor Michael Reisman.[7] First, Reisman identifies America's "prophetic and reformist role", under which, since the late 19th Century: "...the United States has seen its destiny as linked to the reform of international politics...This sense of mission has led it to conceive and support the establishment of international institutions endowed with formal decision-making procedures, in which, as in its domestic experience, law and legal symbols figure prominently". It was in this role, of course, that Wilson led his failed crusade for a "peace without victory" and League of Nations. And it was the reformist and prophetic spirit that animated American leadership in creating a United Nations Organisation after World War II. Second, he describes an "infra-organisational role" under which the United States, like other nations, works within international organisations to pursue its own national interests. "Yet U.S. behaviour is magnified by virtue of its preponderant power, and is aggravated by the apparent inconsistency of actions taken in pursuit of specific interests with its prophetic and reformist role".

Third, there is a "domestic-pressure reactive role" under which the United States, like other countries, pursues a foreign policy that is influenced by many different domestic political constellations and interest groups. Here again, U.S. behaviour is arguably not so different from other nations. Yet there is a much larger disconnect (as David Calleo notes in Chapter 1), between American pretensions and responsibilities as a global power, and the fractiousness of its federal system. *The Economist* once observed that America's founding fathers wrote the U.S. constitution with the conscious goal of preventing the new republic from becoming a world power. But the founders' intent was short-circuited in the mid and late 20th Century: Overcoming the fractiousness inherent to American federalism and the separation of powers was another service rendered by the false clarity of the Soviet threat. In the 1990s, however, fractiousness exploded: In the bitter impeachment of President Clinton; and now in an unnervingly close and fiercely litigated presidential election of the year 2000. Foreign observers may be mystified that legislation authorising Washington's payment of arrears in its UN dues could be held up for years by seemingly trivial "riders" attached by Congressional abortion foes. From the perspective of U.S. domestic politics, however, there is nothing trivial about the abortion fight – it goes to the heart of a very bitter struggle about what kind of nation the United States is, and is becoming. The secular-religious divide can be as bitter in other countries. Yet it is the world's misfortune that, because of the ubiquitous global presence of the United States, such struggles over the American identity are inevitably exported.

Finally, there is what Reisman considers America's "custodial role" for preserving world order. François Heisbourg, no knee-jerk supporter of U.S. leadership, has described this role in even more flattering terms:

> However reluctant some of America's allies may be to trumpet the fact, leaders and, to varying degrees, public opinion in allied countries have a fairly clear perception of America's role as a key element of what measure of international order may exist; and furthermore that the United States remains the only credible ultimate guarantor of that order. Economic analysts may talk of the International Monetary Fund as the lender of last resort. In the security realm, the United States is the guarantor of last resort, the only global-scale exporter of security.[8]

It is in this fourth role – as the "only credible ultimate guarantor" of world order – that the United States can make the most convincing case that it is sometimes called upon to use military force without UN sanction. Certainly this author finds the case convincing. However, every such use of military force is not just controversial, but controversial in a way that shakes the structural credibility of the UN system (already weak enough). And the prevailing American disdain for that system informs the carelessness with which American officials justify – or do not even try to justify – American actions. Such carelessness in turn aggravates the strain on the transatlantic consensus (if only a tacit consensus) that is required to sustain America's global security role. This strain was evident in two recent examples: The spring 1999 air war over Kosovo and the December 1998 bombing campaign against Iraq.

The Kosovo War

In the run-up to NATO's Kosovo bombing campaign of spring 1999, European governments were increasingly uneasy about an obvious American reluctance to accept the role of the Security Council as the only source of legitimacy for using military force outside of self-defence. In the end, the same European governments agreed with Washington that the Security Council had to be by-passed. But their unease did not go away.

This anxiety was grounded in a broad criticism of NATO's Kosovo intervention: That the war was illegal under international law; a violation of Belgrade's recognised sovereignty over Kosovo; damaging to a UN-regulated system for authorising the use of force; and thereby dangerously unsettling to international relations in general. It is important to emphasise that this critique does not depend on denying the fact of Serb brutality toward Kosovar civilians; indeed, the heart of the argument is that some evils must be accepted for the sake of a broader order. For its persuasive power, what the argument *does* depend on is evidence that other international players opposed the NATO action not merely out of a lawyerly desire to score points, but in genuine alarm that U.S.-led "vigilantism" threatens global stability and their own legitimate interests. Unfortunately, such evidence is abundant. Governments representing a sizeable share of the world's population have voiced this alarm, including India and China.[9] The most serious concern was that of Russia. On the substance of the Kazoo dispute, Russian diplomacy through summer 1998 had been in line with other members of the Contact Group. When it came to air strikes, however, Moscow seemed truly alarmed at the prospect of NATO military action beyond the borders of its members. For NATO to act without a Security Council mandate implied a devaluation of one of Moscow's last remaining Great Power platforms. And after Moscow had grudgingly accepted NATO enlargement to Central Europe, the Kosovo air campaign could only reinforce Russian awareness of how constricted its strategic space had become. As one Moscow analyst put it: "All we know is that, in a period of one month, NATO took in three new members, finished its New Strategic Concept, and went to war against Yugoslavia". A Russian member of the *Duma* asked: "Who can guarantee that, if not Russia, then somebody else close to Russia will not be punished in the same way?"[10]

This Russian reaction heightened the anxieties among various NATO members about the legitimacy of their action. The consensus for air strikes, in March as well as for the earlier Activation Order of October 1998, does not diminish the reality of fundamental allied disagreements about acting without a UN mandate. The American view, shared to a lesser extent by the British, was that legitimacy should not be confused with the formal mandate of a UN Security Council that is still too divided to judge that legitimacy. Rather, protecting Albanian civilians from Serb brutalities was inherently legitimate, grounded in moral principle and a revived tradition of humanitarian law.[11] The French government took the view that while a UN mandate for military intervention should be required in principle, the humanitarian emergency justified violating that rule in practice. Germany and Italy, "civilian" powers with deep cultural and constitutional inhibitions about using force anyway, were most troubled by the precedent being set. German Foreign Minister Klaus Kinkel toyed with the argument that European standards for protecting human rights, as codified in

OSCE documents, were especially high, and therefore implied a correspondingly low threshold for intervention.[12]

The successor SPD-Green government took several steps back from this theory. Clearly, however, it was a general sense that – after the experience of Bosnia – the same outrages could not be tolerated again in the European space that persuaded most European members of NATO to swallow their scruples about infringing on Yugoslav sovereignty. And Belgrade, of course, made it much easier for NATO to agree on and justify its intervention. The vast ethnic cleansing of Kosovo was organised and systematic; it repeated the pattern of killings and expulsions that marked the onset of Serb attacks in both Croatia and Bosnia. And the act of driving out an entire ethnic population makes one thing very clear: In Milosevic's Kosovo there was no place for Albanians.

If the international community was not willing to accept that proposition, then it had to embrace its opposite: Belgrade, through its actions, had forfeited its sovereignty over the province. But if the "international community" is considered to be represented by the UN security council, the Russian and Chinese vetoes meant, in effect, that an Albanian-free Kosovo would be accepted. With greater or lesser degrees of enthusiasm, all European members of NATO agreed that this was an intolerable prospect. They therefore accepted that NATO would have to act without Security Council mandate.

For Europeans this moment was something like a Catholic acknowledgement of the inevitability of sin.[13] But the same Europeans became very nervous about an American Protestant fervour, which seemed to contain the idea that Americans have a direct line to God, who tells them when it is justified to use military force. While accepting, and sometimes even welcoming, the American readiness to act outside the UN framework, Europeans might be more comfortable with Washington's occasional unilateral moments if they had faith that Americans believed in the restraining benefit of multilateralism in principle.

Desert Fox

"Operation Desert Fox", the air campaign of 15-18 December 1998 against Iraq, marked a decisive moment in the slow unravelling of the UN coalition of countries that had participated in – or to varying degrees supported – the earlier war to eject Saddam Hussein's forces from Kuwait. The unravelling has continued to the point where the new Bush administration's first military action – a limited strike against Iraq's air-defences on 16 February 2001 – provoked fierce criticism not only across the Arab world but also from ally France.[14] France's progressive estrangement from the British-American actions in Iraq has been one of the most corrosive factors within NATO, just as Russian and Chinese (and again French) dissent has more or less destroyed the brief period of post-Cold War hope that the UN Security Council might actually be able to function as its creators intended. This dissatisfaction with the U.S. policy is no doubt fuelled by a number of factors, including national commercial interests and genuine concern about the humanitarian consequences of a sanctions regime that has lasted a decade. But there is also an anxiety, similar to that aroused by the Kosovo war, about the consequences for world order of the United States, together with Britain, taking upon itself to unilaterally enforce UN Security Council Resolutions that were undoubtedly being violated by Iraq, but just as undoubtedly, did not explicitly authorise the use of force. Washington and London insisted that the air strikes were necessary to enforce the "will" of the Security Council as expressed in numerous resolutions concerning the dismantlement of weapons of mass destruction. A European critic of this claim answered thus:

> It is obvious that a general right of states to appoint themselves the executors of the "will" of the Security Council would lead to very significant instability. To appreciate this point, one only needs to flick through the 1,000-plus Security Council resolutions and identify the numerous situations where the "will" of the Council has not been fully and unconditionally complied with. Even in relation to the significantly smaller number of demands of the Council made in the context of Chapter VII, this theory would be immediately rejected by the United States and UK if it were advanced by other states…In fact, it would be very difficult for the Security Council to adopt any sort of resolution at all, if the very fact of the expression of the "will" of the Council were taken to imply a mandate to enforce it militarily.[15]

These concerns are serious. Yet the critique does not quite do justice to the predicament of American power as it stands somewhat in tension with international law but also in support of it.

It is not just that the United States and Britain seem to assess the Iraqi threat rather differently from other permanent members of the Security Council. It must be remembered that the air strikes had been threatened repeatedly, and that they had actually been ordered to begin a month earlier. The previous February, UN Secretary-General Kofi Annan came back from Baghdad having negotiated with Saddam a deal for the inspection of so-called "Presidential sites". Since the deal would not have been possible without earlier U.S. and UK threats to use force, Annan praised Clinton and Blair as the consummate "peace-keepers". While this praise may be taken to be a realistic appraisal of his need for continued support from key members of the Security Council, it was also a recognition of a fundamental truth about the relationship between diplomacy and the threat of force. And what the Americans and Britons, for some reason, seem better able to understand is that an "international community" cannot keep threatening force without, at some point, making good on its threat. The notion that the Security Council authority can operate without resorting to a credible threat of force is a semi-pacifist illusion. This illusion is probably more damaging than America's careless disregard for UN legitimacy.

The American Ideology

Transatlantic differences about the United Nations are tied up with transatlantic differences about the use of force. Although such generalisations often risk being oversimplified, there is little doubt that, on balance, the American leadership is less inhibited about using force than most European leaderships. This difference derives, in part, from different experiences of war. The fundamental American experience of war has been of military and moral success. Although introduced in 1917 to the European battlefield, Americans were largely spared the post-war disillusion and despair that haunted the European consciousness. The real American introduction to world responsibility came with the war against Hitler. Thus, the post-war generation of American leaders (and every post-World War II president until Bill Clinton) was conditioned by a war of historical singularity. Almost universally, by losers as well as winners, World War II was judged a "just" war. More important, it ended in a peace that was successful beyond the wildest Allied hopes. It is not only the famous cautionary lesson of Neville Chamberlain's appeasement, but also the enormity of this post-war success that leaves its imprint on the American consciousness. The elder George Bush, for example, as he went to war in the Persian Gulf, knew from personal experience that war need not lead inexorably to disaster. (This conviction survived, tarnished but essentially intact, the anguish of Vietnam.) Small wonder, then, that many American elites lack what might be called a "European" appreciation of the tragic dimensions of the exercise of power. Not that they love war, or are blind to its human costs, but rather that they have a diminished perception of tragic hubris – the sense that catastrophe can result not only from appeasement of evil, but also sometimes from overconfidence in defending good. Many Europeans, of course, have had a much more disastrous experience of war. They may also have been confused somewhat by a different form of success. In the early 1990s, it was perhaps inevitable that problems of European security would be viewed through the prism of the end of the Cold War. Europeans were generally happy to agree with William Pfaff's observation that "it was the magnetism of the democracies' co-operative successes which irresistibly drew Eastern Europe and the Soviet Union towards western political values".[16] The European Union constitutes the apotheosis of multilateral organisation – and indeed, "multilateral" is an inadequate expression for a form of successful interstate organisation that is truly unprecedented in history. Its success may have inspired a certain overconfidence in the scope for multilateral co-operation, as suggested by the early failures of European governments in dealing with the break-up of Yugoslavia. Many European leaders seemed ill prepared, morally and intellectually, for what Pierre

Hassner describes as "the encounter between a world based on the search for peace, prosperity, and individual fulfilment and one which has not abdicated the search for glory, community, or territory".[17] In one of the most insightful accounts of Yugoslavia's break-up and the international response, two other authors observed that West European leaders: "...sometimes behaved as though all they had to do was to persuade the belligerents of the folly of war. They failed to recognise that, in some circumstances, the resort to war was far from irrational".[18]

Cycles of Disillusion

If Yugoslavia was the field where a number of European illusions were indulged, it was also where European governments and societies learned a greater realism about the occasional necessity of defending interests and values with force. In theory, their mastery of this learning curve should make an effective transatlantic partnership more feasible. But they have to contend with unpredictable swings in America's own willingness to be effectively engaged.

Driving these oscillations were some intimately connected American attitudes towards Europe, on the one hand, and towards international organisation, on the other. The link can be seen clearly in the emblematic failure of Wilson's effort to secure American participation in the League of Nations. This involved Wilson trying to convince the U.S. Senate that League membership need not result in American policing of the Balkans. "If you want to put out a fire in Utah, you do not send to Oklahoma for the fire engine", Wilson assured senators. "If you want to put out a fire in the Balkans...you do not send to the United States for troops".[19] Then, as now, the uncertainties of U.S. engagement posed a problem for European allies. Harold Nicolson, with the British delegation to the 1919 peace conference, observed at first hand this distinctively American combination of lofty ideals, immense power and inconstant application:

> Mr. Wilson had not invented any new political philosophy, or discovered any doctrine, which had not been dreamed of, and appreciated, for many hundred years. The one thing that rendered Wilsonism so passionately interesting at the moment was the fact that this centennial dream was suddenly backed by the overwhelming resources of the strongest Power in the world.[20]

Wilsonian ideals raised immense expectations in inter-war Europe and at home in the United States. The disappointment was mutual. On the European side, for example: "France had been persuaded to abandon her claim to a buffer state between herself and Germany in return for a guarantee of armed support from the United States".[21] That this support was not forthcoming reinforced the fearful and vindictive application of the Versailles treaty. Such enduring enmity in turn helped convince many Americans that the quarrels in Europe were quarrels between various kinds of rogues.

Throughout the 20th Century, therefore, a genuine – if limited – isolationist impulse in the United States was driven mainly by political and cultural currents that ranged from ambivalence to open hostility towards alliances with the major European powers. For half a century after Pearl Harbor, the anti-European element at the heart of classic isolationism became dormant, even if it did not entirely vanish. But with the end of the Cold War, a traditional anti-European isolationism became mixed with a bizarre antipathy to the United Nations as an institution. Over the past three decades, American disillusion with the UN became manifest in three distinct stages: A "neo-conservative" disillusion of the 1970s and 1980s, a "liberal" disillusion of the 1990s, and the "neo-isolationist" Republican Congressional class of 1994. Sadly, the three stages have been cumulative, so that the American discussion of UN issues now occupies some very hostile terrain.

Neo-conservative Disillusion in the 1970s and 1980s

In the early years of the United Nations, Washington enjoyed the comfortable illusion that it would always be able to count on a majority in the General Assembly. In 1950, for example, the United States introduced the General Assembly's "Uniting For Peace" Resolution during the Korean War, and American officials did not worry too much about the precedent of circumventing the Security Council.[22] Over the next two decades, however, as further de-colonisation fed into a supposedly "Non-Aligned Movement", the struggle for Third World "hearts and minds" did not appear to go well for the United States, or for the West in general. From an American point of view, the General Assembly became a kind of Frankenstein's monster lashing out at its American creator. In 1967, at the end of the Arab-Israeli Six Day War, it was Moscow that tried to go to the General Assembly with the "Uniting For Peace" trick. This time Washington resisted, in the name of the Security Council's pride of place in the UN Charter.

The U.S.-Israel relationship, ever more intimate after the Six Day War, increasingly became a lightning rod for Third World anti-Americanism and, simultaneously, the source of considerable transatlantic tensions.[23] A low point, as far as the United States was concerned, came in the 1975 General Assembly Resolution equating Zionism with "racism".[24] This resolution was, indeed, an outrageous piece of demagoguery, and it coincided with the stirrings of a critically important neo-conservative movement in American foreign policy – one that was directed at the Soviet Union, the United Nations and America's European allies, in what seemed, at times, to be equal measure.[25]

In broad terms, neo-conservatism provided much of the intellectual and ideological vigour of the rightward movement of American politics that helped carry Ronald Reagan into the presidency. As such, it is reasonable to apply the term to a large number of Republicans and Democrats, including Reagan himself. Neo-conservatism was a distinct worldview, in particular, a pronounced pessimism about the Soviet threat. More strictly defined, however, neo-conservatives were former liberal Democrats (some remained Democrats) and, in a few cases, Marxist leftists who fiercely repudiated their earlier ideology. Such former liberals as Jeanne Kirkpatrick and Max Kampelman, Minnesota associates of Hubert Humphrey, became disgusted with trends that they associated with Humphrey's defeat in the 1968 presidential election: Anarchic student counter-culture and "McGovernite" isolationism in their own party. Many of these converted liberals were Jews, often refugees or children of refugees from Europe. They were concerned with the fate of Israel and therefore particularly angered by the European embrace of a romantic Third Worldism at the moment when Third World governments equated Zionism and racism.

Since European governments and populations tended to be more critical of Israel (if not positively pro-Arab), and since they also tended towards a more benign view of Soviet power, the neo-conservative world view came to imagine a rather sinister triangle: The Soviet Union, the United Nations and Western Europe. The latter was accused very directly by U.S. neo-conservatives of having developed the reflexes of appeasement. Although this disdain for the European allies never really went away, it could not very well be indulged by a Reagan administration that needed to shore up the Western Alliance. Today certainly, even as they decry what they see as Western Europe's continued tilt against Israel and continued social-democratic delusions, most neo-conservatives accept the need for a strong transatlantic partnership. They make no such allowance for the UN.

Liberal Disillusion in the 1990s

Yet, it must be said that it was a Republican administration – that of the older George Bush – that came closest to placing a transatlantic partnership at the centre of successful, UN-legitimised foreign policy. The 1991 Persian Gulf War contained all the elements necessary to marry a realistic view of American primacy with more idealistic expectations about a UN system of global governance. It was directed against a clear and particularly ruthless case of cross-border aggression. It was explicitly sanctioned by the UN Security Council, with the active support of Russia and China. It was carried out by a "coalition of the willing" that included a number of Arab states, but which was – in more substantial reality – the leading NATO powers employing NATO equipment and doctrine. U.S. forces played the leading and indispensable role. Finally, and notwithstanding the world's continuing problems with Saddam, the war was successful in the terms set out by the United Nations: Kuwait was liberated from Iraqi occupation.

Thus, as the Clinton administration came to power promoting a distinctly American approach of "assertive multilateralism", it had the opportunity to build on a certain successful momentum behind the idea that U.S. leadership, transatlantic co-operation and UN governance could be complementary elements of a viable world order.[26] Bill Clinton was a self-styled "New Democrat" and part of the minority in his party that had supported President Bush's war to eject Iraqi forces from Kuwait. He was also energetically open to European models and European ideas: The Centre-Left "Third Way" was truly a transatlantic project. In its combination of liberal idealism and pragmatic respect for power, the new administration seemed ideally suited to continue the rejuvenation of U.S.-UN ties that the elder Bush had started. Sadly, however, the Clinton administration's relationship with the United Nations quickly turned sour.

The first cause of this souring was another UN project initiated by the first Bush administration – the Somalia debacle. The deaths of 18 American Rangers – and the public dragging of several of their corpses through Mogadishu's dusty streets – inflamed several sources of American neuralgia. It inspired the American right-wing battle cry against allowing American troops to serve under UN command (a rather eccentric obsession, since the Rangers had been very much under American command). It started the bitter feud between Clinton administration officials and UN Secretary-General Boutros Boutros-Ghali, which culminated in the United States' vetoing Boutros-Ghali's bid for a second term.[27] Following the Mogadishu disaster, the rapid withdrawal of U.S. troops from Somalia promoted the world-wide image of a United States that was unwilling to accept casualties for any mission that did not serve the most vital of American national interests. Most critically, Somalia stoked the U.S. armed services' already deep distrust of Clinton and his aides, and stiffened the military's resistance to being involved in the "mission creep" inherent to "nation-building" and UN peacekeeping. The Clinton team was, to a very similar degree, chastened: This was what its own "Vietnam" could look and feel like.

All of these sources of neuralgia were prominent in the most important episode of liberal disillusion with the UN: The war in Bosnia. Here, the conflation of transatlantic tensions and American-UN tensions became most evident. French and British UNPROFOR commanders answered to two masters: The United Nations Secretariat and their own respective national governments. Both sources of authority were reluctant to use force, and their reluctance was mutually reinforcing. UN officials complained that their organisation became a scapegoat for key Security Council members who were themselves unwilling to confront the Serbs. The complaint was accurate enough, but it also constituted a convenient alibi: for the UN had its own institutional philosophy, influence and responsibility, as acknowledged in a 1999 UN report – a stunning institutional *mea culpa* – from Kofi Annan, Boutros Boutros Ghali's successor as UN Secretary-General. While unsparing in its criticism of other international players, the report also dissects the role of the Secretariat itself at the centre of an international response that Serb leaders quickly learned how to paralyse. It examines the fall of Srebrenica, and the Serb massacre of some 8,000 unarmed men and boys there, as the most grievous consequence of a host of UN policy errors: A ludicrous "dual-key" command arrangement for authorizing the use of force (which usually meant blocking it); a "prism of "moral equivalency" through which the conflict…was viewed by too many for too long"; and a "failure to fully comprehend" that "civilian inhabitants of the enclaves were not the incidental victims of the [Serb] attackers; their death or removal was the very purpose of the attacks upon them".

> In the end, these Bosnian Serb war aims were ultimately repulsed on the battlefield, and not at the negotiating table. Yet, the Secretariat had convinced itself early on that the broader use of force by the international community was beyond our mandate and anyway undesirable. A report of the Secretary-General to the Security Council spoke against a "culture of death", arguing that peace should be pursued only through non-military methods…The cardinal lesson of Srebrenica is that a deliberate and systematic attempt to terrorize, expel or murder an entire people, must be met decisively with all necessary means. In the Balkans, in this decade, this lesson has had to be learned not once, but twice. In both instances, in Bosnia and in Kosovo, the international community tried to reach a negotiated settlement with an unscrupulous and murderous regime. In both instances it required the use of force to bring a halt to the planned and systematic killing and expulsion of civilians.[28]

European "appeasers" and "pacifist" UN bureaucrats are the kinds of stereotypes easily thrown about in the American political discourse. Regarding Bosnia, they were thrown about in a manner that seemed blithely to assume that the United States – the most powerful member of the Security Council, not to mention NATO – had only limited responsibility for the course of Western policy. This assumption was, of course absurd: The story of Western abdication in the face of Bosnia's agonies was, in large measure, the story of the reluctance of the Bush and Clinton administrations to become involved militarily. Still, the UN itself would come to acknowledge that the American-liberal critique of the UN and European reluctance to use force against the Bosnian Serbs, however selectively focused, was also valid.

The Republican Right

Both the neo-conservative and the liberal disillusion with the UN were grounded, then, in a serious – if not always nuanced – assessment of the institution's real practical and moral failings. From the mid-1990s, however, the American critique of the United Nations was injected with another powerful element that can only be described as bizarre.

In the 1994 mid-term elections, Republicans took control of both Houses of the U.S. Congress. Exploiting public disenchantment with the first two years of the Clinton administration, the Republican victory was spearheaded by then House Minority Leader Newt Gingrich on the basis of his much-vaunted "Contract With America." This rather gimmicky document promised that 10 pieces of legislation would be passed in the first 100 days in office of the new Congress. Only one, "The National Security Restoration Act", made any mention of foreign policy; its first words, as presented in the "Contract", were: "No U.S. troops under UN command...".[29]

The Republican Right that took control of Congress 1994 defined itself by the iconic ideology of Reaganism, but it was far less internationalist than Reagan and his administration. To be sure, labelling any American political party "isolationist" runs into a logical trap: the United States, the most powerful nation on earth, its presence and influence ubiquitous, lacks any real isolationist option. Yet there is no question that deep neo-isolationism informed much of the rhetoric and mentality of this new Congressional majority. The United Nations was attacked, incredibly, as a threat to American sovereignty: At least one member of the new Republican majority peppered her speeches with references to the UN "black helicopters" that – in right-wing conspiracy theorists imaginings – threatened American freedoms. As with traditional isolationism, this neo-isolationism carried a harsh anti-European element.

Also mixed up with their fervent insularity was a burning hatred of President Bill Clinton. Much of the American policy debate was refracted through this hatred, so that it often became difficult to discern the motives of the Administration's UN diplomacy. When the United States, in arrears with its UN dues, tried to negotiate a reduction in its assessments, or when it took issue with the mandate of the very International Criminal Court that it had so prominently helped to establish, one could assume two motives: (1) A serious pursuit of American interests as the Clinton administration genuinely perceived them; but (2) also a need to appease the Republican Congress and, particularly, the unique procedural power of Senate Foreign Relations Committee Chairman Jesse Helms. But unfortunately, due to the Republicans' relentless personal enmity towards the President, the Congress was not appeaseable. Thus, America's European allies found the U.S. positions on UN matters not just objectionable, but also highly unpredictable.

Probably the most egregious consequence – because the stakes for humankind are so huge – stems from the American mixture of indifference and outright hostility to the United Nations Framework Convention on Global Warming and its Kyoto Protocol. The science of global warming is no longer in doubt. Nor is there any question about the disproportionate responsibility of a

United States that, per capita, produces 2.5 times the carbon-dioxide emissions of the average West European level, and eight times the Chinese level. There may, however, be some doubt about how much the United States as such will suffer from global warming; it is certainly plausible that immense human suffering, deaths, population movements and resulting conflict will be confined to the world's warmer and poorer regions. Thus, when the Republican Senate, again led in this matter by Helms, displays its trademark hostility to all such multi-lateral regimes, and refuses to ratify the Protocol, it demonstrates one area where U.S. isolationism may, indeed, be a plausible – albeit profoundly immoral – option.

The Second Bush Administration

On the face of it, the coming to power of a Republican administration reduces the prospects for transatlantic consensus on the UN and global governance. There are substantial reasons for pessimism. George W. Bush took over a country that experienced a staggering expansion of wealth in the previous eight years. Yet far from hinting at any need for sacrifice, Bush's central campaign promise was a massive tax cut. One of his central foreign-policy ideas was that America's military forces were "over-extended"; his only proposed concrete cure was to suggest withdrawing U.S. peace-keeping forces from the Balkans.

In defeating Al Gore, moreover, Bush defeated the author of *Earth in the Balance*, one of the first serious policy books to warn of global warming, and to call for "global Marshall plan" to deal with it. Bush's victory constitutes unilateralism's defeat of multilateralism in other ways as well. In stark contrast to Bush, Gore was forthright in defending the use of American military forces for humanitarian and "nation-building" missions. Indeed, Democrats and Republicans seem to be reverting to their foreign-policy postures of half a century ago. In that age before Vietnam, Democrats were the party of expansive, liberal internationalism. Democrats tried in the campaign to label the Bush campaign as "isolationist". For reasons already suggested, this was an exaggeration. However, if Bush does not represent so much the Republican isolationism of the pre-World War II variety, his administration certainly seems to be an emblem for the conservative scepticism expressed by such Republican leaders as Robert Taft at the outset of the Cold War. And the critical question for world governance is how that scepticism will combine with the real isolationist impulse of the Republican right wing.

Perhaps the answer is that only a Republican President can tame that isolationism. It can at least be counted on that foreign-policy initiatives no longer will be automatically weighed down by the heavy baggage of the Republican Congress' personal dislike of the President. As one European analyst puts it:

A Republican administration could provide an opportunity for transatlantic burden sharing to be put on a more secure footing. The Clinton administration has often been hampered in international negotiations by its difficult relationship with the Republican majority in Congress. A Bush Presidency, by contrast, may be more able to sustain a wider domestic consensus in support of international commitments.[30]

As the Bush administration took office, there were already some hopeful signs. Helms, the United Nations' chief American nemesis, was praising the UN secretariat for its reform efforts, and finally agreeing to the repayment of America's dues arrears.[31] Colin Powell, the new administration's Secretary of State, is certainly no unilateralist, and has expressed a respect for multilateral regimes that is certainly at odds with the prevailing attitude in Congress. Indeed, the new Bush administration contains many figures from the old Bush administration, whose foreign policy triumph was a coalition war very much wrapped in a UN mantle. Times have changed, however: The cumulative effect of three decades of UN-bashing has shifted the centre of gravity of U.S. debate well to the right. At best, the internationalism of the second Bush administration looks likely to be more constricted than that of the first.

Conclusion: A Tacit Transatlantic Bargain?

It is a much-noted irony that the United States actively parented the world's two most important multilateral institutions. One, the European Union, has been successful beyond the wildest dreams of its founders: Yet its organisation, culture and ideology now encounters non-comprehension among most American elites. The second, the United Nations, has been far less successful, and it inspires something closer to actual antipathy among important members of the American governing class. As noted above, there is no reason to expect that the Bush administration will go out of its way to stoke transatlantic divergence and resentment on questions of global governance. Bush was no doubt sincere when he called during the campaign for the United States to present a more "humble" face to the world (and a certain style of conservatism may be better suited to such humility, in contrast to Clinton-era liberal internationalism which, to foreign critics, sometimes seemed indistinguishable from American triumphalism).

But humility is not the same thing as constructive engagement. During the campaign Bush also expressed hostility to the Kyoto global-warming, calling it "unfair to America".[32] Upon taking office, he immediately reinstated President Reagan's "Mexico City" policy of denying U.S. foreign aid to any health programs that dispense advice on abortion (a ban that the Clinton administration had lifted). And the new administration has announced a thorough-going review of defence spending with the aim of "skipping a generation" in military technology. In practice, this probably means that the U.S. armed services are not going to be configured or equipped for involvement in peacekeeping or humanitarian interventions. These are all signs that the divergence in transatlantic views and priorities is likely to widen.

American attitudes, unlikely to change, will leave a gap in practical support for the United Nations. This hard reality leaves just one outstanding question: Will the European Union and its leading powers be in any position to fill that gap? In theory, as the world's most successful multilateral institution, with a culture and acquired habits of wielding soft power, the European Union should be ideally placed to become the "engine room of the United Nations" – as a prominent former European envoy to the UN has put it.[33] This European solution is only realistic, however, if the Europeans maintain a realistic sense of its limits. Soft power is no substitute for hard power; nor can Europe replace or even challenge the United States on the world stage. What the Europeans can do is to promote a re-configuration of the transatlantic bargain to put it more in the service of UN governance. Such a reconfiguration – more tacit and ad hoc than explicit and systematic – would require three elements.

First, the Europeans would need to recognise that the U.S. role as "guarantor of last resort" of global security is not, strictly speaking, reconcilable with a formal UN-based system for regulating the use of force. Regarding the Persian Gulf, the three other permanent members of the Security Council are increasingly at odds with American and British determination to enforce sanctions against Iraq and, occasionally, to strike militarily. Yet, the U.S. and UK determination remains the only hope for buying time: A few more years of containment against Saddam Hussein's dangerous aspirations to acquire weapons of mass destruction. Likewise, in East Asia, the U.S. security role means a possible intervention of defence of democratic Taiwan, which is to say, a possible war over what one permanent member of the Security Council considers its sovereign territory. It is hard to reconcile this prospect with a UN system that places the Security Council at its apex, and it is hard to imagine many European ships joining the United States in such a naval action. But it is equally difficult to believe that the Asia-Pacific would be a more secure or peaceful place if the U.S. security presence disappeared. Part of the challenge for European governments will be to restrain their own irritation and that their publics with American indifference in such cases to international law. This does not require the Europeans to abandon aspirations for a law-based system of international order, but it does mean accepting that the U.S. attitude will remain relatively unconstrained. The UK government – an intimate partner to both the United States and continental Western Europe – can continue to play the leading role in mediating the tensions that the situation will inevitably create.

Second, the EU should recognise that its own hard-power aspirations – for a 60,000-strong rapid-reaction force and a measure of defence autonomy – are going to create new expectations for its role in the world. In the first instance, this means a greater responsibility for European security, and most European nations probably do not conceive of any enhanced European military capabilities being deployed beyond the Balkans. But, as one prominent UK newspaper editor has pointed out, intervention forces are a scarce resource in the world, and new supply may well create new demand.[34] As implausible as it may seem from today's perspective, the "international community" (if such a thing can be said to exist and to be constituted by the United Nations) may yet decide that Africa's deepening miseries cannot be ignored. If the response entails interventions by professional, well-equipped armies and police, these are more likely to be European than American.

Third, the Europeans will have to take the lead in injecting multilateral *fora* with new life and purpose. This may require relaxing the by-now reflexive assumption that burdens should be shared across the Atlantic. In terms of the most important international regime, for global co-operation against global warming, European states should unilaterally commit themselves to stay under the emissions targets that were discussed, but not agreed, at the November 2000 Hague World Climate Conference. And, as Malcolm Chalmers has argued, they should accept what they rejected at the Hague – the Clinton administration's proposal to take credit for so-called "carbon sinks", such as forests, in meeting U.S. emissions targets. This is not a great deal for the Europeans, but they will be lucky if they can coax the same offer out of President Bush.[35]

Taken together, these three elements may not appear to add up to a good bargain for the Europeans. Yet it would be a bargain that reflected not just reality, but also a certain rough justice. The U.S. global security role is so fundamental that it may be taken for granted. And whatever corrosive harm may be done by American unilateralist attitudes toward the United Nations, a broader global order is still served by the U.S. role. The Europeans' challenge will be at once practical and moral: Of "promoting multilateralism by showing how it delivers in practice".[36] European governments can hope that this example will have a positive pedagogical effect on the United States. But they should avoid the frustration of actually expecting the United States to change.

Notes

1   See Alan S. Milward, *The Reconstruction of Western Europe, 1945-1951* (Berkeley: University of California Press, 1984), passim.

2   John Lewis Gaddis, *Strategies of Containment: A Critical Appraisal of Post-war American National Security Policy* (New York: Oxford University Press, 1982), pp. 10,11.

3   Robert Kagan, "The World and President Bush", *Survival* 43, no. 1 (Spring 2001), p. 6.

4   Ibid., p. 6.

5   Ibid., p. 5.

6   For an early warning of this danger, see David P. Calleo, *Beyond American Hegemony: The Future of the Western Alliance* (New York: Basic Books, 1987).

7   All Reisman quotes from W. Michael Reisman, "The United States and International Institutions", *Survival* Vol. 41, No. 4 (Winter 1999-2000), pp. 63-4.

8   Francois Heisbourg, "American Hegemony? Perceptions of the US Abroad", *Survival* Vol. 41, No. 4 (Winter 1999-2000), pp.15-16.

9   India denounced the attacks as a "flagrant violation" of the UN Charter that constitutes interference in the internal affairs of a sovereign state. See Ian Black, James Meek, and Ian Traynor, "Russia and China lead International Protests", *The Guardian*, 26 March 1999, available at http://newsunlimited.co.uk/Kosovo/Story/0%2C2763%2C37728%2 C00 .html. China had more direct reason to fear the possible precedent for US intervention on behalf of the Chinese "province" of Taiwan (and this before the fiasco of NATO's mistakenly bombing Beijing's embassy in Belgrade, with loss of three Chinese lives).

10   Transcript of the Plenary Session of the Russian State Duma, 3 February 1999, cited in Oksana Antonenko, "Russia, NATO and European Security after Kosovo", *Survival* Vol. 41, No. 4, Winter 1999-2000, p. 133.

11   See Prime Minister Tony Blair, "Doctrine of the International Community", speech delivered in Chicago on 22 April 1999; available at: http://www.number-10.gov.uk/public/info/index.html; and President Clinton, television address, 24 March 1999, published in *Washington Post*, 25 March 1999, p. A34.

12   Claus Gennrich, "Im Angesicht der Not im Kosovo baut Kinkel neue juristische Brueken", *Frankfurter Allgemeine Zeitung*, 14 October 1998.

13   An analogy I have borrowed from my IISS colleague Gilles Andreani.

14   Joseph Fitchett, "Bombing of Iraq 'Illegal', Paris Says", *International Herald Tribune*, 20 February 2001, p.1.

15   Marc Weller, "The US, Iraq and the Use of Force in a Unipolar World", *Survival* Vol. 41, No. 4 (Winter 1999-2000), p. 89.

16   William Pfaff, "Is Liberal Internationalism Dead?", *World Policy Journal*, Vol. 10, No. 3, Fall 1993, p. 5.

17   Pierre Hassner, unpublished paper as quoted in Leo Tindemans et. al., *Unfinished Peace: Report of the International Commission on the Balkans* (Washington D.C.: Carnegie Endowment for International Peace, 1996), pp. 57-58.

18   Laura Silber and Alan Little, *The Death of Yugoslavia* (London: Penguin, 1995), p. 175.

19   Adam Roberts, "Communal Conflict as a Challenge to International Organization", in Danchev and Halverson, eds., *International Perspectives on the Yugoslav Conflict*, pp. 176-177.

20   Harold Nicolson, *Peacemaking 1919* (London: Methuen & Co, 1964), p. 191.

21   Ibid, p. 207.

22   See W. Michael Reisman, "The United States and International Institutions", op. cit., p. 70.

23   For my own extended discussion of the role of Israel and the UN in transatlantic tensions, see Dana H. Allin, *Cold War Illusions: America, Europe and Soviet Power, 1969-1989* (New York: St. Martin's Press, 1994), pp. 27-50.

24   United Nations General Assembly Resolution 3379, 10 November 1975.

25   See Allin, *Cold War Illusions,* op. cit., pp. 51-77 and passim.

26   See Remarks of Anthony Lake, Assistant to the President for National Security Affairs, "From Containment to Enlargement", Johns Hopkins University School of Advanced International Studies, Washington D.C., 21 September 1993, http://www. mtholyoke. edu/ acad/intrel/lakedoc.html.

27   The bitterness of the feud was evident in the title of Boutros-Ghali's memoir: *Unvanquished: A U.S.-U.N. Saga* (London: I.B. Tauris Publishers, 1999).

28   *Report of the Secretary-General Pursuant to General Assembly Resolution 53/35 (1998): "Srebrenica Report"* [paragraphs 465-506].

29   Rep. Newt Gingrich, Rep. Dick Armey, and the House Republicans, "The Contract With America". http://www.freedom.gov/scoreboard/contract.asp.

30   Malcolm Chalmers, "A Transatlantic New Deal: What Europe should pay to promote US engagement", The Foreign Policy Centre Policy Brief No. 2 (London: 2001), p. 5.

31   Eric Schmitt, "Senator Helm's Journey: From Clenched-Fist UN Opponent to Fan", *New York Times*, 23 December 2000.
32   Douglas Jehl, "The 2000 Campaign: The Environment", *The New York Times*, 3 November 2000.
33   Former UK envoy David Hanney, conversation with author.
34   Martin Wollocot, Assistant Editor, *The Guardian*, conversation with author.
35   Malcolm Chalmers, "A New Transatlantic Deal", op. cit., p. 19.
36   Ibid, p. 7.

11 New Challenges for Transatlantic Economic Relations[1]

BERNHARD MAY

Introduction

Bill Clinton was elected president in November 1992. His winning campaign mantra was: "It's the economy, stupid!" The elected President Clinton promised to focus like a laser beam on solving America's domestic economic problems to make the United States strong again. The Clinton Administration put economics high on both the domestic and foreign policy agendas. It was an irony that Bill Clinton was elected in November 1992 – after a successful campaign focusing on economic issues – at a time when the so-called "Bush recession" was over and the economy grew again. But the American people did not believe it. The figures about the growing American economy were published one week after the elections – but not by coincidence but because that is what the law requires.

George W. Bush Jr. moved into the White House ironically at a time when many experts were forecasting a slowdown, or even a recession, of the American economy – after a so-called eight year "Clinton boom". Some even argued that President George W. Bush may have inherited a "Clinton recession" or that his presidency will begin with a "George-W. recession"[2] that he is not responsible for.

President Clinton brought about a profound change, putting economics high on his domestic and foreign policy agenda. But this profound change in respect to giving economics a much higher priority could also be observed in many other countries and in world politics. This fundamental change was an essential part of the so-called "post-Cold War era" – a transition period between the collapse of the Cold War system and the emerging Global Age. Whereas the United States focused on military containment during the Cold War era, the focus shifted to economic competition on a global level in the "post-Cold War era". A second profound change helped to speed-up this development: the process of globalisation became an ever more complex and more important one in world politics.

There is another irony. Bill Clinton was elected because he promised to the people to focus on economic problems. But when President Clinton moved into the White House, he could forget his campaign promises because the American economy had turned around and started – as we know now – the longest economic upturn in American history. Instead President Clinton was forced by international developments to become a "foreign-policy-president"– as many American Presidents did before him. It is interesting to see that President Clinton during the last couple of years in office tried very hard to leave a legacy as a successful American President in foreign policy matters.

I will, first, discuss the history of transatlantic relations and argue that it is a myth to believe that there could have ever been trouble-free transatlantic relations. Second, I will examine the new realities of a partnership of economic superpowers. Third, I will analyse the most important current disputes in transatlantic economic relations. Fourth, I will discuss the transatlantic dilemma of being a partner and a competitor at the same time seen in the framework of global governance and transatlantic responsibility.

The Myth of Trouble-Free Transatlantic Relations

Transatlantic relations have always been difficult. From the beginning in 1949 until today, there have been profound differences in terms of interests, power and style. Transatlantic relations had to go through a series of disputes and crises. And at times it really looked like a troubled partnership on the way to breaking up. But the United States and Europe – Western Europe for most of the time – always fought it out and worked out a compromise. Looking at transatlantic relations as an observer from Asia or Africa, it would be true to state that transatlantic relations have always been difficult, but for most of the years since 1949 transatlantic relations have been much more important and much better than relations with other regions of the world – and that is true for the United States as well as for Europe.

Looking ahead and wondering about new challenges for transatlantic relations, it is important to keep in mind a realistic picture of the past. Robert J. Lieber put it succinctly: "Tensions between Europe and America are nothing new. Virtually from the time of its inception in 1949, the Atlantic alliance has weathered a wide range of internal disputes not only over strategy, but economics and politics as well".[3] There are a long list of non-military disputes in transatlantic relations like trade frictions, economic competition, agricultural issues, cultural conflicts, and disagreements about policy toward Cuba and China for example. Some of those conflicts were fought fiercely and got labels like: "Chicken-War" or "Spaghetti-War". But the most difficult and most dangerous transatlantic economic conflict with political and military implications was the "pipeline-embargo-crisis" in the years 1980-84. This dispute was about the: "American attempts to block the construction of the trans-Siberian Pipeline, which the United States believed would make Europe dependent on Soviet energy, thus giving the Soviet Union a source of leverage over Europe, while providing it with an infusion of hard currency earning that would bolster its economic and military potential".[4]

All those transatlantic disputes proved the deep-seated differences concerning interests, power and style between the United States and Europe. But the alliance survived all those disputes because of the threat posed by the Soviet Union that kept it together. Especially Western Europe – and even more so West Germany - depended on the American nuclear umbrella and, therefore, at least in some disputes gave in to American demands "in order to preserve an unambiguous American guarantee".[5]

After the end of the Cold War this very special glue that kept the alliance together – the Soviet threat – disappeared and many observers were afraid that this would lead to a steady weakening and to the break-up of the alliance. Experts like John Mearsheimer[6] expected more instability in Europe after the end of the Cold War and a distancing between the United States and Europe not only in security policy, but in respect to a range of economic issues as well.[7]

And indeed, a profound change has taken place on both sides of the Atlantic concerning transatlantic relations. In Europe: "France has become the most strident critic of American power and the most avid in seeking ways to increase its own autonomy and to steer the European Union toward a more independent course". Near the end of his life, President Mitterrand is quoted in a biography by Georges Marc Benamou as having said: "France does not know it, but we are at war with America. Yes, a permanent war, a vital war, an economic war, a war without death. Yes, they are very hard, the Americans, they are voracious, they want undivided power over the world".[8] Mitterrand died in 1996. And the current French foreign minister Hubert Vedrine just recently proclaimed: "We cannot accept (...) the unilateralism of a single hyperpower".[9] France was the most outspoken European critic of "American hegemonic behaviour". And in discussions about transatlantic relations, the famous book title was quoted more often: "The arrogance of power".

At the beginning of the 1990s and throughout the last decade, especially military experts worried about a weakening foundation for the transatlantic alliance and looked for an alternative reason to keep the Americans in Europe, after the threat of the Soviet Union was gone. And they found that the election campaign mantra of Bill Clinton in 1992 could also be the new underpinning to preserve and strengthen transatlantic relations: "It's the economy, stupid!" Those military experts did not – and some still do not – understand that economic relations cannot be managed like military relations – and that is even more true in a "globalising" world.

The New Realities of a Transatlantic Partnership of Economic Superpowers

The candidate Bill Clinton promised the people that he would focus on solving domestic economic problems. But the elected President Clinton had to focus on foreign policy issues and especially in the first two years invested a lot of "political capital" in successfully concluding international trade negotiations. It was not President Clinton's choice but instead it was the agenda waiting for him. Even though international economic negotiations were not high on the agenda of the elected President Clinton, and not all of his advisers were sure he should make it his priority, President Clinton worked very hard in the first two years to successfully finish the ongoing negotiations concerning world trade negotiations, the so-called Uruguay Round, in respect to the creation of the World Trade Organization (WTO) as well as finalising the North American Free Trade Agreement negotiations (NAFTA). Without President Clinton pushing for it, all of those successes would not have been possible. It helped that there was at least a "silent majority" in Congress in favour of those international economic agreements. It is fair to say that President Clinton in his first two years achieved some of the most important successes of his legacy.[10]

W. Bowman Cuttler put it succinctly: "The first two years of President Clinton's first term were the most successful two years in terms of international economic accomplishments since the creation of the original post-war economic community in the years immediately following World War II. But the growing hostility in both parties to international economic agreements, and the election of Republican majorities in both houses of congress in 1994 meant that little additional progress could be made thereafter".[11]

Two profound changes occurred during the 1990s: First, the United States moved from an active supporter of international economic negotiations – see, for example, the important leadership role played by three American Presidents, i.e. Reagan, Bush and Clinton, during the so-called Uruguay Round[12] – to a kind of road block for further international negotiations in several fields such as trade, investment, climate change, environmental problems, and the International Court of Justice. The problem was – as Cuttler pointed out – that after the elections in 1994, the Republicans won the majority in both houses and a "divided government" became a reality for many years. Furthermore, Congress denied President Clinton "fast track authorization" for trade negotiations. There are three reasons explaining this profound shift in the United States in the 1990s: President Clinton did not make those issues his first priority; divided government created a gridlock situation in terms of getting Congressional support for any American leadership role in international economic negotiations. Furthermore, there was a decreasing interest in international affairs at a time of a strengthening opposition against transferring American sovereignty to international organizations like WTO.

The second profound change of the 1990s was an astonishing revival of the American economy that made the United States the undisputed superpower. Sandy Berger, the long-time security adviser to President Clinton in the White House, put it this way: "America today is by any measure the world's unchallenged military and economic power".[13] What a difference a decade can make! In the fall of 1987, Paul Kennedy published his famous book: *The Rise and Fall of the Great Powers* – analysing the rise and fall of the Spanish and British Empire and arguing that the United States would decline because of what he called the problem of "imperial overstretch". The reason for the fall of the Spanish and British Empire was because they were unable to sustain the material cost of greatness.[14] *Newsweek* wrote at the time about Kennedy's book: "Kennedy gives epic meaning to the nation's relative economic and industrial decline". (The publisher put this quote on the back of the paperback edition in 1989.)

During the presidential election campaign in 1988, when Vice President George Bush, the father of the current American President, was a candidate, a heated debate took place about American decline and what to expect from the next president to avoid such a development.[15] After the Berlin Wall came down, and Germany moved toward unification, newspapers and even some experts wrote that the new superpowers, Germany and Japan, would, to a certain degree, replace the United States. But then Saddam Hussein sent his troops into Kuwait on 2 August 1990 and forced the world to stand up to this military occupation. It was immediately clear which country would have to show leadership to fight Saddam Hussein – and, of course, it was the "old" superpower, the United States, and not the "new" superpowers, Germany and Japan. In the end, Germany and Japan did not even take part but paid a large share of the bill to liberate Kuwait.[16]

Looking back, some people say, Kennedy got it totally wrong implying – without forecasting or predicting it – that the United States would decline like other empires before because of the problem of "imperial overstretch". And, of course, in that sense Kennedy was totally wrong. Over the last decade, the United States did not decline in economic and industrial or military and political terms. Just the opposite happened: There is just one superpower nowadays and that is the United States. But there is another group who argues that Kennedy was right – but he just got confused with the names because he really wanted to write about the Soviet Union – and in that sense his forecast became reality even though there is still a kind of "imperial overstretch" problem in Russia today.

During the late 1980s and early 1990s, at the time when there was a heated debate about an American decline in the United States, there was a kind of euphoria in Europe: Europe looked like the next superpower. There was a kind of over-optimism in Europe that led people to believe that Paul Kennedy could be, and would be, right in forecasting an American decline. And, of course, the United States had to go through difficult years in the 1970s and 1980s. But Europeans underestimated the kind of painful structural changes that were implemented during the 1980s to lay the groundwork for the revival of a strong

American superpower in the 1990s. Europe did not do its homework during those years. Just one example to show the extraordinary turnaround: Whereas European leaders lectured the Americans until the beginning of the 1990s at the annual G-7 summit about solving their economic and deficit problems, it is now the American President who is telling the Europeans to bring their economic house in order. Euphoria at the end of the 1980s was replaced in Europe of the 1990s by Euro-pessimism. Europe wasted a lot of time in the 1990s. But it looks like Europe is turning around and is moving into a much brighter future in the first decade of the new Millennium.

Leaving aside all those transatlantic disputes, all those false predictions, and all those mistakes that have been made on both sides of the Atlantic, the fact of the matter is that Europe and the United States became two superpowers who depend upon each other. They have common interests and to a certain degree a common value system, they are both important actors in a complex system of interdependence. They are competing with each other on the world markets and they are allies at the same time. This is the new reality of transatlantic relations.

The European Union and the United States have very good reasons for cooperation and for improved relations without aiming for a trouble-free partnership. The EU and the United States enjoy a high degree of economic integration. The two economies (taking the EU as one economy even though the EU is not yet a single market like the United States) are the leading participants in international trade, accounting for 37 per cent of world merchandise trade, and 45 per cent of world trade in services. The EU and the United States are also each other's single largest trading partner – taking goods and services together – and each other's most important source and destination for foreign direct investment. Europe and the United States depend even more on each other in terms of managing the world economy, as well as global financial markets.

Robert Lieber sums it up nicely: "Europe and the United States find themselves needing to cooperate through the International Monetary Fund, Group of Seven, WTO, and other groupings, not only to resolve mutual problems, but to cope with global financial and economic dangers".[17]

Current Disputes in Transatlantic Economic Relations

Despite the fact that the United States and the European Union are their most important economic partners, and despite an impressive record in economic integration, there are currently some potentially serious trade disputes between the two transatlantic partners making the headlines and creating a potentially serious political backlash on both sides of the Atlantic. Even though these trade disputes make up only about one per cent of the total transatlantic trade volume, if these problems are not solved in a timely and acceptable fashion, these minor disputes could create a major transatlantic crisis with global implications. And it is not yet clear if both sides are willing to work out a compromise.

The most prominent trade conflicts are some old ones like the Banana import regime of the European Union and the "hormone beef case", but there are also new disputes such as the Foreign Sales Corporations (FSC) conflict, the clash over genetically modified organisms (GMO), and a renewed dispute over subsidies. The European Union's present banana regime was found to be against WTO rules in favouring its traditional suppliers. This dispute goes back to the year 1993 when the EU introduced its banana regime. This regime is supposed to protect the banana producers within the EU – even though there are no banana producers on the continent – as well as banana exporters in the so-called ACP-countries. The European Union has special relations because of historic reasons – French and British colonialism – with those countries in Africa, the Caribbean and Pacific (ACP).

The European Union is arguing that this banana regime would be a special kind of foreign aid for poor countries. And if that is the case, no one can deny that poor ACP-countries are the winners. The losers are European consumers and banana exporters from countries not belonging to the ACP-group who are trying to export bananas to the EU. This is the reason why the United States brought the banana case to the WTO. There are no banana producers in the United States either, but the two largest banana exporting companies are American ones: Chiquita and Dole. Therefore, the dispute is actually between "ACP bananas" and "Dollar bananas". Those "dollar bananas" are produced in Central American countries especially in Costa Rica, Guatemala, Honduras, Nicaragua and Panama. But the fundamental argument of the American administration always was that the banana regime of the EU would be a typical kind of protectionism not allowed under WTO rules. And, therefore, the aim would have to be to fight protectionism and defend open markets.

The WTO ruled in 1997 that the EU banana regime would be against WTO rules and told the EU to open the European banana market.[18] In response, the EU changed its banana regime in January 1999, but the WTO ruled in April of 1999 a second time against the EU and allowed the United States to put punitive tariffs on European products in the amount of 191 million dollars per year. The European Union proposed in its latest plan in October 2000 to resolve the long-running trade dispute over bananas by implementing a tariff-only regime for banana imports by the year 2006.[19] It is not yet clear if all parties involved will accept this compromise to end the banana dispute.

The WTO ruled also against the European Union in the so-called "hormone beef case". American cattle farmers use hormones to produce beef. The European Union is prohibiting the import of American "hormone beef" because of health risks for the consumers. The American administration is arguing that this is protectionism and brought the case to the WTO. The EU lost at the WTO but refused – as in the banana case – to open up the market, but instead accepted punitive tariffs placed upon European exports to the United States. The "hormone beef case" is, in comparison to the banana case, a much more difficult one because it raises a fundamental question: Who should make decisions about health hazards in a case where scientific evidence cannot be produced but consumer attitudes are against such a product? The European Union could not produce any scientific evidence to prove their claim that "hormone beef" is a health hazard. But the European consumers are overwhelmingly against "hormone beef". And the "mad-cow-disease crisis" in Europe will not resolve the "hormone beef dispute" with the United States. On the contrary, consumers are even more worried about "unhealthy beef" and unhealthy food in general.

That is also the fundamental conflict behind the so-called GMO-dispute. GMO stands for "genetically modified organisms". The dispute is about GMO food and food products. Whereas GMO food is part of everyday life in the United States, most EU member states are not allowing the production and distribution of GMO food because of health hazards as the EU is arguing. And consumers in most EU member states are vehemently against GMO food, sometimes even boycotting companies and shops if there are reports about GMO food. The GMO-dispute is just beginning – and it will be very difficult for the European Union and the United States to settle it.[20]

A new and potentially disastrous conflict between the United States and the EU broke out in February 2000 when the WTO ruled against the United States and told the U.S. to scrap an offshore tax-haven plan, the so-called Foreign-Sales Corporations (FSC), an American tax scheme that allows U.S. companies to save at least 3.9 billion dollars a year by exporting through offshore tax havens.[21] In money terms, the FSC-ruling is by far the biggest case the WTO has ever settled. The WTO decision was seen as handing the EU a big stick to prod the U.S. into dropping more than 300 million dollars worth of trade sanctions imposed on the EU over the bananas and hormone-treated beef disputes in 1999.

The United States changed the FSC tax-break system for exporters and signed replacement legislation on 16 November 2000. But the European Union does not believe that the changed system would comply with the WTO ruling. The EU, therefore, asked the WTO to set up a panel to review the changed American system. And the EU asked the WTO to authorize sanctions worth up to 4.043 billion dollars against the United States in the FSC-dispute. The European Union is showing flexibility, but wants to see results as well. European Trade Commissioner Pascal Lamy put it this way: "While wishing to de-escalate this dispute, our aim is to see the WTO-incompatible FSC export subsidies removed".[22]

Now both sides have to await the WTO's verdict. If the WTO rules again against the United States, this would most likely create the most dangerous challenge for transatlantic economic relations as well as for the WTO as an international organization itself. Both sides have good reasons and are responsible for working out a compromise acceptable for both sides to make sure that this "worst case trade-war scenario" will not happen.

The latest transatlantic conflict arose with the launch of the European Airbus Superjumbo program in December 2000. The day before the formal industrial initiation of the A380, President Bill Clinton warned French President Jacques Chirac at the EU-U.S. summit meeting in Washington that if the financing of the Airbus Superjumbo was not on commercial terms, it could create "a serious problem affecting the U.S.-EU relationship". This American challenge over subsidies for Airbus threatens to turn into the most serious trade dispute yet between the United States and the EU. The European Commission said it would retaliate against any possible U.S. action over about 2.5 billion dollar in loans from four European countries for the project. The financial support in the form of repayable loans from France, Germany, the UK and Spain is being challenged by Washington as an unfair subsidy. But the decision about how to respond was left to the incoming Bush administration.[23]

What to Expect from the Bush Administration: Back to the Future?

It was a long election campaign and it seemed to last forever until the American people and the world learnt – a decision the Supreme Court had to take – that George W. Bush was the new president. All along Europeans worried about possible changes in transatlantic relations and trade policy after the Clinton administration would move out. There was little doubt that a Gore administration, heavily dependent upon the trade unions, would have been more protectionist. Yet what about a Bush administration? Would President Bush try to turn back the clock and disengage the United States from world politics? Would he try to return to the old concepts of containment and unilateralism and focus on the old issues of military and security concerns, leaving out the new issues of economic interdependence and global governance?

Those anxieties became more vocal when President-elect Bush announced who the important people in his foreign policy team would be: Colin Powell, Secretary of State, Paul O'Neill, Treasury Secretary, Donald Rumsfeld, Defence Secretary, Don Evans, Commerce Secretary, and Condoleezza Rice as National Security Adviser. All of them were considered men and women of the Bush administration in the 1980s who had a lot of experience from the Cold War era. People on both sides of the Atlantic were afraid that Bush Junior would copy his father's foreign policy, by appointing so many of his father's team as members of his cabinet.

When the news leaked out that the Bush transition team would think about abolishing the U.S. trade representative, as well as the National Economic Council (NEC) in the White House, and give the authority for trade negotiations either to the State Department or to the Department of Commerce while including the NEC-team in the National Security staff. It all looked as if the President-elect was an individual who still thinks in terms of Cold War confrontation and who does not understand the challenges of globalisation.

What a relief it was in Europe, and other parts of the world, when President-elect George W. Bush named a veteran of the last Bush administration as his choice for U.S. trade representative, and stressed that free trade would be at the heart of his foreign policy priorities.[24] It was the substance of the decision and the name of the new USTR that led many people to believe that the new Bush administration would continue what the Clinton administration had started – and that is "the beginning of a foreign policy for the global age" and "a doctrine of globalisation".[25]

When President-elect Bush introduced Robert Zoellick as the new trade representative on 11 January 2001, he announced that Zoellick would hold cabinet rank, and that he would be the key adviser to the president on trade policy. The President-elect stated: "A successful economic strategy must include a confident, assertive trade policy. We will open new markets for products grown and made in America. That will be one of our foremost goals. We will ensure that trade agreements are enforced and that American farmers and workers and entrepreneurs are treated fairly. Bob (Bob Zoellick, the author) and I also understand that we now are in a global economy and that trade will not only mean a good economy at home, trade will mean a good economy with our trading partners".[26]

Bob Zoellick as the new USTR was welcomed in the United States. and in Europe as an excellent choice due to the fact that he was "an experienced public servant, a veteran diplomat, a good negotiator, and a man of great skill and energy" – as President-elect Bush put it. Bob Zoellick was one of the chief architects of the U.S. policy to encourage the unification of Germany. But Bob Zoellick is also known to be a committed and tough negotiator. He has a "daunting task in building bridges, both with U.S. trading partners and with a restive U.S. Congress"[27] before him. It may help that Bob Zoellick knows Pascal Lamy, his opposite number in the European commission, quite well – some even say they are friends. Even though friendship may help in the process of working out solutions for problems, friendship alone will not solve problems. And there are formidable economic problems ahead confronting the transatlantic relationship.

The new USTR Bob Zoellick needs the support of the President and the important people in the Bush foreign policy team and he has to work very closely with Congress if he wants to become a successful USTR. Bob Zoellick has a vision on trade and international economic policy – and he has the support of the President and the key people in the Bush administration. President Bush not only made him the key adviser to the president on trade policy, but President Bush is very grateful to Mr. Zoellick for his decisive role he played in the Florida recount in the weeks after the election until George W. Bush was announced President-elect. He held senior positions in the Treasury and State departments under James Baker. And he obtained the support of Vice President Dick Cheney because they both worked in the first Bush administration and know each other very well. Also both Condoleezza Rice and Colin Powell made it clear as well that they too understand that global trade and international economic relations are important elements of U.S. foreign policy in a globalised world.

The most difficult challenge for the Bush administration in terms of trade policy and transatlantic economic relations is the new Congress and even more so the evenly split Senate. Without a fast-track authorization granted from Congress, the Bush administration cannot convince the European Union and other major trading partners to launch a new WTO trade round. And it will be difficult to get a fast-track authorization – something Congress denied the Clinton administration several times. It is true, however, that the Bush administration will not depend on the support of unions and environmental groups and is therefore more flexible. Furthermore, the Bush administration can count on the support of the business community if there is a renewed interest in trade negotiations by business people.

Considering the growing resistance against globalisation, and especially global trade, which was one important factor responsible for the failure in Seattle to launch a new WTO trade round in December 1999, it will be difficult for the Bush administration to overcome those problems and obtain the necessary support for an active trade policy. But there are also good reasons for optimism that are often overlooked. First, a slowing American economy will create more support from the business community to move on with liberalizing world trade. Second, the American people are not that strongly supportive of a new isolationism as many seem to believe.[28] Furthermore, trade policy depends on the leadership role of the President and President Bush committed himself to implement an active trade policy, whereas President Clinton did not invest a lot of political capital in trade policy in the last couple of years.

So the good news is that there is a new USTR, Bob Zoellick, a competent and confident USTR, an experienced and knowledgeable person – and a tough negotiator who knows Europe very well. And there is President Bush who has declared trade policy to be an essential part of his foreign policy. But no trade policy can be successful without Presidential leadership on the one hand and congressional support on the other hand. And congressional support is missing.

Even worse, Congress is deeply divided and the old bipartisanship in foreign policy and trade policy is no longer guaranteed. And it is quite unlikely that President Bush could restore a bipartisan foreign policy, as James Lindsay predicts. He expects more problems for the Bush administration: "The new partisanship in foreign affairs reflects deep currents in American society that will shape the politics of U.S. foreign policy for years to come". Lindsay then states a paradox: "The rise of the new partisanship has created a paradox: The United States enjoys unparalleled power on the world stage but presidents are finding it harder to mobilize support for their foreign policies. They can no longer assume that Congress and the public will follow their lead".[29]

When President Clinton moved into the White House in January 1993, many experts on both sides of the Atlantic were very worried if the new administration would work hard enough to conclude the trade negotiations that were started by the Reagan and Bush administrations. Looking back, the first two years of the Clinton administration were the most successful ones in terms of trade policy. In the following years, a growing Congressional and popular hostility to international economic agreements, a growing resistance against globalisation, and especially trade liberalization – coupled with the lack of an active leadership role on the part of the president, all are partially responsible for the fact that trade policy in the last couple of years of the Clinton administration could no longer achieve any major success.

In January 2001, President Bush moved into the White House. Once more, many experts on both sides of the Atlantic have been worried about policy changes in the new administration concerning trade policy and transatlantic relations. With a competent and convincing foreign policy team, the Bush administration got off to a good start. If they keep in mind that we are now living in a world characterized by interdependence and globalisation, and if the Bush administration continues the policy of the Clinton administration of making economic relations an essential part of foreign policy, and if President Bush engages himself in a leadership role to support the USTR and especially to win the support of Congress, then the Bush administration has a good chance to avoid protectionism both at home and abroad and to initiate and launch new trade negotiations. In respect to transatlantic relations, the Bush administration will have to focus on some alarming economic disputes and should follow the old Clinton campaign mantra: "It's the economy, stupid!"

Global Governance and Transatlantic Responsibility

Transatlantic relations are facing three major challenges. First, there is the challenge of adapting and strengthening transatlantic relations to the new realities of a post-Cold War world. Second, transatlantic relations are facing the challenge of global governance. Third, Europe and the United States not only have to cope with the challenges of globalisation in a cooperative manner in terms of their own interests but also in terms of their responsibility concerning transatlantic relations and global governance.

Transatlantic relations are still in a state of transition. Ever since the end of the Cold War, the partners on both sides of the Atlantic have been searching for a new framework. There have been many ideas, proposals, initiatives in the 1990s about how to strengthen transatlantic relations after the threat of the Soviet Union disappeared.[30] Many proposals were discussed concerning ways to strengthen transatlantic economic relations – from TAFTA (Transatlantic Free Trade Area),[31] to an Atlantic marketplace, to creating a Transatlantic Economic Area, to the proposal for a Transatlantic Marketplace.[32]

This discussion led to the signing of two transatlantic documents at the European-American summit in Madrid on December 3, 1995: the New Transatlantic Agenda (NTA) and the Joint EU-U.S. Action Plan.[33] The NTA provides the framework for the specific tasks laid out in the Joint EU-U.S. Action Plan. A wide range of issues is covered in these documents: Political cooperation in promoting peace, stability, and democracy around the world; responses to global challenges, such as population growth, drugs, and organized crime; economic cooperation in expanding world trade and the creation of a New Transatlantic Marketplace (NTM); and closer cultural and educational ties in order to strengthen the people-to-people links.

At the Madrid summit in 1995, the Trans Atlantic Business Dialogue (TABD) was launched in an effort to engage corporate leaders on both sides of the Atlantic in identifying and helping to resolve barriers to trade and investment. The NTA was followed by the Transatlantic Economic Partnership (TEP) initiative of May 1998 with the aim to deepen the economic dialogue, both on bilateral and multilateral issues.

All those efforts to strengthen the "transatlantic institutional links and mechanisms of regulatory and trade policy cooperation on different levels that have been established through the New Transatlantic Agenda and the Transatlantic Economic Partnership may prove to be highly beneficial to global economic integration". Scherpenberg concludes his assessment with an optimistic outlook: "By taking a constructive attitude towards the new symmetry of transatlantic economic bipolarism, both sides might be able to move forward to a broader, deeper, and ever more symmetric strategic partnership in order to achieve a non-hegemonic, rule-based multilateral framework for the globalised economy".[34]

No doubt, the United States and the European Union are now the two economic superpowers. The "OECD-world" is, first of all, a transatlantic world. The United States and the EU both represent a more or less similar share of global GDP and of global trade and investment, and in global financial institutions. Furthermore, the United States and the EU maintain a highly balanced bilateral relationship in terms of bilateral trade in goods and services as well as in direct investments. The economies of the EU and the United States are highly inter-linked; in fact the Euro-Atlantic area could be called the most economically integrated region of the world.

All of that is true and is encouraging, but an important and difficult part of transatlantic relations is the fact that the United States and the European Union are each other's main, sometimes even the only, global, economic rivals. And this fact represents a complex challenge of political rivalry and commercial competition. When IBM is competing with Sony in the European market – that is commercial competition and should not create political problems. But if Airbus is fighting with Boeing to get a bigger market share, this is much more than commercial competition and involves political rivalry as well. The Airbus subsidies case is such an issue, as was mentioned above, that could lead to a major "trade war". It is because of those kind of conflicts that more and more people have been arguing for a better and more efficient "early-warning-system" in transatlantic relations. The latest proposal came from Guillaume Parmentier who proposed to create a "Euro-Atlantic Political and Economic Forum" with the only aim to allow dialogue at senior working level to avoid trade wars.[35]

The other profound transatlantic rivalry concerns the competition between the dollar and the Euro.[36] The European Union is implementing the last phase of its plan to create a European Economic and Monetary Union (EMU). So far twelve of the currently fifteen EU members are involved and will exchange their national currencies with the Euro beginning in January 2002. Three major consequences of the EMU should be taken seriously: First, the Euro will start a new phase in European integration. This is a major step towards an Economic and Monetary Union with a common market and a single currency. It will be almost impossible to go back to national currencies. That is the economic and political challenge of the Euro. Second, the Euro will, over the coming years, create a common market of a different quality with important benefits for consumers, with benefits and challenges for companies and fundamental changes for investors and capital markets.

Third, the Euro will play a very important role in international financial markets. The dollar will remain the most important currency but it is expected that the dollar will lose ground to the Euro in the coming years. The dollar-Euro exchange market will be, by far, the largest foreign exchange market. Fred Bergsten, the well-known founder and director of the Institute for International Economics in Washington, D.C. put it succinctly: "The Euro will be for the dollar what Airbus is for Boeing". But of course, it took Airbus more than 20 years to become a serious competitor of Boeing. In a few years, the dollar hegemony will be over. The current G-7-coordination will likely move towards a G3-coordination – with three major actors: the Federal Reserve Bank in Washington, DC, the Bank of Japan in Tokyo and the European Central Bank in Frankfurt. The strengthening of the Euro will change the European Union, bring about change for transatlantic relations and possess important implications for global markets.

The second challenge for transatlantic relations is that of global governance. The term global governance still lacks any accepted definition. Aseem Prakash and Jeffrey A. Hart define "governance simply as organizing collective action".[37] David A. Lake defines governance narrower, as "the enforcement of bargains".[38] And the Commission on Global Governance defined global governance as: "The sum of the many ways individuals and institutions, public and private, manage their common affairs. It is a continuing process through which conflicting or diverse interests may be accommodated and cooperative action may be taken".[39]

In terms of transatlantic relations it means that governments are no longer in full control. There is a complex system of a growing number of actors with profoundly different interests that are trying to take part in the bargaining process and that make it more and more difficult to enforce any kind of agreement, assuming an agreement can be reached. Just two examples: In December 1999, the ministerial conference in Seattle that was supposed to launch the new WTO Trade Round broke down. Most participants, observers, members of NGOs, media, and developing countries put the blame on the American government. The Europeans criticized the Clinton Administration; the American government criticized the developing countries; the developing countries criticized the OECD countries – and the NGOs celebrated their most important victory since many years, at least, that is the way some NGOs are presenting their view of what happened in Seattle.

But Seattle taught the United States and Europe two important lessons. First, the decision-making process inside the WTO is nowadays much more difficult because there are so many members inside, as well as opposing groups, outside the WTO. Second lesson: If the United States and the EU do not work closely together, there will not be any progress, neither in regard to a new trade round, nor in regard to any international agreement. [40] But it is also true that neither the United States nor the European Union need to wait for a new WTO Round if they want to open up their markets, for example, offering special agreements to the poorest developing countries – something the European Union just recently did – or else forgiving the debts of the poorest developing countries – something the G-7 countries decided to do.

The second example concerns the World Economic Summits or so-called G-7/8 Summits. The summits have been important meetings in the 1970s and 1980s for transatlantic relations and global events.[41] But over the years the summits have become more and more a kind of media event. There has been a lot of talk, a growing number of journalists, an ever-longer communiqué – but less and less substance in terms of enforceable decisions. And there are now more and more "Global Summits", and "Regional Summits", and even a "UN Millennium Summit" in September of 2000. Political leaders taking part in all those summits seem to like to meet and talk, to discuss and suggest, and to listen and present – but they obviously do not like to decide and implement agreements. This is partially due to the demands of a media-society-democracy, but it is also due to the fact that those leaders are trying to avoid the acceptance the political leadership and political responsibility in respect to bilateral, as well as transatlantic and global issues.[42]

Globalisation is the third challenge for transatlantic relations. The term globalisation lacks – like governance – any accepted definition. There is a vast literature on the subject and almost anybody has a very determined opinion about what globalisation means and what kind of changes globalisation will bring about. For one school of thought globalisation is nothing new, for another school of thought, and it seems that the majority supports this perspective, globalisation is a "completely new ball game".

Globalisation is seen as a new engine for producing prosperity and higher income in many countries. But globalisation is creating a new problem concerning income distribution within countries as well as among countries. Seen in terms of income distribution, globalisation will create "winners and losers of globalisation". It is very well known, that losers will fight hard to stop this process that makes them losers, whereas winners will take what they get without actively supporting globalisation. This is the fundamental challenge for all democratic countries that is being created by globalisation. There will be a growing number of people that will organize all kind of activities to be heard and listened to as new "actors in the game" trying to stop the process of globalisation. It has to be expected, therefore, that the resistance against globalisation will get stronger in the coming years in many countries. And this will also create new and complex problems for transatlantic relations in the future.[43]

Notes

1   This paper was completed in January 2001 as part of a project on "Resistance against Globalization". The latter project is funded by the Otto Wolff Foundation and The German Marshall Fund of the United States. We are very grateful to both foundations for their support.

2   Nicholas Kulish, "Economists Find Difficulty In Defining a Recession. The Use of the Economic Buzzword Causes Controversy", *The Wall Street Journal Europe*, 11 January 2000.

3   Robert J. Lieber, "No Transatlantic Divorce in the Offing", *Orbis*, Fall 2000, pp. 571-584, here p. 571.

4   George E. Shambaugh, *States, Firms, and Power: Successful Sanctions in United States Foreign Policy*, (New York: State University of New York Press, 1999), p. 71. Chapter 3 in this book is a detailed analysis of the pipeline crisis, pp. 71-110: "Maintaining Power in an Alliance Conflict: The Trans-Siberian Pipeline Embargo, 1980-84". For more details about the American embargo policy see also Claudia Wörmann, *Osthandel als Problem der Atlantischen Allianz* (Bonn: DGAP, 1986).

5   Robert J. Lieber, "No Transatlantic Divorce", op. cit., p. 572.

6   John Mearsheimer, "Back to the Future: Instability in Europe after the Cold War", *International Security*, Summer 1990, pp. 5-56.

7   Benjamin J. Cohen, "Return to Normalcy? Global Economic Policy at the End of the Century", Robert J. Lieber (ed.), *Eagle Adrift: American Foreign Policy at the End of the Century*, (New York: Longman, 1997), p. 74.

8   This passage is quoted in Robert J. Lieber, "No Transatlantic Divorce", ibid., p.573.

9   Vedrine is quoted in Charles Krauthammer, "Not for Moi, Thanks", *Washington Post*, November 26, 1999; here quoted from Robert J. Lieber, "No Transatlantic Divorce", ibid., p. 573.

10 The Clinton Presidency is analysed in Steven Schier (ed.) *The Postmodern Presidency: Bill Clinton's Legacy in U.S. Politics* (Pittsburgh, PA: University of Pittsburgh Press, 2000); also: Peter Rudolf and Jürgen Wilzewski (eds.), *Weltmacht ohne Gegner. Amerikanische Aussenpolitik zu Beginn des 21. Jahrhunderts*, (Baden-Baden: Nomos, 2000).

11   Bowman Cuttler, "A New International Economic Order", in Hutchings, Robert L., *At the End of the American Century. America's Role in the Post-Cold War World* (Baltimore and London: John Hopkins University Press 1998), pp. 131-153; p.151f.

12   For a detailed analysis see Bernhard May, *Die Uruguay-Runde. Verhandlungsmarathon verhindert trilateralen Handelskrieg*, (Bonn: DGAP, 1994); and Jeffrey J. Schott, *The Uruguay Round: An Assessment* (Washington, D.C.: IIE, 1994).

13   Samuel R. Berger, "A Foreign Policy for the Global Age", *Foreign Affairs*, November/December 2000, pp. 22-39, here p. 22.

14   Paul Kennedy, *The Rise and Fall of the Great Powers. Economic Change and Military Conflict from 1500 to 2000* (New York: Random House, 1987).

15   Samuel P. Huntington, "The U.S. – Decline or Renewal?" *Foreign Affairs*, Winter 1988-89, pp. 76-97; and: Charles Krauthammer, "The Unipolar Moment", *Foreign Affairs*, Winter 1989-90, pp. 23-33.

16   Bernhard May, *Kuwait-Krise und Energiesicherheit* (Bonn: DGAP, 1991).

17   Robert J. Lieber, "No Transatlantic Divorce, " ibid., p. 580.

18   Steve Peers, "Banana split. WTO law and preferential agreements in the EC legal order", *European Foreign Affairs Review* (London: Summer 1999), pp. 195-214.

19   For more information see EU-Einigung im Bananenstreit. Quoten werden 2006 abgeschafft, in Frankfurter Allgemeine Zeitung, 20 December 2000; and Annäherung im EU-Bananenstreit, in: Neue Zürcher Zeitung, 9 October 2000; and "Commission proposes plan to end banana dispute", http://europa.eu.int/comm/trade, 4 October 2000.

20   For more about the transatlantic biotechnology dispute, see Mark A. Pollack and Gregory C. Shaffer, "Biotechnology: The Next Transatlantic Trade War?" *The Washington Quarterly*, Autumn 2000, pp. 41-54.

21   Geoff Winestock, "WTO Says U.S. Must Scrap An Offshore Tax-haven Plan. Group's Ruling on Foreign-Sales Corporations is Big Victory for Europe. Decision Hands EU a Stick in Fight Over Bananas and Hormone-Treated Beef", *Wall Street Journal Europe*, February 25-26, 2000. It was the headline of this WSJE-copy.

22   For more details see, "EU seeks $4bn sanctions against US", *Financial Times*, November 17, 2000; see also, "Die USA wenden EU-Sanktionen vorläufig ab. Revision des Exportsubventions-Systems", *Neue Zürcher Zeitung*, 14. November 2000.

23   For more details, see Kevin Done, Edward Alden and Deborah Hargreaves, "Airbus launch flies into U.S. challenge over funding", *Financial Times*, 19 December 2000; and "Der neue Airbus entzweit Amerika und die EU", *Frankfurter Allgemeine Zeitung*, 20 December 2000; and Barry James, "Airbus Superjumbo Faces Trade Storm", *International Herald Tribune*, 20 December 2000; and "USA: Clinton warnt vor Handelskrieg", *Wirtschaftswoche*, 19 December 2000.

24   Roy Denman, "Trans-Atlantic Trade: So Much Is at Stake", *International Herald Tribune*, 19 January 2001.

25   Jim Hoagland, "Assessing Clinton Foreign Policy", *International Herald Tribune*, 27 November 2000.

26   "Bush Picks Trade Envoy and Keeps the Post in the Cabinet", *International Herald Tribune*, 12 January 2001.

27   Edward Alden, Richard Wolffe and Stephen Fidler, "Zoellick faces task of building trade bridges", *Financial Times*, 12 January 2001.

28   For an interesting analysis of this myth, I. M. Destler, Steven Kull, Celinda Lake, Frederick T. Steeper, *Misreading the Public: The Myth of a New Isolationism* (Washington, D.C.: Brookings., D.C. 1999).

29   James M. Lindsay, "The New Partisanship: The Changed Politics of American Foreign Policy". http://www.brookings.edu.

30   Robin Gaster and Clyde V. Prestowitz, Jr., *Shrinking the Atlantic. Europe and the American Economy* (Washington, D.C.: ESI, 1994).

31   Horst Siebert, *TAFTA: Fuelling trade discrimination of global liberalization?* (Washington, D.C.: AICGS, 1996).

32   Bruce Stokes (ed.), *Open for Business. Creating a Transatlantic Marketplace*, New York: Council on Foreign Relations, 1996; and Wolfgang H. Reinicke, *Deepening the Atlantic*, (Gütersloh: Bertelsmann Foundation Publishers, 1996).

33   Horst Günter Krenzler and Astrid Schomaker, *"A New Transatlantic Agenda"*, European *Foreign Affairs Review* (London), No.1, 1996, pp. 9-28.

34   For more information see Jens van Scherpenberg, "Europe and America in the World Economy", in Susanne Baier-Allen (ed.), *The Future of Euro-Atlantic Relations*, Baden-Baden: Nomos 2000), pp. 79-93, here p. 93.

35   Guillaume Parmentier, "Let's Give the Atlantic Trade Partners a Forum for Problem-Solving", *International Herald Tribune*, 11 January 2000.

36   Martin Feldstein, "EMU and International Conflict", *Foreign Affairs*, November/December 1997, pp. 60-73; and Steven Everts, *The impact of the euro on transatlantic relations* (London: Centre for European Reform, 1999).

37   Aseem Prakash and Jeffrey A. Hart, "Globalization and Governance: An Introduction", in Aseem Prakash and Jeffrey A. Hart (eds.), *Globalization and Governance* (London and New York: Routledge, 1999), pp.1-24, here p.2

38   David A. Lake, "Global governance. A relational contracting approach", in Aseem Prakash and Jeffrey A. Hart (eds.), *Globalization and Governance* (London and New York: Routledge 1999, pp. 31-53, here p.33.

39   Commission on Global Governance, *Our Global Neighborhood*, (New York: Oxford University Press, 1995), p.2.

40   Bernhard May, Erfolglos in Seattle. *Der Fehlstart der WTO-Runde* (Bonn: Internationale Politik, January 2000), pp. 49-50.

41   Bernhard May, "The World Economic Summits in the Era of the Cold War", in German Historical Institute (ed.), *Germany and the United States in the Era of the Cold War* (Cambridge University Press, Cambridge/New York 2001), pp. 268-281.

42   Christoph Bertram calls this phenomenon "global glossolalia". Christoph Bertram, "The Verbosity of Power. Needed: a cure for global glossolalia", in *Foreign Policy*, November/December 2000, pp. 86-87.

43   Bernhard May, "Globalisation, democracy and trade policy" in Klaus Günther Deutsch and Bernhard Speyer (eds.), *The World Trade Organization Millennium Round: Freer Trade in the Next Century* (London: Routledge, 2001), pp. 72-81.

12 Conclusion: The New Transatlantic Agenda: Whereto?

HALL GARDNER AND RADOSLAVA STEFANOVA

The majority of the contributors to this book would probably agree with the general thesis that the development of a more unified Europe, and of a Common European Defence and Security Policy (CESDP) in particular, would not only benefit Europe, but the U.S. as well. The problem, however, is they may strongly disagree as to the modalities and the precise extent of autonomy that Europe should seek. Many of the authors would also pose the question about whether, and to what extent, *can* Europe create a CESDP? To what extent can the United States and Europe forge a more concerted strategy on the basis of greater parity given the fact that "transatlantic relations are by nature quite confusing and asymmetrical and, as such, manifest a strange mixture of cooperation and conflict" as **Jan Zielonka** has argued?

Building a serious European security and defence capability would benefit not only Europe's own security, but it would also permit the United States to put its own house in order and re-focus its attention and resources more upon its own domestic and foreign policy. As **David P. Calleo** has argued, a stronger Europe would also prompt the re-examination of the increasingly disjointed foreign policy decision making process of the American system itself, and the reversal of the traditional Cold War logic. Instead of Europeans following the American lead, it is time that United States begin to learn something from the European approach and that of Europe's history and diplomacy. Along somewhat similar lines, **Yves Boyer** takes perhaps an even more critical view of NATO-EU relations in asserting the necessity for "*L'Europe puissance*". As he argues, many issues which are now afflicting European security will require new flexibility in areas that are no longer solely the domain of military force. In that sense, only a more unified Europe can help to contain American unilateralism at the same time that the EU seeks to tame the potentially destabilizing processes of globalisation.

While the above arguments in support of a more powerful Europe appear logically valid, there are still a significant number of practical obstacles to overcome—and **Anne Deighton**'s warnings about the potential negative side effects of EU "militarisation" should not go unheeded. Most practically, will EU member states develop the political will to spend more on defence in a time of generally decreasing budgets? Can NATO and the EU forge a truly concerted foreign and security policy (CSFP) at the same time that the EU seeks a more "autonomous" defence capability, and hence a greater degree of "parity" with the

United States? Can the two sides find a happy compromise over issues in regard to "power" and "responsibility" sharing?

Karsten D. Voigt sustains a qualified optimism in regard to the capability of Europe to forge a CESDP. He believes that we are living through the birth pangs of a new Atlanticism, but points out that consensus building is still difficult on many aspects of EU-NATO relations, as "nothing is agreed until everything is agreed". While the European Council at the December 2000 Nice summit endorsed the proposals for CESDP, and the North Atlantic Council (NAC) welcomed the EU's proposal on permanent EU/NATO arrangements in its December 2000 ministerial session, the EU's demand for assured and automatic EU access to NATO planning capabilities did not meet the approval of all Allies. Consequently, Voigt notes that while all states that participate in a EU-led operation are to be granted co-decision rights within the framework of the day-to-day management of the operations, there are still problems as to the structural modalities and extent of those co-decision rights and as to exactly how and when EU members and non-EU states are to be engaged in EU-led activities. Clearer regulation on the relationship between PSC and Operations Committee is accordingly needed.

For her part, **Anne Deighton** points out that the European Council may also "authorise the Committee [PSC], for the purpose and for the duration of a crisis management operation, to take the relevant decisions concerning *the political control and strategic direction of the operation*". The PSC, an un-elected body, is therefore given considerable authority to act collectively during a crisis. This clause is an important one as, hitherto, there was some doubt about the constitutionality and possible legality of such actions, unless this kind of decision-making procedure for a committee had been incorporated into the Treaty structure. Concurrently, the question of Article 5 of the Brussels pact is still dangling before EU members, as **Deighton** points out, but so is the question of how the EU's article 5 of the 1948 Brussels Treaty might intermesh with that of NATO's Article 5 of the 1949 North Atlantic Treaty as **Hall Gardner** argues.

Jan Zielonka points out a perhaps more fundamental contradiction in the European approach to CSFP which will need to be overcome, if Europe is to achieve greater unity in its political-and military decision-making processes. While EU institutions are becoming the most important means for coping with global pressures and local problems, the problem is that the common policies of the Union do not really enjoy genuine legitimacy. Moreover, the EU is not certain where it is heading, a fact that poses important questions such as: Where will borders of the Union be in ten years time? What division of power is likely to emerge from the current reform process of its government structures? Is the EU likely or not to become an all-round military power? Can the EU resolve its own differences in regard to a clear-cut course of policy formation, if its major actors possess divided political visions?

The December 2000 Nice summit forewarned of a potential rift in Franco-German relations based on what appear to be different visions of the future on the part of the two "core" EU states. Whereas Bonn has sought to create a European federation, France has generally sought a looser relationship, more of a "united Europe of states" than "a United States of Europe". The UK, on the other hand, appears to be calling for a Europe "à la carte". Concurrently, some members of the U.S. Congress appear to be playing the UK versus continental Europe. American calls to bring UK into NAFTA (as pointed out by both **Yves Boyer** and **Bernard May**) raise prospects of a break down in European unity unless the UK can somehow successfully straddle both political-economic camps.

As one moves from intra-EU politics to inter-national politics, even more demanding questions come to the forefront: Can the United States and EU ultimately forge a common policy in regard to Russia—and work with the latter in an entente or alliance relationship? How can the EU and the United States constructively help Russia achieve economic stabilisation, which could then spill over into a more constructive foreign policy? Is WTO membership the appropriate path? Or should Russia work toward a CIS "payments union"[1] as an intermediate step before membership in the WTO?

Can NATO, the EU, and Russia then find a way to compromise over the complex security concerns presently arising in regard to the Baltic region, and Kaliningrad, as well as in regard to Central and Eastern Europe, the Near East and Central Asia, as **Hall Gardner** suggests is possible? Can the U.S. and EU, and ultimately with Russia, formulate and then *sustain* common policies in regard to actual and potential regional conflicts such as those now occurring in Bosnia and Kosovo, Macedonia, Chechnya, Iraq, Central Asia (in regard to the Taliban in Afghanistan, for example.), along the lines of *complementarity* as **Volker Perthes** suggests in relation to U.S.-EU policy in the Middle East? What if civil strife breaks out in Ukraine or Belarus? Will NATO, the EU and Russia coordinate strategy? Will NATO (and the EU) unilaterally extend security guarantees to the Baltic states in spite of Russian threats against such an action? Or can the three negotiate a compromise in the Baltic region involving overlapping NATO-EU-Russian security guarantees?

Given the still inconclusive nature of the Balkan crises (despite the arrest of former Serbian strong man Slobodan Milosevic by the new authorities in Belgrade), are the transatlantic allies ready to re-negotiate a genuine peace settlement for the entire Balkan region, particularly now that the U.S. administration is not faced with a re-election for another four years, as **Radoslava Stefanova** has suggested? Should the United States and Europeans thus engage in a peace process for the Balkans, for example, but this time on an equal footing, in search for a genuine and legitimate peace in Bosnia and Kosovo, while at the same time also mend growing policy divergences in the transatlantic alliance? How might the independence of Kosovo be regarded by the rest of the region? To what extent is such a peace strategy likely to take into account local needs (in which partition should not be excluded as an option) but without raising a regional, if not global, can of worms—of claims against counter-claims? It is clear that the status quo cannot be sustained for too much longer; and it is also clear that the transatlantic community cannot escape its responsibilities. Having now engaged in military action, it must remain engaged in the Balkans for quite awhile.

Can the United States, the EU, and Russia forge a common strategy in regard to Turkey, as well as in regard to rising powers such as Iran, India and China, among other states in an emerging *polycentric* global system characterized by states with highly uneven military and political-economic capabilities? To what extent can Ankara continue to extend its geopolitical and economic interests into former Ottoman former Soviet (and now Russian) spheres of influence and security without causing a Russian backlash? Can Russian and Turkish membership in the EU help to ameliorate actual and potential tensions between these two states? Or, what might happen if the EU ultimately refuses to draw Turkey or Russia into membership? Is the United States expecting too much of the EU to bring both Russia and Turkey in as members—and is the EU expecting too much of itself as it expands into new regions? If, however, NATO, the EU, Turkey and Russia can resolve their differences, how might China react to a closer relationship? Would Beijing seek to obstruct such a relationship or else agree to "bandwagon" by entering into a truly concerted NATO-EU-Russian relationship? Would Russia and China attempt to forge an alliance, perhaps with India and other states? Or could the United States and European Union *separately* seek out an alliance with either Russia or China, among the primary geo-strategic options? Will the major powers then revert to their threats of "encirclement" and "counter-encirclement?"

Another uncertain factor is the global geopolitical consequences of the renewed American push to develop either national or theatre-based Ballistic Missile Defences. Will BMD prove to be a bargaining chip? Or will domestic American lobbies push through its implementation despite its high costs and dubious effectiveness? Will BMD serve to *artificially* block the potential for negotiated settlements between Russia, China, Europe and the United States, among other states, such as North Korea, affected? Or will the EU, Russia, and the United States accept a compromise proposal possibly involving limited theatre boost phase anti-ballistic missile systems? How then would China, and other "states of concern", react to a NATO-EU-Russian BMD system—if such *non-strategic* systems could be developed?

How will the development of the Euro affect the transatlantic relationship? What will happen if the dollar does lose ground to the Euro in the coming years? Will it force the United States to become more fiscally responsible? Will the burden sharing issue become more divisive as **David P. Calleo** suggests? Will the UK, for example, finally be forced to choose between the dollar and the Euro, between NAFTA and the EU? Could the Euro inadvertently draw Kaliningrad and other regions from Moscow's grasp? How might Russia and other non-EU states respond to the burgeoning economic potential of the new Europe? Will non-EU members continue to implement the necessary political and economic reforms to enter the WTO and EU? Or will the politics of backlash dig in its iron heels? Will both Russia and China enter the WTO? What are the implications if China enters, but Russia does not? What will be the outcome of the battle between "winners and losers of globalisation", as **Bernhard May** put it? Are institutional reforms possible at the international and regional levels that might help mitigate the potentially destabilizing political- economic- social- ecological effects of the WTO and globalisation?

Many separate issues are becoming confused in the contemporary transatlantic debate. How will the commercial, biogenetic and ideological battles play in the domestic political debates on each side of the Atlantic? How will disputes over ACP bananas (stemming from Africa, the Caribbean and the Pacific) versus dollar bananas (stemming from Central America); or over American beef hormones and genetically modified organisms versus European 'mad cows'; or over European subsidies for Airbus versus American-backed Boeing; or over the U.S. Foreign Sales Corporation Act; or over American support for the death penalty, plus opposition to gun control versus the general European tolerance for the right to abortion but strict restrictions on firearms; not to overlook American free market libertarianism versus European social democracy, affect the overall U.S.-European relationship?

How will the Bush administration's initial stance against Kyoto and efforts to stop global warming be interpreted and acted upon by the Europeans? Can the U.S. and EU accordingly find a compromise over the significant disputes over commercial interests, such as agriculture and aerospace, which "run the risk of dominating the (transatlantic) debate".[2] Or will, for example, the United States and Europe continue to dispute over issues such as the new oil pipeline from Russia as they did during the Cold War, in effect, making the possibility of a concerted U.S.-European-Russian geostrategic and political-economic strategy null and void?

It is accordingly quite clear from all of these essays that the Americans and European need to address thoroughly, and as soon as possible, their significant disputes that appear increasingly and dangerously divisive. While a number of factors can help hold the transatlantic relationship together, a number of negative factors could also pull it apart. It is certain that the clear and sustained nature of the Soviet "threat" helped to provide some of the glue that held the transatlantic relationship together during the Cold War. From this perspective, it is often asked if the United States and Europe still need a renewed common "threat" to sustain their transatlantic solidarity? Yet what happens if the rise of new, more uncertain, and less clearly defined, "threats" in the contemporary post-1989 era actually prove to be disruptive rather than unifying precisely because they are harder to define and to identify for purposes of a common strategy? The possible revival of

Russia, or increasingly, China as "potential threats", along with those threats posed by "states of concern", may not serve to sustain the coherence of transatlantic relationship, as is argued, particularly if the two sides cannot forge a common strategy toward both Moscow and Beijing in particular in the very near future. Secondly, while Europe and the United States did engage in a number of significant disputes during the Cold war, it is not clear that similar strategic and economic disputes will not reveal new and even deeper ruptures and schisms within the transatlantic relationship—*but only in the absence of a concerted approach to foreign and international economic policy in general.*

Here **John Ikenberry**'s challenge to traditional neo-realist thinking becomes relevant. He argues that the Euro-Atlantic community can be made more durable if it is held together not just by interests, but by a new common identity that is strengthened by conjoint and renewed, institutions. This means that both Europe (already in the process of constructing a new identity out of its past of historical rivalries) and the United States must "continuously act to construct (a) common identity". Such institutions and practices can help channel or restrain American actions, and attempt to prevent the latter from engaging in potentially destabilizing unilateralism. In effect, reversing the Cold War construct, a stronger Europe would help "double contain" a United States with its tendency toward "selected interventionism" (as opposed to isolationism).[3] At the same time, both the United States and EU will need to better coordinate their common interests.

In addition to the need to reform NATO, the EU, the World Bank, IMF, the WTO, etc., what new institutions might be needed to sustain a close transatlantic relationship in post-Cold war circumstances? Here, **Dana Allin**'s analysis focuses on the key case study in regard to the ability of the transatlantic alliance to reform major institutions. What will be the ultimate transatlantic approach to the UN— the organization that, in many ways, was created to legitimise the post-World War II order? Will the U.S. retain its seemingly visceral disapproval of UN activities? Will Washington be more and more willing to engage in unilateralism, or in selected interventions without UN mandates that, at least ostensibly, appear to serve American interests? Or can the United States continue to press for UN reforms but without undermining the institution? Can the United States and the rest of the UN Security Council agree, for example, as to the best way to reform the UN, and ultimately achieve the reform of the UN Security Council itself, for example?

In the process of *constructing a new common transatlantic identity and of formulating a concerted approach to foreign and international economic policy in general*, the book makes a number of proposals that could be considered at the initiation of a serious discussion (i.e. without summitry for the sake of summitry!) about the new transatlantic agenda:

- The formation of a Transatlantic Political-Economic and Strategic Council to co-ordinate global geopolitical and economic strategy at the level of senior advisors and officials, as well as at an expert mid-level.

- The continuation of NATO-EU reforms that permit greater EU power and burden sharing within—if not *outside*—NATO on the basis of greater parity with a recognition of the radical changes taking place in the nature of transatlantic security.

- The formation of a permanent U.S.-EU-Russian dialogue with consideration of a "new" form of Russian membership in NATO and the EU, through practical cooperation in the Baltic region, including the proposal of a Euro-Atlantic Partnership Headquarters, as well as a EU centre, in Kaliningrad.

- Greater U.S.-EU cooperation in regard to Balkans, the Near and Middle East, and China with a more conscious, conscientious and coordinated recognition of the *complementarity* of both the American and EU approaches.

- The re-negotiation of the Dayton and the Kosovo agreements with an eye to a genuine peace settlement for the entire Balkan region, particularly now that the U.S. administration is not faced with a re-election for another four years.

- Consideration of the formation of a Central and Eastern European Defence, Security, and Economic Community (a community within a larger European Union) backed by overlapping NATO, EU and Russian security guarantees, coupled with a re-thinking of the EU approach to Schengen for Central and Eastern European states.

The above rest as suggestions for a not so long term global strategy, and do not necessarily reflect the particular views of each of the authors, but can hopefully serve as general guidelines for policy makers as they must grapple with the complex issues that are presently confronting, and will continue to confront, the new transatlantic agenda well into the foreseeable future.

Notes

1   Jacques Sapir, Lecture (Paris: American Embassy, 21 June 2001).
2   U.S. Ambassador to France, Felix Rohatyn, "France and Europe: Perspectives of a Departing Ambassador" IFRI, Paris, 16 October 2000.
3   See Hall Gardner, *Dangerous Crossroads: Europe, Russia and the Future of NATO* (Westport, CT: Praeger, 1997).